PUBLISHED FOR
JUDAICA RESEARCH AT YALE UNIVERSITY
on the
LOUIS M. RABINOWITZ FOUNDATION

YALE JUDAICA SERIES

EDITOR

JULIAN OBERMANN

ASSISTED BY

Michael Bernstein

Volume IX

THE CODE OF MAIMONIDES

(*MISHNEH TORAH*)

BOOK ELEVEN

The Code of Maimonides

BOOK ELEVEN

THE BOOK OF TORTS

TRANSLATED FROM THE HEBREW BY

HYMAN KLEIN, M.A. (Cantab.)

New Haven and London

YALE UNIVERSITY PRESS

Third printing, July 1964

Printed in the United States of America by
The Murray Printing Company, Forge Village, Mass.

Library of Congress catalog card number: 49-9495

CONTENTS

INTRODUCTION

Book Eleven of the Code of Maimonides and the three following books (already published in this series) form a unit concerned mainly with civil and criminal law—that is, with affairs "between man and his fellowman"—in contrast to the preceding ten books that are given over, for the most part,[1] to the symbolic and ritual observances of the Law, and thus deal with provisions "between man and God." [2]

These four books incorporate most of the material of the Fourth Order of the Mishnah, called *Nĕziḳin*. In appropriating this title for Book Eleven, the first of the four, and designating it *Sefer Nĕziḳin,* Maimonides has followed a precedent set by the Talmud, in which the first tractate of this Fourth Order bears the same name, *Nĕziḳin,* as the whole Order. Its derivation from a Hebrew root meaning "to damage, to injure" [3] makes it also a very suitable title for a legal work on torts. By contrast, only the first of the titles of the five treatises into which Book Eleven is divided is of talmudic origin,[4] the other four titles being framed independently with due regard to the central theme of each treatise. The five treatises and their major topics present themselves as follows:

1) Laws Concerning Damage by Chattels. This treatise deals with the amount and mode of compensation to be paid for damage to persons or property caused by one's chattels (such as livestock) or through one's negligence (in leaving a pit uncovered or in allowing a fire to spread from his premises); and with the ransom to be paid if an animal kills a human being.

1. The chief exceptions are Book IV ("Women") and the parts of Book VII ("Seeds") that deal with the dues payable to the priests and the poor.

2. For Maimonides' views concerning the various spheres of Jewish law, cf. his *Guide of the Perplexed,* III, Ch. 35 (tr. M. Friedlander, pp. 163–168).

3. Whether *Nĕziḳin* really signifies "injuries" or "injurers" is of no consequence since it occurs only as a title.

4. See B. BḲ 4b.

2) Laws Concerning Theft. This treatise deals with fines imposed for theft, fines imposed when a bailee pleads falsely that goods committed to his care have been stolen, protection for a bona fide purchaser of stolen property, the ban on purchase of property likely to have been stolen, weights and measures, theft of human beings, and conditions under which an intercepted thief may be killed.

3) Laws Concerning Robbery and Lost Property. This treatise deals with definitions of robbery, unlawful detention of what is due to another, covetousness, and desire; the obligation to restore property obtained by robbery or to pay compensation; alteration and improvement of robbed property; restitution when the person robbed dies; robbery of land; unauthorized improvement of another's land; the obligation to restore lost property to its owner and provisions appertaining thereto; interim care of lost property; and circumstances under which the finder of lost property may keep it.

4) Laws Concerning Wounding and Damaging. This treatise deals with cases of assault, insult, and insulting behavior; visible and invisible damage caused by human beings; damage caused by an informer; and punishment of informers.

5) Laws Concerning Murder and the Preservation of Life. This treatise deals with cases of deliberate murder, inadvertent homicide, and the rite (of breaking a heifer's neck) incumbent upon the community nearest a person found slain by an unknown slayer; and with various provisions calculated to guard against danger to human life or to assist persons in jeopardy.

As in all the books of the Code, so in the Book of Torts, Maimonides depends primarily on the Mishnah for the scope and substance of the Oral Law. The material of the first four treatises derives largely from the first twelve chapters of the mishnaic tractate *Nĕziḳin,* i.e. from BḲ 1–10 and BM 1–2, other tractates being represented only by occasional isolated paragraphs. For the fifth treatise, however, a wider range of tractates was drawn upon. The actual relationship between the Book of Torts and the Mishnah is indicated by the following table:

Book of Torts	*Mishnah*
Damage by Chattels	BḲ 1–6
Theft	BḲ 7; BB 5; San 8, 11
Robbery and Lost Property	BḲ 9–10; BM 1–2
Wounding and Damaging	BḲ 8; BḲ 3; Giṭ 5
Murder and Preservation of Life	San 8, 9; Mak 2; Soṭ 9; Ter 8; Ḥul 3; AZ 2; BM 2

A detailed discussion of the difference in arrangement between the Mishnah and the Code, however, lies outside the scope of this Introduction.[5]

Again as elsewhere in the Code, the mishnaic material bearing on torts is supplemented by decisions taken from other tannaitic sources, such as the Tosefta, Baraita materials quoted in the Talmud, and halakhic Midrashim, as well as from the Gemara, mainly of the Babylonian—but occasionally also of the Palestinian—Talmud. An interesting case of a law based entirely on sources outside the Mishnah is that of the informer—that dread of all Jewish communities subject to alien rule. Since, however, Maimonides himself describes the Code, in his own introduction to it, as "a compendium of the whole of the Oral Law, together with all the regulations, customs, and decrees introduced from the time of Moses to the compilation of the Talmud," only rarely are decisions in the Book of Torts based on developments of the Geonic period (see Index under *Geonim*).

Beyond occasionally observing that a given law rests merely on the authority of the Sages—rather than that of Scripture—or is an enactment of the Geonim, Maimonides does not identify the particular source of any of the multitude of rulings codified in Book Eleven. Instead he relies on the general survey of the literature employed by him, given in his introduction to the Code. The task of identification is, however, greatly simplified by Maimonides' method of reproducing the actual words of his

5. It is useful to remember that in the Mishnah cases are placed together when the decision or ruling is the same, regardless of differences between the facts. This is a mode of classification especially appropriate in a work intended to be memorized and applied from memory.

source, while most of the sources are in fact already identified by the commentators, above all MM and KM. Even so, the origins of a few of the decisions of our book still remain to be discovered.[6]

Where, exceptionally, a recorded decision is post-talmudic, it is marked by an expression like "this regulation has been accepted in all courts of law" (I, viii, 12) or "Cases of this kind occurred regularly in Spain" (IV, iii, 6). Cases in which Maimonides is offering his own decision are clearly indicated by a phrase like "It is my opinion that" (I, x, 14; III, xiii, 19; IV, ii, 8; V, iii, 7; III, iv, 16).

Quite apart from its importance for the history of Jewish law, Book Eleven contributes its full share to the general—philological and cultural—interest of the Code. The following examples, out of many, may suffice here by way of illustration.

Like other authors of his era, Maimonides combines a preference for the vocabulary of the Bible with an extensive acquaintance with the Aramaic translations of the Hebrew Bible contained in the Targumim. Thus, for tin and lead (II, viii, 4) he uses the biblical forms (cf. Num. 31:22) instead of the neo-Hebrew of his source. For an ox to be fattened (III, xiii, 16) Maimonides uses the biblical *bari* (cf. I Kings 5:3 and Targum), although his source used the aramaicized form of the mishnaic *pěṭam* (cf. Shab 20:4). Again, Maimonides (II, vi, 3; viii, 11) employs the word *peles,* used rarely in the Bible and commonly rendered as "balance, scales," to denote a steelyard or the lever of a goldsmith's scales, rather than scales themselves. Essentially the same meaning of this Hebrew vocable has been suggested independently by modern scholars.[7]

Very striking is Maimonides' exposition (III, v, 11–18) of the provisions under which tax collecting does not fall into the cate-

6. E.g., II, i, 10; iii, 16–17; IV, i, 13; V, iv, 9. Many of the source references omitted by MM and KM are midrashic. Those traced by the translator include examples from P. (I, xii, 3), MRSY (IV, i, 5), SZ (V, iii, 8) and MT (IV, i, 9) as well as the usual halakhic midrashim. For further details see Notes, *passim.*

7. Hebrew *peles* has been combined by P. Haupt with Akkadian *naplasu,* "to watch, observe"; see Gesenius-Buhl (16th ed.), *s.v. PLS.* (I am indebted to Prof. Obermann for this reference.) Cf. YJS, *8,* xlv, n. 11.

gory of robbery, decisive requirements being that the tax imposed is universal and definite—and not directed against individuals or discriminatory in assessment—and that the ruler to whom the tax is paid has been accepted by the consensus of the citizenry. Striking too is the exposition of the law of the informer (IV, viii), especially the provision that although Jewish courts can no longer impose capital punishment as a penalty, it is nevertheless permissible to kill an informer to prevent his denunciation from jeopardizing the life of anyone or from depriving anyone of his property (Secs. 9–10). Although the rules themselves are taken from his sources, they gain considerably from their organization and presentation in the Code.

Maimonides often gives moral reasons for the laws of torts, or states the principle underlying a given law. Where these have not been taken from the rabbinical sources, they may be either at variance with them or be independent suggestions for cases where no reason or principle is given by the sources.[8] An interesting example is afforded by the duty, promulgated in Scripture (Deut. 23:5), of giving assistance to an "enemy" whose "ass" is "lying under its burden," which is dealt with in the Mishnah after the obligation to restore lost property, and could plausibly be connected with it. Maimonides (V, xii, 13–14), however, explains it as one of the commandments to assist those in jeopardy, for the "enemy"—defined here as an unrepentant "evildoer"—may endanger his life in order to save his property; and does not Scripture itself say, *I have no pleasure in the death of the wicked but that the wicked turn from his way and live* (Ezek. 33:11)?

The first draft of this translation of the Book of Torts was prepared during 1939–40 from the Warsaw edition of 1881 for my pupils at Aria College, Southsea (England), for whom the study of Maimonides' Code was intended as a bridge between the Mishnah and the Talmud. In 1948–50, during which my lectures and courses at Liverpool Talmudical College covered the main Tal-

8. For statements of reason or principle taken from the rabbinic sources, cf. I, vii, 7; IV, v, 11. Independent statements, controverted by other authorities, may be found in I, viii, 5; II, viii, 4; III, xvi, 8; V, xii, 5, and elsewhere. See, on this feature of the Code, Ch. Tchernowitz, *Tolĕḏoṯ happosĕḳim, 1,* 287 ff.

mudic sources of the Book, a second draft was made, for which account was taken of the readings of the Berlin edition of 1864, and notes were added. This revised draft was very kindly read by Mr. Maurice Simon, M.A. (Oxon), and a third draft incorporated his many fine suggestions and also took into account suggestions made by the editor, Professor Julian Obermann, after reading a specimen chapter (Laws of Wounding and Damage, Chapter 1). In preparing this draft I also had a photostat of an Oxford manuscript of the Book of Torts kindly placed at my disposal by the librarian of Yale University Library.[9] This third draft was finished early in 1951. In 1952–53 it was edited by Professor Obermann and a new typescript incorporating his numerous editorial suggestions was kindly made by his assistant, Mr. A. Leslie Willson. This typescript was checked with the Hebrew text by a group of young friends (Maurice Cohen, David Jacobson, Emmanuel Klien, Vivian Halpern, and Judith Klein) as well as by myself, and the edited version has been readily accepted by me not only in the many cases in which it was a manifest improvement on my translation, but also in those cases in which I continued to consider my own rendering no less adequate. Others who were of occasional assistance include Rabbi B. D. Klien, M.A., the Rev. J. Halpern, M.A., and Mr. Gerald Abrahams, M.A., Barrister-at-Law. The material for the Index was assembled by Mr. Maurice Rimel, Ll. M., Barrister-at-Law. To all of these it is a pleasure to express here my sincere thanks. To my dear wife I owe a special debt for continual encouragement during a period when prolonged

9. As one of the most widely studied books of the Code, the Book of Torts has a well-preserved text, difficult readings or errors being few. However, a comparison of the editions with this MS is valuable as a check on the readings, especially where Maimonides' Talmud text appears to have differed from our present one as available in the several printed editions (e.g., v, v, 8). Occasionally, however, variants, as well as additional words or phrases do occur in the MS (cf. III, viii, 12) which improve the quality of the Hebrew text, although they may not necessarily affect its meaning in substance. Indeed, the influence of the Oxford codex on the present translation has been considerably greater than may be gleaned from the notes.

Parentheses are used to indicate the translator's insertions in the text.

illness and its aftermath could so easily have meant abandonment of my task.

Finally, I should like to regard my translation of the Book of Torts as a tribute to the scholarly and lay founders of the Tree of Life Talmudical College in London, and as a memorial to my departed teachers of blessed memory (Rabbis Joseph Green, Hirsch Neumann, and Saul Cohen) who ensured that between my twelfth and sixteenth years my Jewish learning was never inferior to my secular learning.

THE BOOK OF
TORTS

COMPRISING FIVE TREATISES IN
THE FOLLOWING ORDER

I. LAWS CONCERNING DAMAGE BY CHATTELS

II. LAWS CONCERNING THEFT

III. LAWS CONCERNING ROBBERY AND LOST PROPERTY

IV. LAWS CONCERNING WOUNDING AND DAMAGING

V. LAWS CONCERNING MURDER AND THE PRESERVATION OF LIFE

Incline my heart unto Thy testimonies,
And not to covetousness. (Psalms 119: 36)

TREATISE I

LAWS CONCERNING DAMAGE BY CHATTELS

Involving Four Positive Commandments
To Wit

1. To administer the law of damage by an "ox";
2. To administer the law of crop destruction;
3. To administer the law of damage by a "pit";
4. To administer the law of damage by a conflagration.

An exposition of these commandments
is contained in the following chapters.

CHAPTER I

1. If any living creature under human control causes damage, its owner must pay compensation because the damage is done by his chattel. When Scripture says, *If one man's ox hurt another's* (Exod. 21:35), the term *ox* includes any other domestic animal, as well as wild animals and birds. Scripture speaks of damage by an ox merely because it is a common occurrence.

2. How much compensation must the owner pay? If the animal causes damage by doing things which are natural and normal to it—for example, if one's animal eats another's straw or hay or does damage with its foot while walking—the owner must pay compensation for the whole of the damage from the best of his property. For Scripture says, *Of the best of his field and of the best of his vineyard shall he make restitution* (Exod. 22:4). If, however, it acts in an unusual way and causes damage by doing things which are not habitual to it—for example, if an ox gores or bites—the owner must pay for half of the damage, (but only) from the body of the injurious animal itself. For Scripture says, *Then shall they sell the live ox and divide the price of it,* etc. (Exod. 21:35).

3. Thus, if an ox worth one hundred *denar* gores an ox worth twenty and kills it and the carcass is worth four, the owner of the ox must pay eight, this being half of the residual damage. Moreover, he is obliged to pay only from the body of the ox that causes the damage, since Scripture says, *Then shall they sell the live ox.* If, therefore, an ox worth twenty denar gores an ox worth two hundred, and the carcass is worth one hundred, the owner of the carcass cannot say to the owner of the live ox, "Give me fifty," but the latter may say to him, "Here is the ox which has caused the damage; take it and go"—even though it may be worth but a single denar. The same rule applies in all similar cases.

4. An animal is called *mu'ad,* "forewarned," with respect to actions which it does normally and habitually, and *tam,* "innocu-

ous," with respect to actions which it does only exceptionally and which are not normally done by members of its species—as, for example, if an ox gores or bites. If an animal, having acted abnormally once, makes it a habit to repeat the abnormal action on numerous occasions, it becomes "forewarned" with respect to the particular action which it has made a habit. For Scripture says, *Or if it be known that the ox was wont to gore* (Exod. 21:36).

5. There are five actions with respect to which an animal is regarded as innocuous and which are such that if an animal makes a habit of any one of them, it becomes forewarned with respect to that action, to wit: an animal is not forewarned from the outset with respect to (1) goring, (2) jostling, (3) biting, (4) squatting upon large articles, or (5) kicking. If, however, it makes a habit of any one of these acts, it becomes forewarned with respect to it.

The tooth, on the other hand, is forewarned from the outset with respect to eating what is suitable for the animal; the foot is forewarned from the outset with respect to breaking things as it walks along; and any animal is forewarned from the outset with respect to squatting upon small pottery jars, or similar objects, and crushing them.

6. Five species of animal are deemed forewarned from their earliest existence with respect to damage they may cause, even when they are tamed. Consequently, if such animals do damage or kill by goring, biting, clawing, or a similar action, the owner must pay for the whole of the damage. These animals are the wolf, the lion, the bear, the panther, and the leopard. Similarly, a snake which has bitten is regarded as forewarned even if it is tamed.

7. In the case of any forewarned creature, the owner must pay for the whole of the damage from the best of his property, while in the case of any innocuous one, he need pay only for half of the damage from the animal itself. This is the rule when the animal enters the premises of the injured party and causes him damage there. If, however, the plaintiff enters the premises of the defendant and the latter's animal causes him damage, the defendant is

exempt from any claim, for he can say to the trespasser, "Had you not entered my premises, no harm would have overtaken you." Moreover, Scripture says explicitly, *And shall let his beast graze and it shall feed in another man's field* (Exod. 22:4).

8. If the damage is caused in a public domain, or in a courtyard which belongs to neither the defendant nor the plaintiff, or in a courtyard which belongs to both of them and in which both have the right to place produce or bring cattle—such as an open field or a similar place—the rule is that if the animal causes damage in a normal way by tooth or foot, its owner is exempt because it had the right to walk there and it is natural for an animal to walk about and feed normally or to break things as it walks along. If, on the other hand, it gores or jostles or squats or kicks or bites, then the owner must pay for half of the damage if it is innocuous and for the whole damage if it is forewarned.

9. If both partners have the right to place produce in a courtyard, but not to bring animals into it, and one of them brings in his animal and it causes damage, he is liable even for damage by tooth and foot. Similarly, if both have the right to bring animals into it, but only one has the right to place produce there, and damage is caused to his produce, then the other is liable for damage by tooth and foot.

10. Three principal classes of injury may be caused by an ox: injuries by the horn, by the tooth, and by the foot. Subspecies of injuries by the horn are jostling, biting, squatting, and kicking. It is a subspecies of injury by the tooth if an animal rubs itself against a wall for pleasure and causes damage thereby, or if it soils produce for pleasure. It is a subspecies of injury by the foot if an animal causes damage with its body while walking along, or with its hair while moving, or by swishing its tail, or with the saddle on its back, the bridle in its mouth, or the bell on its neck; similarly, if an ass walking along causes damage with its load, or a heifer causes damage with the wagon it is pulling. All the above are subspecies of injuries by the foot and the owner is exempt if

the damage occurs in a public domain but must pay in full for damage caused on the premises of the injured party.

11. If, in a public domain, an animal swishes its tail more vigorously than usual and causes damage, or if it swishes its membrum and causes damage, the owner is exempt. If, however, the injured party seizes property of the owner, he may obtain half of the damage from what he has seized. For it is doubtful whether these actions are deemed subspecies of injury by the horn, for which, as we have explained, the owner is liable even in a public domain, or whether they are regarded as subspecies of injury by the foot, for which the owner is exempt if the damage occurs in a public domain.

CHAPTER II

1. The principal classes of injuries and their subspecies have this in common, that if a principal class of injuries is considered habitual to an animal its corresponding subspecies are also so considered, and if a principal class of injuries is considered abnormal, its subspecies are similarly regarded. An animal is considered forewarned from the outset with respect to all the principal classes and each of their subspecies, with the exception of the horn and its subspecies, with respect to which an animal is deemed innocuous initially, and remains so until forewarned, as we have explained.

2. (The compensation payable for damage by) any subspecies and its corresponding principal class is the same, except in the case where pebbles spring from beneath the feet of a walking animal. Although damage by these is a subspecies of injury by the foot—so that the owner, as in the case of the principal class, the foot, is not liable if the damage occurs in a public domain, whereas if it occurs on the premises of the injured party the owner must pay compensation from his finest property as in the case of the principal class, the foot—he nevertheless pays for only half of the damage caused.

3. Thus, if an animal enters the plaintiff's courtyard and treads in such a way that pebbles spring from beneath its feet and break certain vessels, the owner pays for (only) half of the damage, (but) from his finest property. This rule is a law handed down by tradition.

4. Similarly, if an animal is walking along a public domain and pebbles spring from beneath its feet into the premises of the plaintiff and break some articles, the defendant need pay for only half of the damage.

If an animal treads on an article on the plaintiff's premises and breaks it, and this falls upon another article and breaks it, the defendant must pay for the whole of the damage to the first article but for only half of the damage to the second.

5. If, while walking in a public domain, an animal kicks and in the process makes pebbles spring up, and they cause damage in that domain, the owner is exempt. If, however, the plaintiff seizes a quarter of the damage from the defendant's property, we may not take it away from him. For since the animal has kicked, its action should perhaps be regarded as an abnormal one (and a subspecies of the horn) and not as a subspecies of the foot, and so the rule is in doubt.

6. If an animal stamps on the ground on the premises of the plaintiff and as a result pebbles spring up and cause damage there, the defendant must pay for (only) one quarter of the damage, since this does constitute an abnormal way of causing pebbles to spring up. But if the plaintiff seizes one-half of the damage, we may not take it away from him. Even if the animal walks in a place where it would have been impossible for it not to cause pebbles to spring up, and it stamps and so causes them to spring up, the owner must pay for (only) one quarter of the damage, yet if there is seizure by the plaintiff of one half of the damage, this may not be taken away from him.

7. Whenever full compensation is payable, the payment is a monetary obligation that the defendant must pay just as one who

borrows from another must repay a loan. Whenever half compensation is payable, the payment is a fine except in the case of compensation for damage by pebbles, where the half compensation is a traditional law, as we have explained.

8. The general rule is as follows: Whenever the compensation payable is for the actual damage caused, the obligation is deemed a monetary one; but whenever one must pay more or less—such as double compensation, for theft, or only half, for damage caused—the excess over the actual sum involved, or the lesser amount, is deemed a fine. Fines, however, are payable only on the testimony of witnesses, a defendant being exempt if he admits liability in any case in which the penalty is regarded as a fine.

9. If a cock, having inserted its head into the interior of a glass vessel, crows and breaks it, the rule is as follows: If there are condiments or the like inside, and the cock inserts its head in order to eat these, its owner must pay for the whole of the damage to the condiments and for half of the damage to the vessel—(this half damage being a monetary obligation) as is half damage in the case of pebbles—since the cock's action was normal. If the vessel is empty, the action is deemed abnormal and the defendant must still pay for half of the damage, this being then regarded as any other fine.

10. Similarly, if a horse neighs or a donkey brays and in so doing breaks some articles, the owner must pay for half of the damage.

Poultry are deemed forewarned with respect to breaking things as they walk along. But if a thread or a strap is tied to their feet and a vessel becomes entangled in the thread and rolls over and is broken, the owner need pay for (only) half of the damage. This is the rule if someone has tied the thread on. If, however, it has become entangled in their feet accidentally, the owner of the poultry is exempt. If the thread is owned by someone and has not been abandoned, the owner of the thread must pay for half of the damage, since his thread is considered a pit which moves.

11. If the owner of the thread puts it out of the way but nevertheless the poultry tread on it and drag it out and it becomes entangled in their feet and they break articles with it, then even the owner of the thread is exempt because he had no way to prevent the damage.

12. Where poultry in flying from one place to another break articles, the rule is that if they break them with their wings, the owner must pay for the whole of the damage, but if they break them with the wind set up by their wings, he need pay for only half of the damage.

13. If poultry hop about upon dough or upon produce and soil it or peck at it, the owner must pay for the whole of the damage. If they cause damage with earth or pebbles thrown up by their wings or feet, the owner need pay for (only) half of the damage.

14. If poultry peck at a well rope and the rope snaps and the bucket breaks, the owner must pay for the whole of the damage, provided that the bucket has continued to roll down as a result of their action until it fell and broke. If there is food upon the rope and they snap the rope while eating this food, the owner must pay for the whole of the damage to the rope as well.

15. If a dog or a goat jumps down from a roof and breaks some articles, the owner must pay for the whole of the damage, since these animals are deemed forewarned with respect to this action. The same rule applies if they fall down and cause damage, because their ascent to the top of the roof constitutes negligence. For although their fall was accidental, the rule is that the owner is liable in every case where negligence has preceded an accident.

16. If a dog or a goat springs upward, the owner need pay for only half of the damage, provided that the goat has clambered and climbed and the dog has leaped. If, however, the dog has climbed or the goat has leaped, whether upward or downward, the owner must pay for the whole of the damage. Similarly, if a cock jumps, whether upward or downward, the owner must pay for the whole of the damage.

17. If a dog takes a cake from hot coals and proceeds to a cornstack, the rule is as follows: If it puts the cake down on the cornstack and eats the cake and sets the cornstack on fire, the owner must pay full compensation for the cake and the section occupied by the cake, and only half compensation for the rest of the cornstack. However, if the dog drags the cake over the cornstack, eating the cake and burning the cornstack as it moves, then the owner must pay full compensation for the cake and half compensation for whatever the coals have touched; but he is exempt from paying for the rest of the cornstack.

18. This rule applies only if the owner of the burning coals guards his fire by closing the door but in spite of this the dog digs its way in and takes the cake off the fire. If, however, he does not guard his fire, the owner of the fire is liable for the burning of the stack, while the owner of the dog is liable only for the consumption of the cake and for the section of the cornstack occupied by it.

19. If one incites another's dog against a third person he is legally exempt but morally liable. But the owner of the dog is liable for half of the damage caused because, since he knows that his dog bites when incited, he ought not to have left it loose. If, however, one incites another's dog against himself, the owner of the dog is exempt, because whenever anyone who has acted abnormally first (is injured by) another who is acting abnormally, the latter is exempt.

20. If there are two cows in a public domain, one lying down and the other walking along, and the walking cow stamps upon the one lying down, its owner must pay for half of the damage. For although it is normal for it to walk over the other one, it is not normal for it to stamp on it.

CHAPTER III

1. An animal is deemed forewarned with respect to eating produce or green vegetables or the like. If, therefore, it enters the premises of the plaintiff and eats things of the kind that it normally eats, the defendant must pay for the whole of the damage. For Scripture says, *And it shall feed in another man's field, of the best of his field . . . shall he make restitution* (Exod. 22:4). If, however, it eats them in a public domain, the owner is exempt. If the animal benefits, the owner must pay for the benefit received, not for the damage.

2. Thus if an animal enters the premises of the plaintiff and eats a denar's worth of sesame or lotus or the like, the defendant must pay a denar. If, however, it eats them in a public domain and benefits, they are regarded as if they were barley or hay and the defendant must pay only the value of hay or barley at the cheapest (prevailing) rate.

3. If an animal eats foodstuffs harmful to it, such as wheat, the owner is exempt because it has not benefited. If it eats things that it does not normally eat, such as clothing or utensils, the owner must pay for half of the damage whether the damage is done on the premises of the plaintiff or in a public domain, because this is an abnormal act, and it is usual for persons to set their utensils or garments down in a public domain while they take a short rest.

4. If an animal standing on the plaintiff's premises eats there produce it has plucked from a public domain, the rule is a matter of doubt and therefore the owner need pay only for the benefit the animal receives. If, however, the plaintiff seizes the value of the damage, this may not be reclaimed from him, for the animal has eaten on his premises.

5. If a dog enters a courtyard, seizes a morsel of bread or meat, and takes it out into a public domain or into another courtyard and eats it there, the owner must pay for the benefit it receives.

If, however, the dog eats it in a field belonging to the owner of the courtyard from which it was seized, the defendant must pay for the whole of the damage, as though the dog had eaten it in that courtyard, for it eats on the premises of the plaintiff. The same rule applies in all similar cases.

6. If an animal eats foodstuffs that it does not eat ordinarily but may eat when short of food—for example, if a cow eats barley, or a donkey eats vetches or fish, or a pig eats a slice of meat, or a dog laps oil, or a cat eats dates, or the like—the rule is as follows: If the animal eats the foodstuff on the premises of the plaintiff, the owner must pay for the whole of the damage, but if it eats in a public domain, he is exempt. If it has benefited, the owner must pay for the benefit it receives.

7. If a beast of prey enters the premises of the plaintiff, and devours an animal or meat, its owner must pay for the whole of the damage, for this is its normal behavior. But if a dog eats small sheep or a cat eats fully grown chickens, the act is deemed an abnormal one and the owner need pay for only half of the damage.

8. If a donkey enters private premises and finding a basket of bread breaks the basket and eats the bread, its owner must pay full compensation for both the basket and the bread, since this behavior is normal. Similarly, if a goat sees a turnip or the like on top of a jar and clambers up onto the jar, then eats the turnip and breaks the jar, its owner must pay full compensation for both, since just as it is normal for it to eat, it is also normal for it to climb up onto articles in order to eat. The same rule applies in all similar cases.

If, however, the trespassing donkey first eats the bread and then breaks the basket, its owner must pay full compensation for the bread and half compensation for the basket. The same rule applies in all similar cases.

9. If an animal, while walking along or after halting to eat, eats from the middle of a market square, or even turns its head and eats from the sides of the square, the owner need pay for only the

benefit it receives. If, however, it leaves the open square and stands at the side of the square and eats, the owner must pay for the damage it causes. If it eats in the doorway of a shop, its owner must pay for the benefit it receives; if it eats inside the shop, he must pay for the damage it causes.

10. If an animal walks along a public domain and stretches its neck and eats from off the back of another animal, its owner need pay only for the benefit it receives, even if it halts, since it is normal for animals to eat from off each other's backs. If, however, it rears up and eats with its legs upon the other animal's back, its owner must pay for the damage it causes, because the animal's back is here regarded as the courtyard of the plaintiff.

11. If an animal slips on a stone or on its urine and falls into a garden and breaks its fall on produce or vegetables, or eats them, its owner must pay for the benefit it receives. Even if it goes from one vegetable patch to another, or stays in the garden all day long, the owner need pay only for the benefit it receives. What benefit does it receive from falling on the produce? The fact that it finds a soft spot and its limbs are not dislocated.

If, however, it descends in a normal way and causes damage, its owner must pay for the damage it causes. Even if it soils produce with birth fluid, he must pay for the damage it causes, since there is preliminary negligence. Similarly, if another animal crowds it and it falls, the owner must pay for the damage it causes, because he should have taken them past one by one in order to prevent them from crowding each other.

12. If an animal which has slipped and fallen into a garden comes out of it and then returns to it, the owner must pay for the damage it then causes, even if it returns without his knowledge, because he should have taken care of it and prevented its return. For it is certain that once it knows the way to the garden, it will return of its own accord.

13. If a potter takes his wares into a private householder's courtyard without permission and the householder's animal breaks

them, the householder is exempt. If the animal is damaged by them, the owner of the pots is liable. If, however, they are taken in with permission, he is exempt. If the householder agrees to guard the pots, the householder is liable.

14. Similarly, if one takes his produce into a householder's courtyard without permission and an animal belonging to the householder eats it, the householder is exempt. If the animal slips on it and suffers injury, the owner of the produce is liable. If, however, the produce is taken in with permission, he is exempt. If the householder agrees to guard the produce, the householder is liable. If produce is taken in without permission and the householder's animal eats of it and suffers injury as a result, the owner of the produce is exempt because the animal should not have eaten it.

If one takes produce in with permission and the owner of the courtyard leaves him to guard it, and the householder's animal eats of the produce and suffers damage as a result, the owner of the produce is liable. For when he sees the animal eating things harmful to it and allows it to do so, he incurs liability, seeing that the owner of the courtyard is not there to keep the animal away. In an actual case which once occurred, a woman came to bake in a neighbor's oven and, in order not to watch her during the kneading and baking, the neighbor left her and disappeared. The householder's goat then came and ate the dough and died; and the Sages ruled that the woman who was baking had to pay its value. The same rule applies in all similar cases.

15. If one places a cornstack in another's field without permission and an animal belonging to the owner of the field eats of it, the owner of the field is exempt. If the animal slips on the produce and suffers injury, the owner of the produce is liable. But if the animal eats of it and suffers harm as a result, he is exempt.

If, however, he places the stack there with permission, the owner of the field is liable even if he does not agree to guard it. For when a watchman in charge of a threshing floor says to a person, "Set your stack here," it is equivalent to his saying to him, "Set your stack down and I will watch over it."

CHAPTER IV

1. If one brings sheep into a fold and secures them with a door able to withstand a normal wind and a sheep gets out and does damage, the owner is exempt. If, however, the door is unable to withstand a normal wind or if the walls of the fold are weak, he has not secured his sheep adequately and he is liable if a sheep gets out and causes damage. The owner of the sheep is liable in this case even if the sheep burrows its way out, and even if the partition is broken down at night or by brigands. If, however, the partition is a strong one and is broken down at night or by brigands and a sheep gets out and does damage, the owner is exempt. If brigands take a sheep out and it causes damage, the brigands are liable.

2. If one breaks down a fence enclosing his neighbor's animal so that it gets out and causes damage, the rule is as follows: If the fence is strong and firm he is liable, but if it is weak, he is legally exempt but morally liable. Similarly, if one places poison before another's animal, he is legally exempt but morally liable.

3. If one places another's animal in front of standing corn belonging to a third person, he is obligated to pay for the damage the animal causes. Similarly, if one whips an animal so that it goes into another's standing corn and does damage, he is liable.

4. If one entrusts his animal to a gratuitous bailee or a paid bailee, or to a hirer or a borrower, these take the owner's place, and if the animal causes damage, they are liable. This is the rule only if they do not guard it at all. But if they take proper and adequate care of it, and it gets out and causes damage, they are exempt. If less than adequate care is taken of it, a gratuitous bailee is exempt—the owner being liable even if it kills a person—but a paid bailee, a hirer, or a borrower is liable.

5. If an animal is left (in a pen) exposed to the sun, whoever left it there is liable for the damage it causes even if it burrows its way out. For an animal left in the sun becomes distressed and does everything it can to escape.

6. If one entrusts his animal to the care of a deaf-mute, an idiot, or a minor, the owner is liable even if it is tied up, for it is normal for an ox or a similar animal to work a knot loose and get out and cause damage. Even if the deaf-mute, the idiot, or the minor guards it properly and it burrows its way out and causes damage, the owner is liable.

7. If one entrusts his ox to the care of five people and one of them is negligent so that the ox gets away and causes damage, the rule is as follows: If it can be guarded only by the five of them together, the one who neglects his charge is liable. If, however, it can be guarded by those who remain, they are liable as well.

8. If one borrows an animal, presuming it to be innocuous, and it is found to be forewarned, the rule is as follows: If the borrower knows that it has in fact gored previously, the owner must pay for half of the damage it causes, because wherever the animal goes it bears its owner's name, and the borrower also must pay for half of the damage it causes. For even if it were innocuous, as he believed, he would have to pay for half of the damage, since he knows that it has already gored. If, however, he does not know that it has gored, the borrower is not liable at all and the owner must pay for the whole of the damage caused.

9. If one borrows an animal when it is innocuous and it becomes forewarned while in his care, then when he returns it to the owner, it reverts to its innocuous state, for when its domicile changes the forewarning becomes void. The owner then need pay for only half of the damage it causes and the borrower is exempt because he has returned the animal.

10. If a bailee undertakes merely to take care of the animal and not to prevent its causing damage, and the animal does cause

damage, then he is exempt from paying, but its owner is liable. If, however, the bailee undertakes to prevent its causing damage, and it does cause damage, then he is liable. If it suffers injury, the bailee is exempt and the owner must bring a suit against whoever caused the injury.

11. If one bailee entrusts his charge to another bailee, the first must compensate the plaintiff, because a bailee who entrusts his charge to another bailee is liable, since the plaintiff can say to him, "Why did not you yourself look after the animal instead of entrusting it to another? Pay me compensation and bring suit against the bailee to whom you yourself entrusted it." If, however, the bailee entrusted it to his son or to a member of his household or to an assistant, any one of these takes the bailee's place and is liable.

12. If a bailee who has been ordered to pay compensation is without means and the animal that caused the damage is innocuous—in which case payment for half of the damage caused is due from the animal itself—then the plaintiff may take his compensation from the value of the animal, and the amount collected by the plaintiff becomes a debt owed by the bailee to the owner of the animal.

13. If an animal causes damage to growing crops, the damage is estimated on the basis of a sixty-fold area, and whoever is ordered to pay (compensation), whether owner or bailee, must pay this amount. Thus, if an animal eats an area sown with a *sĕ'ah* of seed, an evaluation is made of the previous value of a portion of the same field sixty times this area, and of its present value after an area of one sĕ'ah has been despoiled, and (compensation) must be paid for the difference. Similarly, if an animal eats an area sown with a *ḳab* or a quarter-ḳab or even a single stalk, it is evaluated as part of sixty times its area.

14. If an animal eats fully ripe produce which is no longer dependent on the soil, the owner must pay the value of fully ripe produce; thus, if it eats a sĕ'ah, the value of a sĕ'ah (must be

paid), and if it eats two sĕ'ah, the value of two sĕ'ah (must be paid).

If an animal eats the fruit of a single date palm, or if a person gathers the fruit of another's date palm and eats it, the rule is as follows: If the tree is a Roman or a similar palm, the dates of which are not choice, it is evaluated as part of sixty-fold together with the land. But if it is a Persian or a similar palm, the dates of which are especially choice, the previous value and the present value of the palm itself is ascertained.

CHAPTER V

1. If an animal at pasture strays into fields and vineyards, the owner should be warned three times even if it has done no damage. If the owner of the animal does not take care of it and prevent it from pasturing there, the owner of the field has the right to slaughter the animal in a ritually valid manner and then say to its owner, "Come and sell your meat." For one is forbidden to cause damage willfully, with the intention of paying for the damage he causes. Even to bring about damage indirectly with this intention is forbidden.

2. Because of this, the Sages forbade the rearing of small cattle or small wild animals in the Land of Israel in regions containing fields or vineyards, but allowed it only in the wooded and desert regions of the Land of Israel. In Syria such animals may be reared anywhere.

3. Joshua and his court made ten stipulations when they apportioned the Land (to the Tribes of Israel). To wit:

i. That small cattle may be pastured in woods consisting of large trees, but large cattle must not be pastured there. Neither small nor large cattle may be pastured in a wood of small trees, except with the owner's consent.

ii. That anyone may gather wood from another's field, provided that it is taken from trees of small value, no better than thorns, such as prickly shrubs and thistles, and provided also that the wood is still fresh and attached to the ground, and that he does not tear out the roots. Other wood, however, is forbidden.

iii. That anyone may collect plants growing wild anywhere, except in a field of fenugreek sown for animal fodder.

iv. That one may take a cutting from any tree other than the stumps of olive trees. One may take cuttings from trees only as follows: from the olive tree, as much as the bulk of an egg; from reeds and vines, above the joint; and from other trees, from the side branches but not from the central stem. Moreover, permission is granted to take cuttings only from newly grown twigs not yet producing fruit, but not from old branches producing fruit. A cutting may be taken from only that part of the tree which does not face the sun.

v. That if a new spring begins to flow, the inhabitants of the city in the limits of which it emerges may supply themselves from it even though its source is not in their domain; but no others can demand to be supplied from it with them.

vi. That anyone may catch fish from the Sea of Tiberias, provided he uses only a fishhook. Only members of the tribe in whose territory the lake is found may spread a net or keep a boat there.

vii. That anyone who must relieve himself may leave the road, go behind the nearest fence and evacuate his bowels there, even if it happens to be a field of saffron. He may also take a stone from there and cleanse himself.

viii. That anyone who is lost among vineyards or similar cultivated lands may cut his way through and go up or down until he comes out on his way.

ix. That whenever a public road becomes very muddy or waterlogged, the travelers have the right to go to the sides of the road and walk there, even on privately owned paths.

x. That an unclaimed dead body acquires title to the place where it is lying and must be buried where it is found, provided it is not lying across a boundary or within the border strip of a city. If it is found on a boundary or within such a border, it must be taken to a cemetery.

4. King Solomon decreed that travelers during the summer might walk on privately owned field paths until the falling of the second rains.

5. All the above enactments are in force everywhere, even outside the Land of Israel.

6. In Babylonia it is forbidden to walk on privately owned paths after the dew has fallen.

7. Although small cattle may not be reared in the Land of Israel, it is permissible to keep them for thirty days before a festival or for thirty days before a son's wedding. A butcher may buy small cattle and slaughter them immediately, or buy and keep them and slaughter them over a period of time, provided that they are not allowed to go out and graze with a herd but are kept at home, so that they may not cause damage.

8. The Sages of long ago forbade the rearing of small cattle and small wild animals in Babylonia as if it were the Land of Israel, because in their day most of its fields and vineyards belonged to Israelites.

9. The Sages also forbade the rearing of pigs everywhere, and of dogs unless they were kept chained. To rear dogs in a town near the border was, however, permitted. A dog must be tied up by day but may be untied at night. The Sages said, "Cursed be he who rears dogs or pigs," because they cause substantial and frequent damage.

10. If a herder (raising small cattle or small wild animals) repents, he is not compelled to sell them all at once but may sell them piecemeal. Similarly, if one inherits dogs or pigs, he is not obliged to sell them all at once but may sell them gradually.

CHAPTER VI

1. What is a forewarned animal? One against which testimony has been presented on three separate days. If it gores or bites or lies down or kicks or jostles with its body even a hundred times on a single day, it is not deemed forewarned. If, however, three different sets of witnesses testify against it on a single day, there is doubt whether it is deemed forewarned or not.

2. Forewarning can take place only in the presence of the owner and before a full court (of three), for Scripture says, *And*

warning hath been given to its owner (Exod. 21:29). There can be no forewarning except during a session of the court.

3. If the ox belonging to a deaf-mute, an idiot, a minor, or a person absent abroad gores, the owner is exempt. The court, however, must appoint a guardian to act for such a person and forewarning may take place in the presence of the guardian.

4. If the ox causes damage after evidence has been offered in the presence of the guardian, the rule is as follows: If the animal is still innocuous, payment from the animal itself must be made for half of the damage it has caused, while if evidence is given against it on three days and it then causes damage, payment from the finest land of the guardian must be made for the whole of the damage caused. When orphan minors come of age, they must answer at law to the guardian and must repay him.

5. Oxen used for sport and trained to gore each other are not deemed forewarned with respect to injury to each other. Even if they kill a person, they do not incur the death penalty, for Scripture says, *If an ox gore* (Exod. 21:28), not "has been incited to gore."

6. If an ox which has been forewarned is sold or given away, it reverts to its innocuous state because change of ownership changes its legal status. But if it is lent or entrusted to a bailee, it retains its (forewarned) status. Similarly, if an ox is forewarned in the presence of a guardian and then the deaf-mute becomes normal, the idiot becomes sane, or the minor comes of age, although the guardian's commission is annulled the ox retains its forewarned status. For these oxen are under their owner's authority.

7. If an animal is forewarned and then discontinues the action with respect to which it was forewarned, it reverts to its innocuous state. Thus, if an ox is forewarned with respect to goring and it then recovers and, although it jostles, refrains from goring, it is deemed innocuous with respect to goring. From what point is recovery assumed? When children handle the ox with-

out its goring. Similarly, in the case of other actions with respect to which it has been forewarned, it remains forewarned until children can handle it without its performing those actions.

8. If an ox is forewarned with respect to its own species, it is not deemed forewarned with respect to a species not its own. An ox forewarned with respect to human beings is not deemed forewarned with respect to animals, and an ox forewarned with respect to minors is not deemed forewarned with respect to adults. Consequently, if it causes damage to the species with respect to which it is forewarned, the owner must pay for the whole of the damage, while if it causes damage to another species, he need pay for (only) half of the damage. If it is forewarned with respect to the Sabbath, it is not deemed forewarned with respect to weekdays. Hence, if it causes damage on a Sabbath, the owner must pay for the whole of the damage, but if on a weekday, he need pay for (only) half of the damage. From what point is its recovery assumed? When children can handle it on the day with respect to which it is forewarned without its causing the damage with respect to which it is forewarned.

9. If an ox gores another ox one day, a donkey the next, and a camel on the third, it becomes forewarned with respect to all of them.

If an ox sees another ox one day and gores it, sees an ox the next day but does not gore it, sees an ox the third day and gores it, sees an ox the fourth day but does not gore it, sees an ox the fifth day and gores it, and sees an ox the sixth day but does not gore it, it becomes forewarned for alternate days with respect to oxen. The same rule applies in all similar cases.

10. If an ox sees another ox one day and gores it, sees a donkey the next day but does not gore it, sees a horse the third day and gores it, sees a camel the fourth day but does not gore it, sees a mule on the fifth day and gores it, and sees a wild ass the sixth day but does not gore it, it becomes forewarned for alternate days with respect to all (three) species. If, therefore, on a day on which

it is regarded as forewarned, it gores one of the three species originally gored on alternate days, it is deemed a forewarned animal.

11. If an ox gores on the fifteenth day of one month, on the sixteenth of the next month and on the seventeenth of the third month, it becomes forewarned only after the interval is repeated a third time.

If it gores on hearing the sound of a horn, and does the same a second time and a third, it becomes forewarned with respect to (the sound of) horns. The same rule applies in all similar cases.

12. If one ox gores three other oxen on three consecutive days, gores a donkey on the fourth, and a camel on the fifth, or if it first gores a donkey and a camel on two consecutive days and then gores three oxen on consecutive days, it remains a matter of doubt whether it is deemed forewarned with respect to oxen only, or whether it is deemed forewarned with respect to all three species.

Similarly, if an ox gores on three consecutive Sabbaths and then on Sunday and Monday, or if it gores on Thursday, on Friday, on the Sabbath and on the two following Sabbaths, it remains a matter of doubt whether it is deemed forewarned with respect to Sabbaths alone, or with respect to all three days, two of which are weekdays.

13. In all these and similar cases of doubt, the owner of the ox that causes the damage is required to pay for only half of the damage, but if the plaintiff seizes the value of the whole of the damage, it may not be reclaimed.

CHAPTER VII

1. If one ties up his ox with a halter and shuts it in securely, and it gets out and causes damage, the rule is as follows: If the ox is innocuous, the owner must pay for half of the damage, but if

it is forewarned, he is exempt. For Scripture says, *And he hath not kept it in* (Exod. 21:29), from which it is inferred that if he does guard it, he is exempt, and this ox was guarded. Similarly, if it causes damage by an act with respect to which it is forewarned from the outset, such as by eating things suitable for it, or by breaking things with its feet while walking, the owner is exempt from paying compensation.

2. If an animal is forewarned with respect to its right horn but not its left, and even though it is properly guarded it gets loose and gores, the owner must pay for half of the damage caused, whether such damage is done with its right horn or with its left.

3. If an animal injures a person, whether intentionally or unintentionally, the rule is as follows: If it is innocuous, the owner must pay compensation for half of the injury from the animal itself, whereas if it is forewarned, he must pay for the whole of the injury. He is, however, exempt from payment of compensation for enforced idleness, humiliation, pain, and medical treatment, because the Law has confined liability for these other effects to the case of one human being who injures another. But if an animal injures a human being, the rule is the same as if it had damaged his property, namely, that the owner is liable for the damage alone. Consequently, if one's ox causes humiliation, the owner is exempt, whereas if he himself causes humiliation, he is liable, as will be explained. Again, if one's ox injures his father or his mother or sets fire to another's cornstack on the Sabbath, the owner is liable for the damage, whereas if he himself does these things, he would not have to pay, as will be explained.

4. If one takes his ox into a privately owned courtyard without permission, and the householder's ox gores it or his dog bites it, the householder is exempt. If, however, it gores the ox belonging to the householder, the rule is as follows: If it is innocuous, its owner must pay for half of the damage; if it is forewarned, he must pay for the whole of the damage, as is the rule when an ox gores in a public domain.

5. If an ox falls into a well in the courtyard and fouls its water, the rule is that if it fouls the water immediately upon falling in, its owner is liable for the damage to the water. If, however, it fouls the water after an interval, he is exempt, because the ox is then considered an obstacle classed as a pit, and the water is like any other inanimate object, and the owner of a pit is not liable for damage to inanimate objects, as will be explained.

If, however, the owner takes the ox in with permission, he is exempt. If the householder undertakes to guard it, he is liable for any injury suffered by the ox if it falls into the well.

6. If one takes his ox into a private courtyard without permission and it injures the householder or the householder injures himself on it, or if it burrows pits or trenches or caves in the courtyard, the owner of the ox is liable for the damage to the courtyard, while the owner of the courtyard is liable for damage caused by the "pit," since it is his duty to close it up.

7. If the householder injures the ox, the rule is as follows: If he injures it unintentionally, he is exempt, for he can say to the owner, "Why did you enter without permission? For I did not know of your presence until I injured it inadvertently." If, however, he injures the ox deliberately, he is liable for the whole of the damage because, while he has the right to turn it out of his premises, he has no right to injure it.

8. An evaluation must be made in the case of damages. Thus, if a person or his animal breaks an article belonging to another, one may not say to the person who causes the damage, "Take the broken article and pay the original value of the article"; rather the amount by which the article has depreciated from its original value is estimated, and the defendant must give the plaintiff the whole of the depreciation, if the animal that caused the injury is forewarned, or half of the depreciation, if it is innocuous. For when Scripture says, *And the dead beast shall be his* (Exod. 21:34), it refers to the plaintiff.

Depreciation of a carcass is borne by the plaintiff. Appreciation of the carcass is shared between the plaintiff and the defendant.

9. Thus, if an ox worth two hundred is gored and dies and the carcass is worth one hundred at the time, but by the time the case is tried in court it has depreciated and is worth only eighty, the defendant need pay only one hundred if his animal was forewarned, while if it was innocuous, he need pay (only) fifty from the animal itself.

10. If the carcass appreciates, however, and is worth one hundred and twenty by the time the case is tried in court, then the defendant must pay ninety if his animal was forewarned, while if it was innocuous he need pay (only) forty-five from the animal itself. For the meaning of the scriptural verse, *And the dead also they shall divide* (Exod. 21:35), is that any appreciation of the dead animal is shared by halves.

11. If an ox worth two hundred gores an ox of equal value and lessens its value by fifty, but by the time the case is tried in court the injured ox has appreciated and is worth four hundred—although had it not depreciated because of the goring, it would now have appreciated to eight hundred—then whether it appreciated by being fattened or of its own accord, the defendant need pay compensation based only on the value at the time the damage was caused.

If by the time the case is tried in court the ox has grown lean because of the blow it received and has depreciated to the extent of one hundred, the defendant must pay compensation based on the value at the time the case is tried in court.

12. If the injuring animal has appreciated by the time the case is tried in court, the rule is as follows: If it has appreciated because the owner fattened it, the plaintiff may take compensation based only on the amount it was worth at the time it caused the damage. If, however, it has appreciated of its own accord, he may take compensation for half of the damage from the full value of the animal at the time the case is tried in court.

13. The defendant is responsible for the delivery of the carcass to the plaintiff. Thus, if the ox falls into a pit and dies, he must

raise the carcass from the pit and give it to the plaintiff, and then the depreciation of the carcass is estimated for him. For when Scripture says, *He shall give money unto the owner and the dead beast shall be his* (Exod. 21:34), it means that he must return the carcass to the plaintiff, together with the depreciation from its living state; or if an innocuous animal injured it, together with half the depreciation, as we have explained.

CHAPTER VIII

1. If an ox belonging to an Israelite gores an ox belonging to the Sanctuary, or if an ox belonging to the Sanctuary gores an ox belonging to an Israelite, the owner is exempt, since Scripture says, *The ox of his neighbor* (Exod. 21:35).

The law of compensation for damage does not apply to any consecrated animal subject to the law of sacrilege.

Consecrated animals which have become disqualified are subject to the law of compensation for damage whether they cause damage or suffer injury, since they are redeemable and become profane after redemption.

2. If an animal designated as a peace offering causes damage, compensation may be claimed from its flesh, but no meat can be claimed for the share of damage attributable to the sacrificial portions, since the sacrificial portions of lesser Hallowed Offerings are subject to the law of sacrilege, as we have explained in the Laws Concerning Sacrilege. Similarly, if an animal designated as a thank offering causes damage, compensation may be collected from its flesh, but not from the bread accompanying the offering, since the bread is not part of the meat.

3. How is the compensation taken? The plaintiff and his guests may eat in ritual holiness a quantity of meat equal in value to half of the damage he has suffered.

What is meant by his being unable to collect from the share attributable to the sacrificial portions? If he is entitled to claim a denar's worth as compensation for half of the damage, and the meat together with the sacrificial portion is worth two denar, whereas the meat alone is worth a denar and a half, he may not collect two thirds of the meat but only half of it.

4. Similarly, if an ownerless ox causes damage, there is no liability, because when Scripture says, *The ox of his neighbor* (*ibid.*), it indicates that it must be the property of a specific owner. Thus, if an ownerless ox gores, and someone comes and takes possession of it before the plaintiff can seize it, he is exempt. Furthermore, if an ox with a specific owner causes damage, and the owner dedicates it or renounces his ownership of it after it has caused the damage, he is exempt, for there is no liability unless the ox has an owner both at the time it causes the damage and at the time the case is tried in court.

5. If an ox belonging to an Israelite gores an ox belonging to a heathen, the owner is exempt whether it is innocuous or forewarned. For heathen do not hold one responsible for damage caused by one's animals, and their own law is applied to them. However, if an ox belonging to a heathen gores an ox belonging to an Israelite, the owner must pay for the full damage caused whether his ox is innocuous or forewarned. This is a fine imposed upon heathen because, being heedless of the scriptural commandments, they do not remove sources of damage. Accordingly, should they not be held liable for damage caused by their animals, they would not take care of them and thus would inflict loss on other people's property.

6. If an innocuous ox has caused damage and its owner sells it before the case is tried in court, the plaintiff can collect compensation from it, although the sale is valid, and the purchaser must reclaim from the defendant, who sold it to him. For when an animal causes damage, people know about it and the purchaser should not have bought it before the plaintiff collected his compensation.

7. If the defendant dedicates it, it becomes consecrated, lest people say that dedicated property can become profane without

redemption. If he slaughters it, the plaintiff may collect his compensation from its carcass. If he gives it away as a gift, his act is valid, but the plaintiff may collect compensation from it.

8. If an animal causes damage and the case is tried in court and the owner sells it afterwards, the sale is not valid; if he dedicates it, it does not become consecrated; if he gives it away, his act is not valid. If creditors of the defendant seize the animal first, they do not acquire title to it, whether he contracted the debt before it caused damage or whether it caused damage before he contracted the debt; but the plaintiff may collect his compensation from it. For even if it had belonged to the creditors from the outset and then caused damage, the plaintiff would have claimed compensation from the animal itself.

9. If a forewarned animal causes damage, and its owner dedicates it or sells it or gives it away or slaughters it, his act is valid, whether the case has been tried in court or not. If his creditors lead it away first, they do acquire title to it, whether he contracted the debt before it caused the damage, or whether it caused the damage before he contracted the debt. This is because the plaintiff is paid from the finest of the defendant's property only, and all his property is subject to a lien for compensation for this damage.

10. If the court intervenes to collect compensation for a plaintiff from the property of the defendant, it must collect from his movable property first. If he has no movable property, or does not have sufficient to cover the whole of the damage, it may collect the remainder from the defendant's finest real property. But as long as there is movable property to be found, even if it be bran, the court may not intervene to seize land.

11. If the defendant dies before paying compensation, the court may not intervene to collect movable property of the orphan heirs, but may seize only land. It should seize inferior land for the plaintiff, because he now has the legal status of a creditor, and movable property is not subject to lien by creditors. If, however,

the plaintiff has seized movable property during the lifetime of the defendant, the court may attach this property for the plaintiff after the defendant's death.

12. The Geonim have made a regulation permitting a creditor's claim to be enforced against movable property, and this regulation has been accepted in all courts of law. Consequently, compensation for damage may now be collected by the court for the plaintiff from the movable property of orphans. If, however, the defendant has left no movable property, the court must collect for the plaintiff from the inferior land, because, as we have already explained, if one seeks to collect compensation from the property of orphans, he can collect it only from inferior land.

13. Unless there is clear proof from witnesses eligible to testify, compensation for damage may not be paid a plaintiff, liability for ransom may not be collected, nor may the animal be killed. One must not think that because only slaves, shepherds, or similar persons are generally found in horse stables, cattle stalls, or sheep pens, these should be heard if they testify that one animal has caused damage to another, or that children or women should be relied on if they testify that one person has wounded another or if they testify about other types of damage. This is not the case. No one may ever be required to pay compensation on the evidence of witnesses unless they are eligible to give evidence in other cases and a court decrees that the defendant must pay.

14. If an ox is grazing on the bank of a river, and a dead ox is found at its side, then even if the dead ox has been gored and the live ox is forewarned with respect to goring, or even if the dead ox has been bitten and the live ox is forewarned with respect to biting, we do not say it is certain that the live ox bit or gored the other. Even if a camel runs amuck among other camels and one is found dead beside it, we do not say the amuck camel definitely killed the other unless eligible witnesses saw it do so.

CHAPTER IX

1. If an animal about to calve causes damage, compensation for half of the damage may be collected from both it and its calf, since the latter is part of its body. If, however, a hen causes damage, compensation cannot be collected from its egg, because the egg is not deemed part of its body, but is separate and distinct from it.

2. If an animal about to calve gores, and its calf is found by its side, and it is uncertain whether it calved before it gored or afterwards, the owner must pay for half of the damage from the cow, and the plaintiff cannot collect at all from the calf unless he presents proof that the animal was still in calf at the time it gored. For the burden of proof rests with the person who seeks to extract money from another.

3. If an ox gores a cow in calf and the calf is found aborted at its side, and it is uncertain whether the cow dropped the calf before it was gored or as a result of the goring, compensation must be paid for the damage to the cow but not for the damage to the calf, since the burden of proof rests with the person who seeks to extract money from another.

4. If an ox gores a cow in calf and the calf is aborted, the depreciation of the cow and that of the calf are not estimated separately; rather an estimation is made of how much the cow was worth when in calf and healthy and how much it and the aborted calf are now worth. The owner of the ox must then pay for the depreciation, or for half of it if the ox was innocuous.

5. If the cow belongs to one person and the calf to another, the payment for the shrinkage of the body of the cow belongs to the owner of the cow, and the remaining depreciation is shared between the owner of the cow and the owner of the calf, and the aborted calf belongs to its owner.

6. If an ox pursues another ox which is later found injured, and the owner of the injured ox says, "Your ox caused the damage,"

while the other replies, "I do not know, but your ox may have hurt itself on a stone," then the burden of proof rests with the one seeking to extract compensation from the other, even though the plaintiff says, "I know for certain," and the defendant says, "I do not know."

If the plaintiff asserts, "You know for certain that your ox caused the damage," the defendant must swear an oath of inducement that he does not know. This is the rule if the ox is forewarned. If it is innocuous, he is exempt even from an informal oath because he would also be exempt even if he admitted of his own accord, since payment for half of the damage is regarded as a fine, and the rule is that one who admits a charge entailing the penalty of a fine is exempt.

7. If two oxen pursue another, and witnesses testify that one of the oxen causes damage but they do not know which one it was, the rule is as follows: If one owner says, "Your ox caused the damage," and the other says, "Your ox caused the damage," both owners are exempt. If, however, both oxen belong to a single person, he must pay compensation from the less valuable of the two animals. If both oxen are forewarned, the owner must pay for the whole of the damage from his property.

8. The above rule applies when both oxen can be produced. If, however, one of them is dead or lost, and if either of them is innocuous, the owner is exempt even if both belong to him. For he can say, "Bring proof that the one here is the one which caused the damage and I will pay you."

9. If one of the two pursuing oxen is large and the other is small and the plaintiff says the large ox caused the damage while the defendant says the small one caused the damage, or if one ox is innocuous and the other forewarned and the plaintiff says the forewarned animal caused the damage while the defendant says the innocuous animal caused the damage, the burden of proof rests with the one seeking to extract compensation from the other.

10. If there is no clear proof that a particular animal has caused the damage, but witnesses testify that it was one of two oxen, the defendant must pay in accordance with his own admission. If, however, the plaintiff pleads, "You know for certain that this particular ox caused the damage in your presence," the defendant must take a scriptural oath and pay whatever he admits, seeing that he has admitted part of the claim.

11. If there are two injured oxen, one large and one small, and two injuring oxen, one large and one small, and the plaintiff says that the large ox injured the other large one and the small ox the small one, while the defendant says it is not so but that the small ox injured the large one and the large one the small one; or if one ox is innocuous and one forewarned, and the plaintiff says that the forewarned ox injured the large one and the innocuous ox injured the small one, while the defendant says that the innocuous ox injured the large one and the forewarned ox injured the small one, then the burden of proof rests with the person seeking to extract compensation from the other. If there is no clear proof, the defendant is exempt. For this is similar to the case of one who claims wheat from another person who admits owing barley, in which the rule is that the defendant must take an oath of inducement and is exempt from paying even the value of barley, as will be explained in the Laws Concerning Pleading. If the plaintiff has seized the oxen, he may take compensation for the smaller ox from the larger and for the larger ox from the smaller, this being the damage admitted by the defendant. If, however, he has not seized the oxen, nothing at all may be extracted from the defendant.

12. If, after goring one ox, an ox gores a second one, the owner of the first gored ox and the owner of the goring ox are regarded as co-owners of the goring ox. Thus if an ox worth two hundred gores another ox worth two hundred, and the carcass of the gored ox is worth nothing at all, then the plaintiff is entitled to receive one hundred and the defendant one hundred. If the ox now gores another ox worth two hundred, and the carcass of the gored ox

is worth nothing at all, the second plaintiff is entitled to receive one hundred and the first plaintiff and the defendant receive fifty *zuz* each. If the ox now gores another ox worth two hundred, and the carcass of the gored ox is worth nothing at all, the third plaintiff is entitled to receive one hundred, the second plaintiff fifty, and the first plaintiff and the defendant twenty-five each. And division is continually made in this manner.

13. If a plaintiff seizes the animal which has caused damage, in order to collect from it half of the damage he has suffered, he is deemed its paid bailee with respect to future damage, so that if it strays and causes more damage, he is liable and the owner is exempt. Thus if an ox worth two hundred gores and inflicts a loss of two hundred, and the plaintiff seizes it to collect one hundred compensation from it, and it then gores again and inflicts a loss of one hundred and forty, then the second plaintiff is paid seventy, the first plaintiff—who seized the ox—is paid the remainder of the amount due to him as compensation for the damage he suffered, which is thirty, and the original owner retains one hundred. This rule applies in all similar cases.

14. If two innocuous oxen cause each other (different) injuries, half compensation of the surplus must be paid (for the more severe injury). If both oxen are forewarned, or if a forewarned animal and a person injure each other, full compensation of the surplus must be paid. If one ox is innocuous and the other is forewarned, the owner of the forewarned ox must pay the owner of the innocuous ox full compensation for the surplus, or the owner of the innocuous ox must pay the owner of the forewarned ox half compensation for the surplus.

Thus if an innocuous ox causes another innocuous ox a loss of one hundred, and the latter in turn causes the former a loss of forty, the owner of the former must pay the owner of the latter thirty. If both oxen are forewarned, the owner of the first must pay sixty. If the first is forewarned and the second is innocuous, the owner of the first must pay eighty. If the first is innocuous and the second is forewarned, the owner of the first must pay ten.

CHAPTER X

1. If an ox kills a person anywhere, whether an adult or a minor, a slave or a freeman, it incurs death by stoning whether it is innocuous or forewarned. However, if it kills a heathen, it is exempt in accordance with heathen law.

2. It makes no difference whether it is an ox or another domestic animal, or whether it is a wild animal or a bird—if any of these kills a person, it incurs death by stoning.

What difference is there between an innocuous animal which kills a person and a forewarned animal which kills a person? Only that the innocuous animal does not entail the payment of ransom, whereas the forewarned one entails payment of ransom provided that it is forewarned with respect to the killing of humans.

3. Since any domestic or wild animal or any bird which kills a person is to be stoned, how can any be found forewarned with respect to the killing of humans, so that its owner would be obligated to pay ransom? It is when an ox kills three heathen first and then kills an Israelite, seeing that an animal forewarned with respect to killing heathen is also forewarned with respect to Israelites; or when one kills three fatally ill Israelites and then kills one in good health; or when an ox has killed previously and escaped and is caught after a fourth killing, for the owner is not liable for payment of ransom unless the ox is to be stoned. Similarly, an ox which mortally injures three human beings at one time, or which kills three animals, becomes forewarned with respect to killing, and its owner must pay ransom.

The same rule applies if witnesses identify the owner of an ox but do not identify the ox on the first, second, or third occasions, and on the fourth they see an ox belonging to the same owner kill, without knowing whether this is the ox which killed on the three previous occasions or is another ox: for since the owner has been warned that he has an ox in his herd which has killed three times, it is his duty to keep guard over all his animals, and since he does not keep guard, he must therefore pay ransom.

4. Concerning the law of Scripture, *And its owner also shall be put to death* (Exod. 21:29), it is learned from tradition that this pronouncement refers to death at the Hand of Heaven, but if the owner pays ransom for the person killed by his ox, this will be his atonement. Although the ransom is merely in the nature of atonement, the court may forcefully exact bond from anyone liable to pay ransom.

5. If an ox belonging to two partners kills, each must pay the full ransom, for each needs complete atonement.

6. If the ox has an owner, the trial cannot be concluded except in the presence of the owner. If, however, it has no owner, as, for example, a wild ox or an ox of the Sanctuary or the ox belonging to a proselyte who has died without heirs, it must be stoned if it kills, and the trial is concluded even though it has no owner. Similarly, an ox belonging to a woman, or to orphans, or to guardians, must be stoned if it kills. Guardians need not pay ransom, because ransom is a form of atonement, and minors, deaf-mutes, and imbeciles are not legally culpable and do not require atonement.

7. If an ox with an organic defect kills a person, or if the ox belongs to a person who has an organic defect, it is not stoned, for the verse in Scripture, *And its owner also shall be put to death* (*ibid.*) makes the death of the ox analogous to the death of the owner. Since the owner is here regarded as if he were dead and thus need not be put to death, the ox is exempt.

8. If one incites a dog against another person and it kills him, the dog is not to be stoned. The same rule applies if one incites a domestic or a wild animal against another person and it kills him. If, however, one incites a serpent, or even if he causes the serpent to bite a person, and it kills him, the serpent is stoned, for the serpent expels its deadly venom of its own accord. Consequently, the one who has caused the serpent to bite is exempt from the death penalty at the hands of the court.

9. An animal that kills is not stoned unless it has intended to injure a victim for whose death it would be condemned. If an ox intends to kill an animal but kills a human being, or intends to kill a heathen but kills an Israelite, or intends to kill a prematurely born infant but kills a living child, it is exempt from the death penalty. If it is forewarned, the owner is obligated to pay ransom, or to pay a fine if it kills a slave, even if it kills without intention, since it is forewarned with respect to this deed.

10. If an animal is forewarned with respect to tumbling onto human beings in pits, and it notices green vegetables in a pit and tumbles into the pit on account of the green vegetables, but there is a person in the pit and he is killed, or if it is forewarned with respect to rubbing its body against walls and causing these to fall on human beings, and it rubs itself against a wall for its own pleasure and causes it to fall upon a person, and he dies, then the ox is exempt from the death penalty because it has had no intention to kill; but the owner must pay ransom, because the animal was forewarned with regard to tumbling onto people in pits or causing walls to fall upon people.

How can one know that the ox was rubbing itself for pleasure? If it goes on rubbing itself after it has caused the wall to fall and kill.

11. No owner need pay ransom unless his animal kills outside his premises. But if it kills on his premises, then although it is liable for stoning, the owner is exempt from paying ransom. Thus if one enters a privately owned courtyard without the owner's permission—even if he enters to collect wages or a debt from the owner—and the householder's ox gores him and he dies, the ox must be stoned, but the owner is exempt from paying ransom since the victim had no right to enter another's premises without the owner's consent.

12. If one stands at the entrance and calls to the householder, and the householder answers, "Yes," and he then enters and is gored by the householder's ox and dies, the owner is exempt, for

"Yes" means no more than "Stay where you are until I speak to you."

13. If an animal enters the courtyard of the plaintiff and while walking it treads upon a child and kills it, the owner must pay ransom, because the foot is deemed forewarned to cause damage while the animal is walking, and the owner is responsible also for damage by tooth and foot in the courtyard of the plaintiff, as we have explained.

Thus it is clear that if a forewarned animal kills intentionally, it must be stoned and the owner must pay ransom; but if it kills unintentionally, it is exempt from the death penalty, although the owner must still pay ransom. If, however, an innocuous animal kills unintentionally, it is exempt from the death penalty and the owner need not pay ransom; but if it intends to kill, it must be stoned, although the owner is still exempt from paying ransom and, similarly, from the fine payable for killing a slave.

14. It is my opinion that although the owner of an innocuous animal which kills a slave or a bondwoman intentionally is exempt from the fine of thirty *sela'* prescribed by law, he must pay half the value of the slave or half the value of the bondwoman from the animal itself if it kills unintentionally, exactly as he would if it killed another's ox or donkey.

CHAPTER XI

1. What is the amount to be paid as ransom? Whatever the judges consider to be the value of the person killed. Everything depends on the value of the person killed, because Scripture says, *Then he shall give for the redemption of his life whatsoever is laid upon him* (Exod. 21:30).

The ransom for slaves, whether adults or minors, male or female, is the fine fixed by law, thirty sela' of fine silver, whether the slave is actually worth one hundred *mina* or only a denar.

The killing of a slave whose document of manumission has

been delayed does not entail payment of the fine, since he has no master, for he has acquired his freedom.

2. To whom is ransom to be given? To the heirs of the person killed. If a woman is killed, the ransom goes to the heirs on her father's side and not to her husband. If an ox kills one who is half slave and half free, half of the fine must be paid to his master; the other half should properly be paid also, but there is no one entitled to receive it.

3. If an ox gores a pregnant woman and her offspring comes forth prematurely, the owner is exempt from paying for the value of the child, even if the ox is forewarned with respect to goring. For Scripture imposes liability to pay the value of such infants on humans only.

4. If an ox gores a pregnant bondwoman and her child comes forth, the owner must pay the value of the child, for this is as if the ox gored a she-ass about to foal. If the ox is innocuous, its owner must pay half the value of the child from the ox itself.

5. How is the value of the child assessed? We estimate how much the bondwoman was worth when she was pregnant and how much she is worth now. Her master must then be given the depreciation caused, or half of it, as the case may be. If the ox kills the bondwoman, its owner must pay only the ransom fixed by law, as we have explained.

6. If an ox intending to gore an animal gores a person—although, as we have explained, its owner would be exempt if it killed him—the owner is responsible for damage if it wounds him. If the ox is innocuous, its owner must pay for half of the damage from the ox itself, and if it is forewarned, he must pay for the whole of the damage.

7. If an innocuous ox kills and also causes damage, it must be tried on the capital charge and not on the money charge. If, however, a forewarned animal kills and causes damage, it must be tried first on the money charge and then on the capital charge. If

it is tried first on the capital charge, it must be tried nevertheless on the money charge as well.

8. From what is payment made? From the profit obtained by the labor of the animal after its trial is concluded. For once the trial is concluded with the sentence of stoning, the animal has no legal owner to be held responsible for the damage it has caused. If it is tried on the capital charge and escapes (from custody), it may not be tried on the money charge.

9. If an ox kills a person and its owner dedicates it, it does not become consecrated. Similarly, if the owner relinquishes his ownership of it, it does not become ownerless. If he sells it, the sale is not legally valid. If a bailee returns it to its owner, this return is not recognized by law. If the owner slaughters it, no benefit may be had from its meat. This rule applies after the trial has concluded with the sentence of stoning. Before the trial has concluded with the sentence of stoning, however, if the owner dedicates it, it becomes consecrated; if he relinquishes his ownership of it, it becomes ownerless; if he sells it, the sale is legally valid; if a bailee returns it to its owner, the return is recognized by law; and if its owner slaughters it, it may be eaten.

10. If an ox whose trial has not been concluded becomes mixed with other oxen, all are exempt, because the trial of an ox can be concluded only when the ox is present, exactly as is the rule concerning the trial of a person. If its trial has been concluded and it then becomes mixed with other oxen—even with a thousand others—all must be stoned and buried and are forbidden for use, as is the rule concerning any animal condemned to be stoned.

11. If a cow in calf kills a person, and, so too, if a sexual offense is committed with such an animal, the unborn calf is analogous to the mother: both mother and unborn calf gore; both mother and unborn calf are abused.

12. If a cow gores and kills and then becomes pregnant, the rule is as follows: If it becomes pregnant before its trial is concluded

and also calves before the conclusion of the trial, benefit from the calf is permissible. If, however, it calves after the conclusion of the trial, benefit from the calf is deemed forbidden, since an unborn calf is regarded as part of its mother.

If the calf becomes mixed with others, all must be kept in confinement until they die.

13. If an ox is condemned to be stoned by the testimony of witnesses who are proved guilty of conspiracy, the rule is that whoever seizes the ox first becomes the owner of it, for immediately after the trial is concluded, the owner relinquishes his ownership. If, however, witnesses testify that the owner has abused it and they are subsequently proved guilty of conspiracy, the ox still belongs to the original owner, and if anyone else seizes it, he does not thereby acquire ownership, for since the owner is aware that he did not sin and that these are false witnesses, and he hopes to be able to prove them conspirators, he has not relinquished his ownership.

CHAPTER XII

1. If one digs a pit in a public domain and an ox or a donkey falls into it and dies, the owner of the pit must pay for the whole of the damage caused, even if the pit is full of wool shearings or the like. For Scripture says, *The owner of the pit shall make it good* (Exod. 21:34). This rule applies whether it is an ox or an ass or any other domestic animal or wild animal or bird. Ox and ass are mentioned in Scripture only because they are the usual cases.

2. Whether one digs a pit in a public domain, or on his own property and opens it onto a public domain or onto another's premises, or digs or opens a pit on his own premises and then declares his premises ownerless but does not declare the pit ownerless, he is liable for the damage it causes. If, however, he declares both premises and pit ownerless, or declares the pit inside his premises ownerless or consecrates it, he is exempt. For when Scripture

says, *The owner of the pit shall make it good* (*ibid.*), it indicates that this law applies only to a pit that has an owner. Here the pit is ownerless; moreover, when he first dug the pit, he had the right to do so since he dug it inside his own domain.

3. Whether one digs a pit deliberately or whether it has been formed of itself or by a domestic or a wild animal, the owner is liable for the damage it causes, since it is his duty to fill it up or cover it and he has not done so. It makes no difference whether one digs a pit or purchases it or is given it as a present, for when Scripture says, *The owner of the pit shall make it good* (*ibid.*), it means every case in which the pit has an owner.

4. It makes no difference whether one digs a pit or whether one uncovers a pit that was covered, for Scripture says, *And if a man shall open a pit—or if a man shall dig* (Exod. 21:33). If one covers it properly, he is exempt even if the cover becomes worm-eaten on the inside and an ox falls into the pit and dies. For Scripture says, *And he does not cover it* (*ibid.*), implying that if he covers it, he is exempt.

If one covers a pit with something that can bear oxen but cannot bear camels, and camels walk over the cover and weaken it and then oxen walk over it and fall into the pit, the rule is as follows: If camels are unusual at that place, he is exempt, because this is deemed an accident; but if camels do come there, even at intervals, he is liable.

5. If the cover becomes worm-eaten on the inside and oxen fall into the pit, he is exempt even though camels are always present at that place and he was thus negligent with respect to camels, seeing that it was on account of the cover being worm-eaten that the oxen fell in. The same rule applies in all similar cases.

6. If one finds a pit and covers it and then uncovers it again, the owner of the pit is liable and the finder is exempt. If the finder fills it up with earth and then removes the earth, he is himself liable, because as soon as he fills it up with earth, the act of the original owner is deemed undone.

7. If a cistern is jointly owned by two persons and one of them (draws from it and) leaves it without covering it, and then the other leaves it without covering it, the first one continues to be liable until he has handed his bucket to the second. Once he has handed the bucket to his partner to draw water from the pit, he becomes exempt and his partner becomes obligated to cover it. If the first one does cover it and the second comes and finds it uncovered yet does not cover it, it is he who becomes liable. How long does the second one alone remain liable? Until the first learns that the pit is uncovered and has had time to engage workmen to cut down cedars and cover the pit. For any fatal accident that occurs within that time, only the second is liable; for any fatal accident that occurs after that time both must pay compensation, since both were negligent with regard to the pit.

8. If one entrusts his pit to a bailee, the bailee is liable for any damage it causes. If one entrusts it to a deaf-mute or an imbecile or a minor, the owner is liable even if it is covered, for a pit is likely to become uncovered and these have not the sense to guard it.

9. If one covers his water pit with another person's lid, and the owner of the lid comes and removes it, the owner of the pit is liable for any damage occurring thereafter.

10. A single rule applies whether one digs a pit or a trench or a cave or a ditch. The reason why Scripture mentions a pit is to teach that it must be deep enough to kill. What is considered deep enough to kill? A depth of ten handbreadths. If, however, it is less than ten handbreadths deep, and an ox or other domestic or wild animal or a bird falls into it and dies, the owner is exempt. If any of these suffers injury only, the owner of the obstacle must pay full compensation.

11. If the depth of the pit is nine handbreadths and one of these is under water, the owner is liable, because one handbreadth of water is deemed equivalent to a depth of two handbreadths of dry soil. If it is eight handbreadths deep and two of the eight are under water, or if it is seven handbreadths deep and three of the

seven are under water, and an ox or the like falls into it and dies, we do not require the owner of the pit to pay compensation. If, however, the plaintiff seizes compensation, it cannot be reclaimed from him, because in these cases the rule is in doubt.

12. If one digs a pit ten handbreadths deep, and another person comes and increases its depth to twenty, and yet another comes and increases its depth to thirty, all are liable. If one digs even one handbreadth less than ten and another comes and completes ten handbreadths, the second person is liable whether he digs the additional handbreadth or builds a rim a handbreadth high around its edge. If he fills in the handbreadth that he has added or demolishes the handbreadth that he has built, the rule is in doubt whether or not the act of the first person is deemed undone.

13. If one digs a deep pit and another comes and broadens it, and an ox falls into it and dies, the rule is as follows: If the ox dies as a result of the asphyxiating atmosphere of the pit, the second person is exempt because his action has rendered the atmosphere less asphyxiating. If, however, it dies as a result of concussion, he is liable since he has increased the likelihood that the pit will cause this damage. Similarly, if the ox falls in on the side on which the second person has broadened it, he is liable even if it dies as a result of the asphyxiating atmosphere, since he has increased the likelihood that the pit will cause this damage. If, however, it falls in on the side dug by the first person, the latter is liable, since the second person has rendered the atmosphere of the pit less asphyxiating.

14. Scripture prescribes liability for damage by a pit even if the animal dies solely because of the asphyxiating atmosphere, the case of death as a result of concussion being self-evident. If, therefore, the depth of the pit is the same as its breadth across, it has no asphyxiating atmosphere and, consequently, if an animal does not suffer concussion in it but nevertheless dies, the owner is exempt. If, however, the depth is greater than the breadth, the pit has an asphyxiating atmosphere, and so if an animal dies in it, the

owner is liable even if it does not suffer concussion on the floor of the pit.

15. If one raises a mound on a public domain, and an animal runs into it and dies, the rule is as follows: If the mound is ten handbreadths high, the owner must pay compensation; but if it is less than ten handbreadths, he is exempt from liability for the animal's death. If, however, the animal is merely injured, the owner must pay for the whole of the damage caused, however small the height of a mound or the depth of a cavity. For damage by an obstacle of small size is a common and well-known phenomenon, whereas death because of a small obstacle is not common and is regarded as due to an accident.

16. Similarly, one is not liable for an animal's death in a pit or for the concussion a mound causes to it unless the animal is small or deaf-mute or witless or blind or it falls in at night. If, however, it is a normal animal and it falls in by day and dies, he is exempt, because this is like an accident, since animals usually see obstacles and avoid them. Likewise, if a person falls into it and dies, even if he is blind or falls in at night, the owner is exempt, whether the victim is a freeman or a slave. If, however, a person or a normal animal is injured by the pit, the owner must pay for the whole of the damage, as we have explained.

17. If an ox, (redeemed from dedication after it has become) unfit for sacrifice, falls into a pit and dies, the owner is exempt, for when Scripture says, *And the dead beast shall be his* (Exod. 21:34), it refers to a dead animal which has an owner and so excludes this case, in which use of the carcass is forbidden and it must be buried.

18. If one is digging inside a pit and because of the noise of the digging an animal falls into it and dies, the rule is as follows: If it falls forward, the owner is liable, but if it falls backward, as when it is startled and moves backwards on its haunches and falls and dies, he is exempt. For Scripture says, *And there fall* (Exod. 21:33), meaning that it must fall in the normal manner. If it falls

forward outside the pit because of the sound of the digging and it dies, the court cannot require the owner to pay, but if the plaintiff seizes compensation, it cannot be reclaimed. If, however, the animal falls backward outside the pit and it dies or is hurt, the owner of the pit is exempt.

19. If an ox pushes an animal into a pit and it dies, the rule is as follows: If the ox is forewarned, the owner of the pit must pay half and the owner of the ox must pay half. If it is innocuous, however, the owner of the ox must pay one quarter from the animal itself, and the owner of the pit must pay three quarters from his best property. For the owner of the carcass can say to the owner of the pit: "You owe me for the depreciation of this dead animal; for since it was pushed into the pit, even though it was full-grown and normal, its case is the same as though it fell in at night. Whatever I am able to get from the owner of the ox I shall extract from him, but you must pay the rest."

20. Similarly, if one places a stone near the mouth of a pit and an ox coming along stumbles over it and falls into the pit and dies, the one who has placed the stone there must pay half and the owner of the pit must pay half.

21. So, too, if a privately owned ox and a dedicated one which has become unfit for sacrifice (and is unredeemed) gore at one time, the rule is as follows: If the privately owned ox is innocuous, its owner must pay for half of the damage, but if it is forewarned, he must pay for the whole of the damage. For the plaintiff can say to its owner, "I could extract whatever I am able to get from the other party, and the remainder would come from you. But since the other ox is Temple property and is exempt, you must pay me the whole amount due."

22. If one is digging a pit in a public domain and an ox falls upon him and kills him, the owner of the ox is exempt. If the ox dies also, the owner of the ox can exact payment for the value of his ox from the heirs of the owner of the pit.

CHAPTER XIII

1. If articles fall into a pit and are broken, the owner of the pit is exempt. For since Scripture says, *And an ox or an ass fall therein* (Exod. 21:33), the Sages learned from tradition that *ox* implies "but not a human being," and *ass* implies "but not articles." Even if an ox wearing its trappings falls in and dies and the trappings are broken, the owner of the pit is liable only for the animal and is exempt from payment for the trappings.

2. The pit is included among the principal classes of injuries, and its subspecies are, like itself, deemed forewarned from the outset. If one sets down an obstacle, this is deemed a subspecies of pit, and if a person or an animal is injured by it, the one who set down the obstacle must pay for the whole of the damage done, whether he renounces his ownership of the obstacle or not. However, if articles are damaged by it, he is exempt.

3. Thus if one deposits a stone or a knife or a pack or straw or stubble or the like on a public domain, and a person or an animal is hurt by it, he must pay for the whole of the damage. The same rule applies if one deposits such articles on his own premises and then renounces the ownership of the premises but not of the articles. If a person catches his foot in the ground and falls against such an obstacle and is hurt by it, the owner of the obstacle is liable. If, however, articles are damaged or are soiled by such an obstacle, he is exempt.

4. If one takes his ox into a privately owned courtyard without permission and it drops excrement on which the householder's articles become soiled, he is exempt. For the excrement is deemed a subspecies of pit, and we do not find that a pit entails liability for damage to articles.

5. If one sets down a jar on a public domain, and a pedestrian stumbles against it and breaks it, he is exempt, because it is not usual for persons to keep their eyes on the road when they are

walking. If the pedestrian is hurt, the owner of the jar is liable for the damage, even if he renounces ownership of the jar. For even though one renounces articles capable of injuring in a place where he has no right to install them at the outset, he is as liable as if he had not renounced his ownership of them.

6. If one deposits a jar in a place where he has a right to deposit it, such as in the corners of wine presses or the like, and another stumbles over it and breaks it, the latter is liable. If a pedestrian is injured by it, the owner of the jar is exempt, because the pedestrian should have looked where he was going. If, however, it is dark, or if a whole passageway is filled with jars, the pedestrian is exempt if he breaks one, and if he stumbles against one and is injured, the owner of the jar is liable. The same rule applies in all similar cases.

7. If one's jar (full of water) is broken in a public domain and a person slips on the spilled water or is injured by the shards of the jar, the owner is legally exempt because he is the victim of circumstances beyond his control, but he is morally liable because he did not remove the shards. The shards and the water are in effect abandoned property, but the owner does not renounce ownership of them until he is the victim of circumstances beyond his control, and he is therefore exempt.

If the owner intends to retain possession of the shards and a person is hurt by them, he is liable. The same rule applies if one's camel falls down and he does not raise it, and in all similar cases. If articles are damaged in any of these instances, the owner is exempt whether he has renounced ownership or not, as we have explained.

8. If two potters are walking along a road, one behind the other, and the first one stumbles and falls and the second one stumbles against the first, the rule is as follows: If the first potter could have risen but did not do so, he is liable for the injuries of the second. For although he is a victim of circumstances beyond his control when he falls, he is no longer a victim of such circumstances when

he is lying on the road and is able to get up. If, however, he could not have risen, he is exempt, even if he does not warn the person who stumbles over him because of his anxiety about himself.

9. The rule that the first potter is liable for damage done to the second applies only if the second suffers personal injury. If, however, his utensils are damaged, the first is exempt, for he is not liable for damage to utensils by a pit, and every obstacle is deemed a subspecies of pit, as we have explained.

10. If potters or glass makers or similar craftsmen are walking, one after the other, and the first one stumbles and falls, a second stumbles over the first, and a third over the second, and each can rise but does not do so, the rule is as follows: The first person is liable for the personal injuries of the second, whether he is hurt by the body of the first as he lay on the ground or whether he is hurt by his pack. The second is liable for the personal injuries of the third, if he is hurt by the body of the second. If, however, the third is hurt by the pack which the second drops, the second is exempt. For since the first person caused the second to fall down with his pack, the second can say to the third, "I myself did not dig the pit represented by my pack." If, however, they warn each other, all are exempt.

11. If the first person falls down and is lying across the road, and one person stumbles over his head, another over his legs, and a third over his trunk, he is liable for damage done to any of them, because he could have risen and did not do so.

12. If one pours out water into a public domain and another is injured because of it, he is liable for the damage. If, however, another's clothes are soiled, he is exempt, as we have explained. If the water is soaked up by the ground and the ground remains slippery and another person slips and falls and hurts himself on the ground, the first person is liable for the other's injuries.

13. Those who open their gutters and rake out their caves have no right to pour the water onto a public domain in the summer

but have the right to do so in the winter. Nevertheless, if a person or an animal is hurt by the water, they must pay full compensation.

14. One may not set out his straw or his stubble on a public domain in order that it should be trodden down and turned into fertilizer for him. If he does place it there, the Sages fine him by declaring it derelict, so that the first person to take possession of it, once it has been trodden down and improved in value, becomes entitled to it. If, however, one takes possession of it as soon as it is set out, it cannot be taken from him. And even though it is deemed ownerless, if a person or an animal is hurt by it, the one who has set it there must pay compensation.

15. Anyone has a right to place his manure and animal droppings on a public domain during the season for putting out manure and to heap it there for thirty days in order that it should be crushed by the feet of men and beasts. Yet, if it causes injury, the owner is liable. The law forbidding robbery applies to this dung, for the Sages did not fine the owner in this case, since there is no improvement in value when it is trodden down.

16. Mortar must not be soaked on a public domain, nor may bricks be made there. Mortar, however, may be kneaded on a public domain, while bricks may not be.

17. If one is building beside a public domain, the building stone must be used for construction as soon as it is delivered. If any part of the material causes damage, he must pay for the whole of the damage.

18. If a quarryman hews stone and delivers it to a mason and a person or an animal is injured by it, the mason is liable. If the mason delivers it to an ass-driver, the ass-driver is liable. If the ass-driver delivers it to a porter, the porter is liable. If the porter delivers it to a builder, the builder is liable. If the builder delivers it to a bricklayer, the bricklayer is liable. If it falls and causes damage after being set in its row, the rule is as follows: If the

laborers are working jointly under contract, all are liable. If, however, they are (independent) wage-earners, the last one is liable and all the others are exempt.

19. If a wall or a tree falls into a public domain and causes damage, the owner is exempt from payment of compensation even if he has not renounced ownership. For these objects are not similar to a pit, since they do not cause damage in their original state. If they are defective, the court should fix a time within which the owner must cut down the tree or demolish the wall. The length of the time is thirty days. If they fall down within this time and cause damage, the owner is exempt; if after this time, he is liable because he let them remain.

20. If one covers up thorns or (pieces of) glass, or makes a fence of thornbushes, and they protrude onto a public domain and injure someone, he must pay for the whole of the damage. If, however, one makes a fence of thornbushes precisely on the border of his own domain, he is exempt, because it is not customary for people to brush against walls.

21. If one deposits thorns or (pieces of) glass in another's wall, and the owner of the wall demolishes it and these articles fall onto a public domain and cause damage, the rule is as follows: If the wall is defective, the one who deposited the articles there is liable. If, however, the wall is sound, the owner of the wall is liable.

22. Pious men of old used to cover up their thorns and (pieces of) glass in their fields, burying them three handbreadths deep in the ground in order that the ploughshare could not bring them to the surface again. Others used to incinerate them. Still others used to throw them into the sea or into a river, in order that no one should be injured by them.

23. One may not throw stones cleared from his own premises onto a public domain. Nor may one make a cavity beneath a public domain, nor (may he make) cisterns or trenches or cellars,

even if a wagon loaded with stones is able to pass over them. For it may become defective underneath without his knowledge.

However, it is permissible to dig a pit for public use.

24. One may not allow the ledges or balconies of his house to project over a public domain unless they are higher than a camel and its rider, and even then they must not darken the way for users of the public domain. If the owner wishes, he may move his wall into his own domain and then let such objects project. If he desires to move the wall without letting them project, he may let them project at any future time. He may never, however, restore the wall to the original limit, for it is forbidden to interfere with any boundary which the public has occupied.

25. If one buys a courtyard from which ledges or balconies project over a public domain, they are presumed to be there legitimately, and if the building falls down, he may rebuild it as it was.

26. If a tree overhangs a public domain, the owner must cut off enough to allow a camel and its rider to pass.

A vacant space must be left on both sides of a river, wide enough for boatmen to disembark and use their arms to pull their boat along. Any tree found within this space may be cut down immediately without warning the owner, since it hinders those who tow ships.

27. If one has a public road crossing his field, and he takes possession of it and grants the public a new road at the side, what he gives the public is a valid gift to which they acquire title, but the road he has taken from them does not become his. The minimum width of a public road is sixteen cubits.

CHAPTER XIV

1. If one kindles a fire in another's field and the fire spreads and causes damage, he must pay for the whole of the damage, for Scripture says, *If fire break out and catch in thorns so that shocks*

of corn or the standing corn . . . are consumed, he that kindles the fire shall surely make restitution (Exod. 22:5). Conflagration is deemed one of the principal classes of injuries.

2. If one kindles a fire in his own domain, he must do so at a distance from the boundary sufficient to prevent it from spreading to his neighbor's field. The actual distance depends on the height of the conflagration. If one does not remove the fire an adequate distance, and it spreads and causes damage, he must pay for the whole of the damage done. If he has removed it an adequate distance, and it nevertheless spreads and causes damage, he is exempt, because this is deemed an act of God. Similarly, if it spreads across a river or a watercourse which contains water and is eight (or more) cubits wide, he is exempt.

3. If a kindled fire spreads across a hedge, the height of the hedge, the height of the conflagration, and the wood or thorns normally found in the vicinity are taken into consideration. If the fire ought not to have spread across, the owner is exempt, but if it was likely to spread across, he is liable. This rule applies to a fire which is burning steadily. If, however, the fire is burning with a great flame which rises up and curls over at the top, and wood is usually found in the vicinity, no such consideration is necessary, and the owner is liable even if the fire spreads across a thousand cubits.

4. If one's courtyard catches fire, and a fence falls down independently of the fire and it spreads into the next courtyard, the rule is that the owner is liable if he could have restored the fallen fence but failed to do so. This is analogous to one's ox getting out and causing damage, in which case the owner is liable, for he ought to have taken care of it but failed to do so.

5. If one spreads a fire through the agency of a deaf-mute, an imbecile, or a minor, he is legally exempt but morally liable. This rule applies when one hands such a person a hot coal and the person fans it into a blaze, for a coal usually goes out of its own accord before it can spread and cause a conflagration. If, however, one

hands such a person a flame, he is liable, because his own actions cause the damage.

6. If one spreads a fire through the agency of a normal person, this person is liable and the one who sent him is exempt. So, too, if one leaves a bailee to take care of a fire, the bailee is liable.

7. If one person provides the fire and a second the wood, the one who provides the wood is liable. If the first person provides the wood and the second the fire, the one who provides the fire is liable. If another person comes and fans it, he is the one liable. If an unusual gust of wind fans it, they are all exempt. If both a person and the wind fan it, the person is liable because he is partly responsible for the damage, and whoever is partly responsible for damage must pay full compensation from his best property, as do all who cause damage.

8. If a fire spreads and consumes wood or stones or earth, the one who has kindled it must pay compensation, for Scripture says, *And catch in thorns . . . or the field* (Exod. 22:5). If it consumes a cornstack or the like, and there are articles concealed inside the cornstack, the rule is as follows: If these articles are threshing sledges or ox harnesses or similar objects that farmers normally conceal inside a cornstack, the one who has kindled the fire must pay for them. If, however, the articles are clothes or glassware or the like, he is exempt from paying for them.

9. The above rule applies to one who starts a fire in another's field. If, however, one starts a fire in his own field and it spreads to another's field, he is exempt from liability for any article that may be concealed in a cornstack. He must, however, pay proportionately for the space occupied by such articles, the space being regarded as if it were filled by the wheat or barley of the stack.

10. If one kindles a fire in another's field, and the fire spreads and consumes a cornstack and also burns a goat tied to the stack or a slave close to it, the kindler of the fire is liable, for this is a normal use for a cornstack. If, however, the slave is tied to it or the goat is near it and they are burned with the stack, he is exempt.

11. If one lends another a place for a stack and the other makes a cornstack and hides articles in it, and the lender lights a fire and burns the cornstack, he need pay only for the value of the cornstack. If one lends another a place on which to stack wheat and the other stacks barley, or a place on which to stack barley and he stacks wheat, or if he stacks wheat but covers it with barley, or stacks barley and covers it with wheat, the lender need pay only for the price of barley.

12. If one sets fire to another's building, he must pay for everything in it, since it is customary for people to keep all their utensils and all their goods in their houses. The householder must take an oath for whatever he claims, holding a sacred object, and then he may exact payment. This oath is on the authority of the Scribes, as will be explained. It is administered, however, only if one claims articles that he is considered likely to own or likely to have in his possession as bailments.

13. If a camel loaded with flax is walking through a public domain, and the flax juts out into a shop, catches fire from the shopkeeper's lamp and sets the whole building aflame, the owner of the camel is liable because he made the load excessive. This is the rule whether or not the animal halts.

If the shopkeeper leaves his lamp outside, he is liable even for the value of the flax, because he has left the lamp outside. Even his Ḥanukkah lamp it is his duty to sit and guard.

14. If one bends another's standing corn towards fire so that it catches alight, the rule is that if the fire can reach it only if driven by an unusual gust of wind, he is legally exempt but morally liable.

If one conceals another's standing corn by covering it with earth or straw, and a fire spreads and burns it, the one who concealed the corn is legally exempt, but he is morally liable because the one who kindled the fire does not have to pay for the concealed corn.

15. If a fire spreads and harms a person by burning him, the one who has kindled it is liable for the injury of that person, for his enforced idleness, his medical treatment, his pain, and the humilia-

tion he suffers, just as if he had injured him with his own hand. For although the fire is the kindler's chattel, he is regarded as one who has caused injury with a missile. If, however, one's animal or pit injures a person, he is liable only for the damage suffered, as we have explained.

16. Every subspecies of fire entails the same legal liability as does fire. Thus if one places a stone or a knife or a parcel on top of his roof, and one of these is blown down by a normal wind and does damage, he must pay for the whole of the damage, since all these and like objects are deemed subspecies of fire. However, if one of these falls as a result of an unusual gust of wind and does damage, he is exempt.

TREATISE II

LAWS CONCERNING THEFT

Involving Seven Commandments,
Two Positive and Five Negative

To Wit

1. Not to steal anyone's property;
2. To administer the law of the thief;
3. To keep accurate balances and weights;
4. Not to act corruptly with measures and weights;
5. That no one possess pairs of diverse weights or measures, even if he does not employ them for buying and selling;
6. Not to move a boundary mark;
7. Not to abduct human beings.

An exposition of these commandments
is contained in the following chapters.

CHAPTER I

1. Whoever steals property worth a *pĕruṭah* or more transgresses the prohibition: *Ye shall not steal* (Lev. 19:11). Breach of this prohibition is not punished by flogging, since theft must be repaid, Scripture having condemned the thief to make restitution. It makes no difference whether one steals the property of an Israelite or the property of a heathen, or whether one steals from an adult or from a minor.

2. On the authority of Scripture, it is prohibited to steal an object of however small a value. It is also forbidden to steal in jest, or to steal an object with the intention of returning it, or with the intention of paying for it. All these acts are forbidden, lest one become accustomed to practicing them.

3. A thief is one who takes another's property away secretly without the owner's knowledge, as when he puts his hand into another's pocket and takes money out without the owner's awareness, or commits a similar act. If, however, one takes something openly and in public by force, he is not a thief but a robber. Accordingly, if an armed brigand commits theft, he is not deemed a robber but a thief, even though the owner is aware of his action at the time he is stealing.

4. If eligible witnesses testify that a person has committed a theft, he must pay the owner of the stolen property double its value. Thus, if one has stolen one denar, he must pay two, and if he has stolen a donkey or a garment or a camel, he must pay twice its value. He thus loses an amount equal to that of which he wished to deprive another.

5. If a thief confesses of his own accord that he has stolen, he must repay the capital value but is exempt from paying double. For Scripture says, *He whom the judges shall condemn shall pay double* (Exod. 22:8), implying that one who condemns himself

need not pay double. The same rule applies to all fines, namely, if one admits his liability, he is exempt.

6. The fine of double payment applies to all things with the exception of a sheep or an ox; for if one steals an ox or a sheep and butchers it or sells it, he must pay fourfold for the sheep and fivefold for the ox.

7. Whether the thief is a man or a woman, he must pay double or fourfold or fivefold. If the thief is a married woman without money of her own to pay, the double amount of the theft becomes a debt until such time as she is divorced or her husband dies, when the court must collect it from her.

8. If theft is committed by a minor, he is exempt from paying double, but the thing he has stolen must be restored to its owner. If, however, it is lost, the minor is not liable to repay even the capital value of the stolen object, not even after he reaches the age of majority.

9. If theft is committed by a slave, he is exempt from paying double, as is also his master, for one is not liable for damage done by his slaves, although they are his chattels, seeing that they have minds of their own and he is unable to keep watch over them. Moreover, should he be annoyed at his master, a slave might go and set fire to a wheat stack worth a thousand denar or do similar damage. Should a slave become free, however, he must pay double for what he has stolen.

10. It is proper for the court to impose corporal punishment upon minors for theft, the punishment being made in proportion to their strength, in order that they should not become accustomed to stealing. The same procedure should be followed if they do other damage. Similarly, if slaves steal or do damage, they should be severely beaten in order that they should not become accustomed to doing damage.

11. If stolen property, while in the possession of the thief, improves of its own accord, as when a ewe lambs or casts its fleece, the

thief must return the animal itself, together with its fleece and its offspring. But if it lambs or casts its fleece after the owner has abandoned hope of recovery, he need pay only for the value it had at the time of the theft. But if the thief has gone to expense in order to improve it, as for example by fattening it, the improvement belongs to him even before the owner abandons hope, so that when he returns the object stolen, together with the double payment, he can recover the improvement from the owner or else have it subtracted from the double payment.

12. If the stolen object itself is in the possession of the thief and is unaltered, it must be returned to its owner whether he has abandoned hope or not, except that after hope has been abandoned, any improvement belongs to the thief, as we have explained. But if the object stolen has been altered while in the hands of the thief, he acquires title to both the object and the improvement even before the owner abandons hope, and need only replace its value in money.

13. If one steals a lean animal and it grows fat, or a fat animal and it grows lean, he must pay double or fourfold or fivefold the value it had at the time of the theft. If one steals a lamb and it grows into a ram, or a calf and it grows into an ox, he must pay double the value it had at the time of the theft. If he butchers it or sells it after it has grown, the growth constitutes an alteration while in his possession; he has thus acquired title to it and it is his own property that he has butchered or sold, and he is therefore exempt from the fourfold or fivefold fine.

14. If one steals an animal, or a vessel, or the like, worth four (denar) at the time of the theft, but worth only two now at the time of the trial, he must pay as capital value of the stolen object its value at the time of the theft, but need pay as fine to make up the double or fourfold or fivefold payment only according to the value at the time of the trial.

If the stolen object is worth two at the time of the theft and four at the time of the trial, the rule is as follows: If the thief butchers or sells the animal, or breaks or destroys the vessel, he must pay double or fourfold or fivefold its value at the time of the trial; if, however, the animal dies or the vessel is lost, he need pay only double its value at the time of the theft.

15. If one steals a vessel and breaks it or causes it to be depreciated, or it breaks or depreciates of itself, we do not assess the loss of value but, rather, we ascertain the erstwhile value of the vessel and make the thief pay the owner twice that value. The broken vessel then belongs to the thief. The same rule applies in all similar cases. But if the owner prefers to take the broken vessel and have the thief pay him for the depreciation and the fine of double, we do heed him.

16. If one steals an animal and butchers or sells it before the owner has abandoned hope of recovery, he must pay fourfold or fivefold even though the buyer does not acquire title, so that the stolen property itself must revert to the owner directly from the buyer. And it is needless to say that he must pay fourfold or fivefold if he butchers or sells it after hope of recovery has been abandoned, for in this case his action has taken effect, since the buyer has acquired title.

17. If one steals from a thief, he is not obliged to pay double even if the rightful owner has abandoned hope. If he butchers or sells (the stolen animal), he is not obliged to pay the first thief fourfold or fivefold. For under the law the animal itself must be restored to the owner, so that the first thief has not acquired title to it. Nor is the second thief obliged to pay double or fourfold or fivefold to the rightful owner, since he did not steal it from the owner's domain.

18. If one steals an animal and butchers it and then it is stolen from him, the second thief must pay him double because he has acquired title by an alteration in its state, and the first thief must pay the original owner fourfold or fivefold. But if one steals an animal and sells it and then it is stolen from the buyer, the rule is as follows: If the original owner has abandoned hope, the first thief must pay fourfold or fivefold and the second thief must pay

double; but if the owner has not abandoned hope, the second need pay only the capital value of the animal.

CHAPTER II

1. If one steals from a heathen, or if one steals sacred property, he need pay only its capital value, for Scripture says, *Shall pay double to his neighbor* (Exod. 22:8)—*to his neighbor,* but not to the sanctuary; *to his neighbor,* but not to a heathen.

Similarly, if one steals sacrificial animals from the house of their owner, he is not obliged to pay either double or fourfold or fivefold, whether they are of the holiest kind or of a lesser degree of holiness, and whether the owner is responsible for their replacement or not. For Scripture says, *And it be stolen from the house of the man* (Exod. 22:6), but not from the house of the sanctuary.

2. So, too, if one steals slaves or bonds or land, he is not obliged to pay double, because Scripture has imposed the liability for double payment only on movable things that have an intrinsic value, for it says, *On an ox or an ass or a sheep or a garment* (Exod. 22:8). Now slaves are legally regarded the same as land, for Scripture says of them, *And you shall bequeath them to your sons* (Lev. 25:46), while bonds have no intrinsic value.

3. If one steals the firstling of an ass before it has been redeemed, he must nevertheless pay double to the owner, for although it does not belong to him at present it is destined to belong to him after redemption.

4. If one steals untithed food and eats it, he must repay its owner the value of untithed food; similarly, if one steals forbidden fat and eats it, he must repay the value of forbidden fat to its owner.

5. If one steals heave offering from a (lay) Israelite who has designated it (to be given to a priest), he is not obliged to pay double, for the owner's only right in it is the pleasure of giving it to whom he pleases, and such a right has no monetary value.

6. If one steals an animal from his father and then butchers it or sells it, and his father dies afterwards, he must pay fourfold or fivefold. If his father dies before he butchers or sells it, he must pay double, but not fourfold or fivefold.

If one steals an animal and then butchers or sells it, and afterwards consecrates it, he must pay fourfold or fivefold. But if he consecrates it first and then butchers or sells it, he must pay double but not fourfold or fivefold, even if he has dedicated it as a sacrifice of the lower degree of holiness. This rule applies only if he consecrates it after the owner has abandoned hope of recovery, but if he consecrates it before this, the consecration is not valid; therefore if he butchers or sells it, he must pay fourfold or fivefold.

7. If the owner consecrates it while it is in the hands of the thief, it does not become consecrated even if he has not yet abandoned hope, because it is not under his control. If, therefore, the thief butchers or sells it, even after the owner's consecration, he must pay fourfold or fivefold.

8. If a thief slaughters a stolen animal and it becomes carrion in the process, or if he stabs it or pulls the throat organs loose, he need pay only double. But if he slaughters it (ritually) for medical purposes or to feed to dogs, or it turns out to be *ṭĕrefah,* or he slaughters it in the Temple courtyard, he must pay fourfold or fivefold. For although it is forbidden to derive any benefit from an animal slaughtered in the Temple courtyard, he must nevertheless pay fourfold or fivefold, because the prohibition rests only on the authority of the Scribes.

9. Similarly, if one steals a hybrid animal deriving from a sheep and some other species, or steals a fatally diseased animal or one amputated or lame or blind, or steals an animal belonging to two partners, and he butchers or sells it, he must pay fourfold or fivefold.

10. If A steals an animal and makes a gift of it to B, or gives it to B to butcher and B does butcher it, or gives it to B to sell and B does sell it, or if A sells it on credit, or barters it for another animal,

or pays a credit account with it, or sends it as a betrothal gift to his father-in-law's house, he must pay fourfold or fivefold.

11. If one steals an animal and sells it with a stipulation that the vendor will again acquire title to it after thirty days, and the thief is discovered during the thirty days, he need nevertheless pay only double.

If he sells all but a hundredth part of the animal, or all but a foreleg or hind leg—or, in general, if he reserves to himself some part which, together with the bulk of the animal, becomes fit for food only through (ritual) slaughter—he is exempt from paying fourfold or fivefold. But if he sells it all except its fleece, or its horns, he must pay fourfold or fivefold, because these are not things that become permissible in consequence of proper slaughtering.

12. If one steals an animal and, after having cut off one of its limbs, sells it, or sells it outright but retains the right to its labor, or sells it outright for all time except a period of thirty days, we do not exact from him fourfold or fivefold payment. But if there is seizure by the plaintiff, we do not interfere.

13. If one steals and sells an animal in which he owns a share, he is exempt from paying fourfold or fivefold.

14. If partners steal an animal and one of them butchers or sells it with the knowledge of the other, they must jointly pay fourfold or fivefold. But if one acts without the other's knowledge, they are exempt from paying fourfold or fivefold, but must pay double.

15. If one steals an animal and is brought to trial and the judges say to him, "Go and give back to the owner what you have stolen," and he goes out but then butchers or sells it, he is exempt from paying fourfold or fivefold. If, however, they say to him, "You are under a liability to give it to him," and he then butchers or sells it, he must pay fourfold or fivefold; for inasmuch as they have not passed judgment, his status as a thief still prevails.

16. If one steals within the owner's premises (and leaves the stolen property there), he need not pay double inasmuch as the

property is still in the domain of the owner. So, too, if he butchers or sells on the owner's premises (an animal stolen there), he need not pay fourfold or fivefold. But if he lifts the object up, he is liable for theft even before he removes it from the owner's premises. Thus, if one steals a lamb from a fold and it dies on the owner's premises while he is pulling it away, he is exempt. But if he picks it up, or takes it off the owner's premises and it then dies, he is liable.

If, while it is still on the owner's premises, the thief gives the animal as firstborn redemption money for his son, or to a creditor, or to an unpaid bailee, or to a borrower, or to a paid bailee, or to a hirer, and it dies while the recipient is pulling it away, the recipient bailee or creditor is exempt. But if the recipient picks it up, or removes it from the owner's premises, and then it dies, the recipient bailee or the creditor is liable, because the thief has not yet taken it off the owner's premises.

17. If one steals a sheep from a flock in the woods, he becomes liable to pay double as soon as he goads the animal and hides it among the trees or the undergrowth. If he butchers or sells it there, he must pay fourfold or fivefold.

18. If one steals an animal within the owner's premises and after the theft is discovered he takes it away and butchers or sells it outside, or if he steals it and takes it outside and then butchers or sells it within the owner's premises, he must pay fourfold or fivefold.

CHAPTER III

1. We have already explained in dealing with the laws of a maiden that if one commits a transgression entailing capital punishment and also a monetary penalty, he need not pay even if he has acted through error. Again, if one commits a transgression for which he is liable for both flogging and a monetary penalty, he is flogged but need not pay, because one is not subjected to both flogging and paying. Consequently, if one acts through error or

without receiving due warning, he must pay but is not flogged.

The above rule applies only if one incurs liability for a monetary penalty and for capital punishment at the same time, or if the liability for a monetary penalty and a flogging is incurred at the same time. But if one first becomes liable for a monetary penalty and afterwards for death or for a flogging, or if he first becomes liable for a flogging or for death and then for payment, he is both flogged and made to pay, or both put to death and made to pay.

2. Thus, if one shoots an arrow on the Sabbath for a distance of four cubits and it tears another's coat in flight, or if one sets fire to another's cornstack on the Sabbath, or if one steals a purse on the Sabbath by dragging it along in such a way that, when it emerges from the owner's domain, which is a private domain, into the public domain, he destroys it there, he is exempt from payment because the breach of the Sabbath occurred at the same time as the theft or the damage. But if one steals a purse on the Sabbath, having picked it up on a private domain, and afterwards takes it out into the public domain and throws it into the river, he must pay double because he is liable for the offense of theft before he is liable for the offense entailing the penalty of death by stoning. The same rule applies in all similar cases.

So, too, if one chops down another's tree on a festival after being duly warned, or if he sets fire to a cornstack on the Day of Atonement after being duly warned, or if he steals an animal and butchers it on the Day of Atonement after being duly warned, he is exempt from the monetary penalty. But if he is not duly warned, he is liable for the monetary penalty and must pay fourfold or fivefold.

3. If one steals an animal and butchers it on the Sabbath or kills it as a heathen sacrifice, even through error, he need not pay fourfold or fivefold, as we have explained.

4. If one borrows a cow and then butchers it on the Sabbath in an act of theft, he is exempt even from paying double, because the breach of the Sabbath and the theft are done at the same time, and

where there is no payment for theft, there can be no penalty for butchering or selling.

5. If one steals an animal and then sells it on the Sabbath or for a heathen sacrifice, he must pay fourfold or fivefold because there is no death penalty for selling. But if a prohibited act of labor is done on the Sabbath in connection with the selling, he is exempt from paying fourfold or fivefold. Thus, a thief would be exempt if he stipulated that ownership was not to be transferred until the animal rested in the courtyard of the purchaser, so that when he took it from one domain to the other the breach of the Sabbath and the act of selling would occur at the same time.

6. If a thief appoints an agent to slaughter an animal for him, and the agent slaughters it on the Sabbath, the thief must pay forfold or fivefold, inasmuch as he has committed no transgression involving the death penalty. We have already explained that a thief who has an animal butchered by an agent must pay.

7. If two persons testify that one has stolen an animal, he must pay fourfold or fivefold, whether they themselves testify that he has butchered it or sold it, or whether others do so. If two persons testify that one has stolen an animal, but only one witness testifies that he has butchered it or sold it, or if he himself confesses that he has butchered it or sold it, he must pay double, but need not pay fourfold or fivefold, because if one confesses in a case in which the penalty is a fine, he is exempt, as we have explained.

8. If one confesses to an offense involving a fine as penalty, and witnesses come forward afterwards, the rule is as follows: If his confession is originally made before a legally constituted court during its session, he is exempt. But if he confesses outside the court or to only two judges, and witnesses come forward afterwards, he must pay the fine on the testimony of the witnesses.

9. Thus, if one confesses in court that he has stolen, and witnesses later testify that he did steal, he is exempt from paying double because he makes himself liable for repaying the capital

value before witnesses come forward. If, however, he says, "I did not steal," thus declaring himself exempt from all liability, and witnesses then testify that he did steal, whereupon he says in court, "I butchered it," or "I sold it," and afterwards witnesses testify that he did butcher it or sell it, he must pay fourfold or fivefold, since he originally denied all liability until the witnesses came forward.

10. If one steals an ox belonging to two partners and butchers or sells it, and then confesses in court to one of them but denies the act to the other, and then witnesses testify that he did steal it and butcher or sell it, he must pay five half oxen or four half sheep to the one to whom he denied his act.

11. The law requires a thief to pay the capital amount and the penalties of double and of fourfold or fivefold from his movable property. If he has no movable property available, the court must attach his real property and collect whatever is due from his finest land, as is the rule in other cases of liability for damage concerning which Scripture states, *The best of his field* (Exod. 22:4). If he has neither land nor movable property, the court must sell the thief and give the money to the plaintiff, for Scripture says, *If he has none, he shall be sold for his theft* (Exod. 22:2).

12. A man may be sold for his theft but a woman may not be, this being traditional law. A thief may be sold only to pay for the principal value of the object stolen, but he may not be sold for the penalties of double or of fourfold or fivefold, which remain a debt against him until he is able to pay.

13. If one steals from a heathen or from the Sanctuary, he may not be sold for the principal amount, but it remains a debt against him until he is able to pay.

14. If the stolen object is worth one hundred (denar) and the thief is worth only fifty, he must be sold and the remainder of the principal amount, together with the rest of the double penalty, becomes a debt against him until he is released in the seventh year and becomes able to pay. If, however, the thief is worth a hundred

and one, he may not be sold, for Scripture says, *And he shall be sold for his theft* (*ibid.*), implying that his whole value must be absorbed in payment for his theft.

15. If one steals and is sold and then steals again, the rule is that if he steals from a different person, he may be sold a second time; even if he steals from a hundred different people, he may be sold a hundred times. But if he steals a second time from the first person, he may not be sold again, rather whatever he has stolen is counted as a debt against him.

16. If one steals from three people, one after the other, all become joint owners of him. If his value is equal to the amount stolen from all three, or is less than this, he is sold and they share the proceeds, while their claims of double payment become a debt against him. But if his value is greater, he may not be sold and their claims remain a debt against him until he is able to pay.

17. If partners steal together, the liability must be divided among them and each may be sold for his share of the original theft. If the value of any one of them is greater than the part of the theft for which he is liable, he may not be sold.

CHAPTER IV

1. If one pleads that an animal entrusted to him has been stolen from his house, the rule is as follows: If he takes an oath (denying theft), and witnesses then testify that he pleaded falsely and that he still had the animal, he must pay double because he himself is like a thief. If he butchers or sells the animal after taking the oath, he must pay fourfold or fivefold. But he need not bring a guilt-offering for his oath as a result of the evidence of witnesses, nor need he add a fifth part, because the fifth part need not be paid when one is liable for double payment. If, however, witnesses come forward before he takes the oath, he need pay only the actual value stolen.

2. The above rule applies if one takes an oath before he tampers with the entrusted animal. But if he first tampers with it and then pleads that it has been stolen and affirms this on oath, and then witnesses come forward, he is exempt from paying double, because as soon as he tampers with it, he becomes responsible for it and acquires title to it.

3. Similarly, if one pleads that an entrusted animal has been lost, and he affirms this on oath, and he then pleads that it has been stolen and affirms this on oath, and witnesses come forward afterwards, then he is exempt from paying double, because the animal has already been withdrawn from its owner's possession in consequence of the first oath.

4. If one pleads that another's lost property which he found has been stolen from him, and affirms this on oath, and witnesses later testify that the lost property is in his possession and that he pleaded falsely, he must pay double, because Scripture says, *Concerning any lost thing* (Exod. 22:8). This rule applies provided that he pleads it was stolen by an armed robber, in which case he would be exempt inasmuch as he was under constraint. If, however, he pleads that it was stolen without duress, he is exempt from paying double because his own plea condemns him to pay for it, since a bailee of found property is deemed a paid bailee, as will be explained.

5. If one pleads that an object deposited with him has been stolen and he affirms this on oath, and afterwards witnesses testify that it is in his possession and he then pleads again that it has been stolen and affirms this on oath, and witnesses again testify that it is still in his possession, he must pay double for each plea even if the same thing happens a hundred times. If, therefore, he swears five times, he must pay six times the value, namely, the original article deposited with him and five times its capital value for the five fines of double payment in consequence of the five oaths.

6. If one pleads theft and takes an oath affirming his plea, and then subsequently pleads loss along with an affirming oath, where-

upon witnesses testify that the object was not stolen, and then he himself admits that it was not lost, the rule is that inasmuch as he must pay double on account of the witnesses, he need not pay a fifth part as a result of the last oath, despite his confession, because the liability which requires him to pay double renders him exempt from paying a fifth part.

7. If one entrusts his ox to two persons who plead theft and affirm their plea on oath, and subsequently one of them confesses guilt and witnesses testify against the other, the rule is that both must repay only the capital value; yet, if the owner of the deposit seizes the fine of double payment, it may not be reclaimed from him. The one who confesses, however, must pay the fifth part, as must all who take an oath denying a deposit and then confess of their own accord.

8. If the owner of a deposit sues the bailee who swears that it was stolen, and subsequently the thief is discovered, is sued by the bailee, and confesses to him that he did steal, whereupon the owner of the deposit sues the thief, who denies the theft, and then witnesses testify that he did steal the deposit, the rule is as follows: If the bailee swore truthfully when he pleaded it was stolen, the thief is exempt from the fine of double payment in consequence of his confession to the bailee. If, however, the bailee swore falsely, the fine of double payment may not be exacted from the thief; but if the owner seizes the double amount, it may not be reclaimed from him.

If an owner sues a bailee and he pays, and subsequently the thief is discovered and is sued by the owner and confesses to him, whereupon the bailee sues the thief, who denies the theft, and then witnesses testify that he did steal the deposit, the rule is that the fine of double payment may not be exacted from the thief; but if the bailee seizes the double amount, it may not be reclaimed from him. The same rule applies to the fourfold or fivefold fine if the thief has butchered or sold the animal.

9. If one pleads that an article deposited with him by a minor has been stolen and affirms his plea on oath, and then witnesses

testify that he has it, he is exempt from paying double even if the plaintiff was a minor only at the time of the deposit and by the time of the claiming has become an adult, because Scripture says, *If a man deliver unto his neighbor* (Exod. 22:6), implying that delivery by a minor is of no account, and that both deposit and claim must alike be made by an adult.

10. If a bailee steals something from his own premises, such as a lamb from a flock deposited with him or a coin from a purse entrusted to him, the rule is that if witnesses testify against him, he must pay double. Even if he returns the coin to its place or the lamb to its flock, he is responsible for them until he informs the owner, because his term of bailment has ceased, and it is regarded as if he has not returned anything at all until he informs the owner.

If, however, one steals a coin from another's purse or an article from his house, and then restores the property stolen to its proper place, the rule is that if the owner is aware of the theft but is not aware of the return, the thief is still responsible for it until the owner has counted his money.

11. If the owner counts the money in his purse and finds it intact in amount, the thief is exempt. If, however, the owner knows neither of the theft nor of the return, even counting is unnecessary, and as soon as the thief returns it to its place, he is exempt from responsibility.

12. The above rule applies only to inanimate objects. But if one steals a lamb from another's flock and the owner knows about it, and the thief then returns it to the flock without the owner's knowledge and it dies or is stolen, he is responsible for it. If, however, the owner counts the sheep and finds them intact in number, the thief is exempt. If, however, the owner knows neither of the theft nor of the return, then even if he counts the sheep and finds them intact, the thief continues to be responsible until he tells the owner so that the latter can guard the stolen lamb, for it may have learned habits different from those of the other sheep in the flock.

CHAPTER V

1. It is prohibited to buy from a thief any property he has stolen, such buying being a great sin, since it encourages criminals and causes the thief to steal other property. For if a thief finds no buyer, he will not steal. Of this Scripture says, *Whoso is partner with a thief hates his own soul* (Prov. 29:24).

2. If one steals an object and sells it and the owner has not abandoned hope of recovery, and subsequently the thief is discovered and witnesses say, "The article that this man sold he stole in our presence," the rule is that the article is restored to its owner, but he must, in the interest of market overt, restore to the purchaser the price he paid the thief. In turn the owner may then bring the thief to trial.

If, however, the thief was a notorious one, the Sages did not apply the rule of market overt and the owner need not pay the buyer anything, but the latter may bring the thief to trial and exact from him the money he paid for the stolen object.

3. If the owner abandons hope of recovering stolen property, no matter whether he first abandons hope and then the thief sells it, or whether he abandons hope after the thief has sold it, the buyer acquires title to it by the owner's abandonment of hope of recovery and the change of ownership, and the buyer need not return the stolen property itself to the owner. The buyer need give the owner only its value if he bought it from a notorious thief, but need give him nothing, neither the property nor its value, if the seller was not a notorious thief, because he has the benefit of market overt.

4. If, when the buyer's suit is against the owner, there are no witnesses to testify concerning the amount paid for the stolen article, the buyer must state on oath, holding a sacred object, what he paid for it and then receive this sum from the owner. Any oath taken by one who receives payment after swearing is on the authority of the Scribes, but it must be sworn while he holds a sacred object, as will be explained in the appropriate place.

5. If the buyer's suit is brought against the thief, and he says, "I bought it for such-and-such an amount," while the thief says, "I sold it to you for less," the buyer must take an oath while holding a sacred object and then receive his money from the thief. For the thief cannot take an oath since he is suspected of aptness to swear falsely.

6. If one steals an object and pays a debt or an account with it, there is no benefit of market overt, rather the owner may take the stolen property without payment and the original debt remains against the thief. If the thief pawns the stolen object, whether for more than its value or for less, the owner must pay the pawnbroker and may in turn bring suit against the thief, unless he is a notorious thief, as we have explained.

7. If one buys from a thief who is not notorious, then whether he buys something worth a hundred for two hundred, or something worth two hundred for a hundred, he can recover this sum from the owner and must then return the stolen property, this being due to benefit of market overt, as we have explained.

8. If a thief owes a debt of one hundred zuz, and he steals an object and brings it to his creditor who then gives him another hundred, the stolen property must be restored to its owner, and the creditor is told, "Go and sue the thief for two hundred, for you did not give him the second hundred merely because he brought you this property. Just as you trusted him with the first hundred, you trusted him also with the second."

9. If A buys property from a thief who is not notorious for a hundred and sells it to B for a hundred and twenty and the thief is then discovered, the rule is that the owner of the property stolen must pay B one hundred and twenty and thus recover his property, and he may then obtain the twenty profit from A and the hundred from the thief. But if the thief is a notorious one, the owner may take the full hundred and twenty from A, who must sue the thief for the original hundred. The same rule applies if the second buyer sells to a third and the third to a fourth and so on even up to a

hundred—the owner may take from each in turn the profit he has made, but must exact the original price from the thief. All these rules apply before the owner abandons hope of recovery, as we have already explained.

10. If a report circulates in town that a householder not given to selling his own property has been robbed and he recognizes his property or his books in the possession of someone else, or if he does frequently sell but the articles that he recognizes are of a kind usually lent or hired out, the rule is as follows: If witnesses testify that these articles belong to the householder, the one who has them must swear, holding a sacred object, what price he paid for them, and, having received this sum from the householder, must restore the property to him.

11. If the householder does frequently sell his property, and the articles in question are not of a type usually lent or hired out, the rule is that although a report spreads in town that he has been robbed and his property is recognized, the householder cannot recover them from the buyer since he himself might have sold them to someone else. But if persons spend the night at his house, and he gets up at night and cries, "My wares and my books have been stolen," and others come and find that a tunnel leading into the house has been dug and that the persons staying there are going out with bundles of wares on their shoulders, and everyone says, "These are so-and-so's things," he is believed and the one who now has the wares must swear, holding a sacred object, what price he paid, and having received this sum from the owner of the stolen property he must restore the wares to him.

12. If a proven and well-known thief entered a person's house and witnesses testify that although the owner was there he came out with articles under his coat, and he says, "I bought them," while the owner says, "They are stolen," the rule is as follows: If the householder is one who does not usually sell his property, and the property is of a kind not usually put under one's coat, and the one who has the property does not usually hide his wares under his

coat, the owner is believed, but he must take an oath holding a sacred object and may then recover his property. If, however, the person was not a proven thief, the householder is not heeded; but the one who has the property must swear an oath of inducement that he bought this property, and he may go his way.

CHAPTER VI

1. It is forbidden to buy anything that can be presumed to have been stolen. Similarly, if the larger part of what is offered for sale is stolen property, it may not be bought. Consequently, wool or milk or young goats may not be bought from shepherds. However, milk or cheese may be bought from them in a desert, though not in a settled region. It is also permitted to buy from shepherds four sheep or four wool fleeces from a small flock or five from a large flock, since there is no presumption in such a case that these are stolen property.

2. The general rule is as follows: If a shepherd wishes to sell something whose loss the owner would notice, it may be bought; but if the owner would not notice its loss, it may not be bought.

3. Wood or produce may be bought from orchard guards only when they sit and sell it and have basket and balance in front of them, for then the transaction is open and public and the property is obviously not stolen. One may buy at the entrance to a market garden but not at the rear of it. If any of the aforementioned persons requests that the purchase be concealed, it may not be bought. It is permissible to buy from a tenant farmer since he has a share in the produce and the wood.

4. Only that property which can be presumed to be theirs with the owner's awareness may be bought from women, slaves or minors—for example, women usually sold linen goods in Galilee and calves in Sharon. If any of the aforementioned persons requests that the purchases be concealed, it is forbidden to buy from them because the property is presumed to be stolen. Eggs or poultry

may be bought anywhere from anyone, but if the buyer is requested to conceal the purchase, it is forbidden to buy such articles.

5. It is permissible to buy from olive treaders a measured quantity of olives or of oil, but not just a few olives or a little oil since this is presumed to be stolen. The same rule applies in all similar cases.

6. Waste wool pulled out by the washerman belongs to him, but that pulled out by the combers belongs to the owner. The washerman may take up to three threads for himself, but more than this belongs to the owner. If there are black threads among the white, he may take them all and keep them.

7. If a tailor has enough thread left to draw a needle through (cloth), or a piece of cloth left that is three fingerbreadths square, he must return it to the owner. Less than this he may keep.

8. The wood fragments that a carpenter chips off with an adze belong to him; those from an axe belong to the employer. If he is working at the employer's house, even the shavings belong to the employer. However, in all these and similar matters, local custom should be followed.

9. If a craftsman sells anything that local usage does not regard as his, as, for example, if a wool comber sells waste wool in a place where the custom is that this belongs to the employer, it is forbidden to buy from him because the goods are presumed to be stolen. But a cushion stuffed with waste wool may be bought from him. If, however, a craftsman sells materials that local usage does regard as his, they may be bought from him. But if he requests the buyer to conceal his purchase, it is forbidden to buy from him.

CHAPTER VII

1. If one weighs with weights that are deficient by the standards agreed upon in his locality, or measures with a measuring vessel deficient by the agreed standards, he violates a negative commandment, for Scripture states, *Ye shall do no unrighteousness in judgment, in meteyard, in weight, or in measure* (Lev. 19:35).

2. Although one who measures or weighs falsely steals thereby, he need not pay double but need only pay for the deficiency in measure or weight. Nor is flogging inflicted for breach of this prohibition, since there is a liability to pay.

3. If one keeps in his house or in his shop a false measure or weight, he transgresses a negative commandment, for Scripture states, *Thou shalt not have in thy bag diverse weights* (Deut. 25:13). It is even forbidden to use a false measure as a urinal, for although one does not buy or sell with it himself, someone who does not know that it is deficient might come and use it for measuring. There is no flogging for breach of this prohibition because it does not involve action.

4. If the measures and weights of the townsmen are stamped with a known mark and a deficient measure or weight has no mark, it may be kept in the house and used for other purposes. Similarly, one may not use a coin that is defective at the edges as a weight or throw it among his scrap metal or pierce it and hang it around his son's neck, lest another come and use it as a weight. It should either be ground up or cut or broken or thrown into the Dead Sea.

5. If a coin is worn away until it is exactly half of its former standard, it may be retained. If it is less than half, it must be clipped and destroyed, and if more than half, it must be clipped until it is half. If it is deficient by less than a sixth, it may be kept to spend but not for weighing, because most people are prepared in business dealings not to mind a deficiency less than a sixth of the value involved.

6. If a coin is worn away in the middle, it may not be sold to a slayer or to an oppressor, because he is apt to use it to deceive others. But one may pierce it and hang it around a child's neck.

7. One may make measuring vessels having a capacity of a sĕ'ah, a half sĕ'ah and a quarter sĕ'ah, a ḳab̲, a half ḳab̲ and a quarter ḳab̲, a half of a quarter and an eighth of a quarter. But one

must not make one of two ḳab̲ because this may be confused with a quarter sĕ'ah, which is a ḳab̲ and a half. Similarly, for liquid measure one may make a *hin,* half a hin, a third of a hin and a quarter of a hin, a *log̅,* a half log̅, a quarter, an eighth, and an eighth of an eighth. The Sages did not forbid the manufacture of both a third of a hin and a quarter of a hin, although these can be confused, because they existed in the Sanctuary from the time of Moses, our Teacher.

8. If one measures or weighs incorrectly in dealing with an Israelite or a heathen, he transgresses a negative commandment and must repay. It is similarly forbidden to deceive a heathen about an account, and one must be scrupulous with him. For since Scripture, even in a case where a heathen is subject to our rule, says, *And he shall reckon with his purchaser* (Lev. 25:50), how much more does this apply to a heathen not subject to our rule. This offense is included in the statement, *For an abomination unto the Lord thy God are all that do such things, even all that do unrighteously* (Deut. 25:16)—that is, in any manner.

9. Similarly, in regard to land measurement, if one deceives another when measuring land, he violates a negative commandment, for when Scripture says, *Ye shall do no unrighteousness in judgment, in meteyard* (Lev. 19:35), *in meteyard* refers to land measurement. The verse must be understood as follows: *Thou shalt do no unrighteousness in judgment,* neither in the law of weight nor in the law of meteyard even in a measure as small as a *mĕśurah.*

10. If members of a group who are strict with one another about their property exchange portions of food, or borrow food from one another and then return it, they transgress the law requiring correct measuring, weighing, and counting, and on a feast day the law forbidding borrowing and repaying on such a day.

11. If one moves his neighbor's boundary mark and brings some of his neighbor's land inside his own border, even if this be only a finger's breadth, he is deemed a robber if he does so by force and a thief if he moves it secretly. If he moves a boundary mark in the

Land of Israel, he transgresses two prohibitions, namely, that of robbery or theft and that of *Thou shalt not remove thy neighbor's landmark* (Deut. 19: 14). The latter prohibition applies only in the Land of Israel, for Scripture continues, *in thine inheritance which thou shalt inherit* (*ibid.*).

12. The punishment for unjust measures is more severe than the punishment for immorality, for the latter is a sin against God only, the former against one's fellowman. If one denies the binding character of the commandment relating to measures, he denies in effect the Exodus from Egypt which was the basis of the commandments; but if one acknowledges the commandment relating to measures, he thereby acknowledges the Exodus from Egypt, which rendered all the commandments possible.

CHAPTER VIII

1. There is a positive commandment to adjust balances, weights, and measures accurately and to calibrate them very carefully at the time of their manufacture, for Scripture says, *Just balances, just weights, a just ephah, and a just hin, shall ye have* (Lev. 19: 36). Similarly, in measuring land great care must be taken to calculate the area of land according to the principles laid down in works on geometry, for even a finger's breadth of land should be regarded as if it were filled with saffron.

2. The four cubits adjoining a ditch should be measured only approximately. Those adjoining a river should not be measured at all because they are public property.

3. A land surveyor should not measure one person's share in the summer and another person's share in the winter because the rope shrinks during the summer. Therefore, if one uses a rod or an iron chain or a similar instrument in measuring, the time of year is immaterial.

4. Weights may not be made of tin or lead or other similar metals because these rust and wear away, but they should be made of polished stone or glass or onyx or the like.

5. A level may not be made of gourd because it will press down too lightly, nor of metal because it will press down too heavily. It should be made of olive wood or of walnut or sycamore or ebony or some similar wood.

6. A level may not be made with one side thick and one side thin. The leveling should not be done too gradually because this causes loss to the seller, nor too rapidly because this causes loss to the buyer.

7. Weights may not be kept in salt so as to make them lighter. Nor may the dealer cause foaming in a liquid measure when measuring, even if the measure is a very small one. For the Law is particular in all measures about the smallest quantity, since it mentions the mĕśurah, a small measure which is one thirty-third part of a loḡ.

8. Vendors of bars of iron or the like must make sure that the balance cord held by the person weighing hangs three handbreadths in the air and that the balance is three handbreadths from the ground. The length of the beam of the balance and the length of the lines should be twelve handbreadths.

9. The length of the cord from which the balance of a wool dealer or a glass dealer is suspended should be two handbreadths and the balance should be two handbreadths above the ground. The length of the beam and the lines should be nine handbreadths.

10. The length of the cord from which the balance of a shopkeeper or a private householder is suspended should be one handbreadth and the balance should be one handbreadth above the ground. The length of the beam and the lines should be six handbreadths.

11. The cord on which a steelyard is hung and, similarly, the cord of a balance for gold or for dealers in fine purple should be

three fingerbreadths long and the balance should be three fingerbreadths from the ground. The length of the steelyard and the lengths of its chains may be deemed optional.

12. How do we know that the vendor must give the buyer overweight when he is weighing for him? Because Scripture says, *A perfect and just weight shalt thou have* (Deut. 25:15). Scripture thus admonishes the vendor, "Be just at thine expense for his benefit."

13. How much should be given as surplus? For liquids one part in a hundred, for dry stuffs one in four hundred. Thus if one sells another ten *litra* of liquid, he must give him as surplus one tenth of a litra. If he sells him twenty litra of dry stuff, he must give him as surplus one twentieth of a litra, and similarly in every sale, whatever the quantity, this proportion of surplus should be maintained.

14. The above rule applies to those localities where it is customary to sell with the scales exactly level. But where it is usual for the scale pan to be allowed to drop, the vendor must let it drop a handbreadth.

15. If one weighs out ten pounds, the buyer may not say, "Weigh out one pound at a time and let the scale drop each time," rather the vendor may weigh all ten together and let it drop just once.

16. In a locality where it is customary to use a small measure, one may not use a large one; where a large one is customary, one may not use a small one; where a level measure is customary, one may not give heaped measure and charge extra; similarly, where it is customary to give heaped measure, one may not level it and charge less, but (in each instance) one must conform to local custom.

17. Townspeople who wish to increase the standards of measures or weights may not increase them by more than a sixth. Thus if a ḳab holds five and they want to make it hold six, they have the right to do so; but they may not make it hold more than six.

18. A wholesale merchant must clean his measures every thirty days, and a householder must clean his every twelve months. A shopkeeper must clean his measures twice a week, clean his weights once a week, and clean his balance each time after it is used, so that they should not rust.

19. If one wants to weigh three quarters of a pound, he must put a pound weight in one scale pan and the meat and a quarter-pound weight in the other pan. For if we allow him to put a half-pound weight and a quarter weight in one scale pan, it is possible that the quarter-pound weight may fall off without the buyer noticing it.

20. It is the duty of the court to appoint inspectors in every province and in every district to visit the shops, adjust balances and measures, and fix prices. If they find anyone with an inaccurate weight or measure or a faulty balance, they have the right to flog him according to his power of endurance, and to fine him whatever sum the court thinks fit, in order to ensure conformity. If anyone forces up the price and sells at a high price, they may flog him and compel him to sell at the market price.

CHAPTER IX

1. If one abducts a human being, he transgresses a negative commandment, for Scripture says, *Thou shalt not steal* (Exod. 20:13). This verse, one of the Ten Commandments, prohibits kidnapping. So, too, if one sells a human being, he transgresses a negative commandment, for this is included in the verse, *They shall not be sold as bondsmen* (Lev. 25:42). There is no penalty of flogging for violation of these two prohibitions, because each is a negative commandment intended as a warning that the violation thereof involves death by order of the court, for Scripture says, *If any man be found stealing any of his brethren,* etc. (Deut. 24:7). The mode of execution for kidnapping is by strangulation.

2. A kidnapper is not liable to death by strangulation unless he abducts an Israelite, takes him onto his premises, makes use of him

and sells him, for Scripture says, *And deal falsely with him and sell him* (*ibid.*). Even if the use to which the kidnapper puts him is worth less than a pĕruṭah—for example, if the kidnapper leans on him or supports himself on him—even though the kidnapped person is asleep, it is regarded as making use of him.

3. If one abducts another and uses him and sells him, but the kidnapped person is still on his own premises and has not been taken onto the premises of the kidnapper, the kidnapper is exempt. If one abducts another and takes him onto his premises and uses him but does not sell him, or sells him before using him, or uses him and sells him to one of the kidnapped person's relatives—for example, if he sells him to his father or his brother—the kidnapper is exempt, for Scripture says, *Stealing any of his brethren . . . and sell him* (*ibid.*), implying that he must separate him from his brethren and kinsfolk by the sale. Similarly, if one abducts a person who is asleep, uses him asleep, and sells him while he is still asleep, the kidnapper is exempt.

4. Similarly, if one abducts a woman and sells her for her offspring alone—for example, if he stipulates with the buyer, "This female slave remains mine, and you merely get her offspring"—he is exempt.

5. If one abducts his own son or his minor brother, or if a guardian abducts the orphan wards in his charge, or if one abducts a member of his household who is supported at his table, or if a schoolmaster kidnaps one of the minors in his class—in any such instance the kidnapper is exempt, even if he uses and sells the kidnapped person, for Scripture says, *He be found in his hand* (Exod. 21:16), thereby excluding the aforementioned persons who are regularly under the kidnapper's authority.

6. If one abducts another—whether the kidnapped person is an adult or a day-old living child, male or female, or whether the kidnapper is a man or a woman—he must be put to death, for Scripture says, *Stealing any person* (Deut. 24:7), meaning of whatever sort. It makes no difference whether one abducts an Is-

raelite, a proselyte, or a freed slave, for Scripture says, *any of his brethren* (*ibid.*), and all these are our brethren in regard to observance of Torah and its commandments. But if one abducts a slave, or a person who is half slave and half free, he is exempt.

7. If a thief enters by *breaking in* (cf. Exod. 22:1) by day or by night, there is no bloodguiltiness for him, and if the owner of the house or someone else kills him, the slayer is exempt. Everyone has the right to kill a thief, either on a weekday or on the Sabbath and in any manner whatsoever, for Scripture says, *There shall be no bloodguiltiness for him* (Exod. 22:1).

8. It makes no difference whether the thief breaks in or is found on one's roof or in his courtyard or in his rear enclosure, whether by day or by night. Why then does Scripture mention entrance by *breaking in?* Because the majority of thieves usually enter by breaking in at nighttime.

9. Why has the Law permitted the life of a thief to be taken although he comes merely to get property? Because it is presumed that if the owner seeks to interfere and offers resistance, the thief might kill him. Consequently, if one enters another's house to steal, he is regarded as is one who pursues another to kill him. He may therefore be killed whether he is an adult or a minor, male or female.

10. If a householder is certain that a thief who has broken in will not kill him and has come only for property, he may not kill him, and if he does so he has committed murder, for Scripture says, *If the sun be risen upon him* (Exod. 22:2), which means, "If it is as clear as day to you that the thief's intentions toward you are peaceful, you may not kill him." Therefore, if a father breaks into his son's premises, he may not be killed, for the father will certainly not kill his son; but if a son breaks in to steal from his father, he may be killed.

11. Similarly, if a thief has stolen and departed, or has not stolen but is found leaving by the way he had broken in, there is blood-

guiltiness for him, seeing that he retreats and does not pursue the householder. So, too, if he is surrounded by people or by witnesses, he may not be killed even if he is still on the premises of the one from whom he came to steal. Needless to say, if he comes before the court, he may not be sentenced to death.

12. Similarly, if one breaks into another's market garden or field or fold or pen, there is bloodguiltiness for him, seeing that he must be presumed to have entered for the sole purpose of taking property, since most owners are not usually found in places of this kind.

13. If a ruin falls upon a thief for whom there is bloodguiltiness, he must be rescued even on the Sabbath. Also, if such a thief breaks articles on entering, he must indemnify the owner. However, a thief for whom there is no bloodguiltiness is exempt from indemnity for articles which he breaks upon entering, as we have explained.

TREATISE III

LAWS CONCERNING ROBBERY AND LOST PROPERTY

Involving Seven Commandments,
Two Positive and Five Negative

To Wit

1. Not to commit robbery;
2. Not to withhold due obligations;
3. Not to covet;
4. Not to desire;
5. To return property obtained by robbery;
6. Not to disregard lost property;
7. To return lost property.

An exposition of these commandments
is contained in the following chapters.

CHAPTER I

1. If one robs another of property worth as much as a pĕruṭah, he transgresses a negative commandment, for it is said, *Thou shalt not . . . rob him* (Lev. 19:13). No flogging is incurred for breach of this prohibition, since Scripture has transformed it into a positive commandment, for if one commits robbery, he is obliged to make restitution, as it is said, *He shall restore that which he took by robbery* (Lev. 5:23), which is a positive commandment. Even if he burns the robbed property, he does not incur flogging, since he is obliged to repay its value, and any prohibition the transgression of which may be repaired by restitution does not entail flogging.

2. On the authority of Scripture, it is forbidden to take by robbery anything whatever (even if its worth is less than a pĕruṭah). Even a heathen must not be robbed nor may money due him be withheld. And if one does rob him or withhold money due him, he must make restitution.

3. Who is deemed a robber? One who takes another's property by force. Thus if one snatches an object from another's hand, or enters another's premises without his permission and takes articles, or if one seizes another's slave or his animal and makes use of them, or if one enters another's field and eats its produce, or commits any similar act, he is deemed a robber, as we find it exemplified in the scriptural verse: *And he plucked the spear out of the Egyptian's hand* (II Sam. 23:21).

4. Who is deemed guilty of unlawful withholding? One who, having come into possession of another person's money with the latter's consent, withholds it forcibly and does not return it upon the other's demand. Such is the case if one who has a loan or wages due him from another claims his due but cannot get it from his debtor because he is an overbearing and hardhearted person. It is of this that Scripture says, *Thou shalt not oppress thy neighbor* (Lev. 19:13).

5. If one commits robbery, he must return the very object he robbed, for Scripture says, *He shall restore that which he took by robbery* (Lev. 5:23). If, however, the object is lost or altered, he must pay its value. But he is liable for the repayment of its capital value only, whether he confesses of his own accord or whether witnesses testify that he took it by robbery. Thus, even if one takes a rafter by robbery and builds it into a structure, by the law of Scripture he must pull down the whole building and give back the rafter to its owner, inasmuch as it has not been altered. The Sages, however, have made a rule for the benefit of penitents, that the robber may repay its value and need not demolish the building. The same rule applies in all similar cases. Hence even if one takes a rafter by robbery and uses it for the booth he builds for the Feast of Booths, and the owner of the rafter comes and claims it during the festival, he need repay only its value. But if it is claimed after the festival, he must return the rafter itself, inasmuch as it has not been altered and has not been built in with mortar.

6. If one robs another of an object valued less than a pĕruṭah, he is not subject to the law requiring the return of robbed property, although he did commit a transgression. But if one robs another of three bunches of vegetables worth three pĕruṭah, and they go down in price so that the three bunches are now worth only two pĕruṭah, and he returns two of them, he must return the third because it was originally worth a pĕruṭah. However, if he robs another of two bunches worth a pĕruṭah and returns one, no significant robbed property remains in his hand, but the commandment to restore such property has not been fulfilled.

7. If one robs another in an inhabited area and returns the robbed property in the desert, the person robbed has a choice: if he wishes, he may accept it, but if not, he may say to the other, "I will accept it in an inhabited area only, lest it be wrested from me here." It thus remains in the possession of the robber and is his responsibility until he hands it back in an inhabited area. The same rule applies when the value of the robbed article is returned.

8. If one robs another and returns the robbed amount indirectly, upon the occasion of settling some account, he has cleared himself. If he puts the robbed amount into a purse of the other containing money, he has also cleared himself. For a person usually examines his purse every now and then, and so the other will count the money that was returned to him, together with his own money, and merely by counting the returned amount, even without awareness of it, he clears the robber. But if he returns it to an empty purse, he has not cleared himself and he remains responsible for the robbed amount until he lets the other know that he has replaced it in that particular purse.

9. If one covets the male slave or the female slave or the house or goods of another, or anything that it is possible for him to acquire from the other, and he subjects the other to vexation and pesters him until he is allowed to buy it from him, then he transgresses the negative commandment, *Thou shalt not covet* (Exod. 20:14), even if he pays him a high price for it. No flogging is incurred for breach of this prohibition, since it does not involve action. Nor does one transgress this prohibition until he buys the object that he covets, as is exemplified by Scripture when it says, *Thou shalt not covet the silver and gold that is on them nor take it unto thee* (Deut. 7:25)—thus implying that the transgression of coveting is effected only when accompanied by action.

10. If one desires another's house or his wife or his goods or any similar thing that he might buy from him, he transgresses a negative commandment as soon as he thinks in his heart how he is to acquire the desired object and allows his mind to be seduced by it. For Scripture says, *Thou shalt not desire* (Deut. 5:18), and desire is a matter of the heart only.

11. Desire leads to coveting, and coveting to robbery, for if the owner does not wish to sell, even when he is offered a high price and is greatly importuned, it will lead the coveter to rob him, as it is said, *And they covet houses and seize them* (Mic. 2:2). Moreover, if the owner should stand up to him to protect his

property and prevent the robbery, this may lead to bloodshed. You can learn this from the story of Ahab and Naboth (cf. I Kings 21).

12. You thus learn that one who covets transgresses one prohibition, and if he acquires the desired object by bringing pressure upon the owner, or by requesting it of the owner, he transgresses two prohibitions, for this is why Scripture says, *Thou shalt not covet* (Exod. 20:14), and, *Thou shalt not desire* (Deut. 5:18). If he then goes on to commit robbery, he transgresses three prohibitions.

13. If one robs another of property worth a pĕruṭah, it is regarded as if he took his life, for Scripture says, *So are the ways of everyone that is greedy of gain, he taketh away the life of the owners thereof* (Prov. 1:19). Nevertheless, if property taken by robbery no longer exists, and the robber wishes to repent and comes of his own accord to return the value of the robbed property, the Sages have ruled that this should not be accepted from him. Instead, he should be helped and forgiven, so as to encourage penitents in the right path. And if one accepts the value of robbed property, he does not act in the spirit of the Sages.

CHAPTER II

1. If an article taken by robbery is unaltered and still in its original state, it must itself be returned to its owner even if he has abandoned hope of recovering it, and even if the robber has died and it is now in the possession of his heirs. If, however, it becomes altered while in the robber's possession, he acquires title to it in consequence of the alteration, even if the owner has not abandoned hope of recovery, and he must pay its value as of the time of the robbery.

2. This law is on the authority of Scripture, which says, *He shall restore that which he took by robbery* (Lev. 5:23); it has been learned by tradition that if the property is still as it was when the

robber took it, he must restore it, but if it has altered while in his possession, he must pay its value. If the owner has abandoned hope of recovery but the property is unchanged, the robber acquires title to any improvement that takes place after hope is abandoned, and he need pay only its value as of the time of the robbery. This rule is on the authority of the Scribes, enacted for the benefit of penitents. When, therefore, a robber returns what he has taken, the improvement is evaluated for him and he recovers this amount from the person robbed.

3. If a robber sells what he has taken or gives it away as a present, the robbed property is not itself recoverable from a buyer even if it is unaltered. For inasmuch as the owner has abandoned hope of recovery, whether he did so before the purchase or presentation or afterwards, the buyer acquires title to it by virtue of the owner's abandonment of hope of recovery and the change of possession.

4. If one robs another of property, improves it and then sells or bequeaths it before the owner has abandoned hope of recovery, the bequest of the improvement, or its sale, is valid. The purchaser or the heir acquires title to the improvement and may exact the value of the improvement from the person robbed, but he must restore the property taken by robbery. The person robbed may in turn exact the value of the improvement from the robber, seeing that he has not abandoned hope of recovery.

Similarly, if the buyer or the heir improves the robbed property, he may exact the value of the improvement from the person robbed.

5. If a robber sells what he has taken to a heathen, it must revert to the owner even if the heathen improves it.

If the heathen, after improving it, sells it to an Israelite, the latter acquires title to the improvements, inasmuch as the robber was an Israelite and the present possessor is an Israelite. If, however, the person robbed seizes the improvement, it may not be reclaimed from him.

6. We have already explained that if an article taken by robbery improves after the owner has abandoned hope of recovery or after it has been altered, the improvement belongs to the robber even if the article improves of its own accord, this being a rule made for the benefit of penitents. Thus if one obtains a cow by robbery and it becomes in calf while in his possession—no matter whether it calves before he is sued for robbery or whether it has not yet calved—or, if he obtains a ewe by robbery and it becomes heavy with wool while in his possession—no matter whether he shears it before he is sued for robbery or whether he has not yet shorn it—he need pay only its value as of the time of the robbery, seeing that the owner has given up hope of recovery. If the cow calves or the ewe is shorn, the fleece and the offspring belong to the robber. If the cow has not yet calved or the ewe is not yet shorn, an evaluation of the improvement is made for the robber, who may exact this amount from the person robbed but must return the animal itself.

7. If one obtains by robbery a heifer in calf and the owner abandons hope of recovering it and then it calves, or if one obtains by robbery a ewe heavy with wool and the owner abandons hope of recovering it and then the robber shears it, he must pay the value of a heifer about to calve or the value of a ewe ready for shearing. If, however, the heifer calves or he shears the ewe before the owner abandons hope of recovery or before there is any change, the fleece and the offspring belong to the owner. Even if the animal becomes in calf or heavy with wool while in the hands of the robber, then inasmuch as the owner has not abandoned hope of recovery and the robbed property has not changed, it is still deemed to be in the possession of its original owner, although the robber is held responsible for all accidents that may befall it.

8. If one steals an animal or robs another of an animal and then declares it dedicated and slaughters it after the owner abandons hope of recovery, it is deemed the property of the robber only from the time that he declares it dedicated, so that a sinner should

not be at an advantage, and all offspring or fleece obtained from the time of the theft to the time of dedication belongs to the owner.

9. The above rule applies only to improvement that is of itself, such as fleece and offspring. But if an animal is lean and the robber fattens it even before hope of recovery is abandoned, he may exact from the person robbed the value of the improvement due to fattening. The same rule applies in every similar case of improvement involving expenditure.

10. An alteration which can be restored to its original state is not regarded as an alteration. Thus, if one obtains wooden boards by robbery and nails them together to make a box, this is not considered an alteration, for he can separate them and they will again become boards.

11. If one obtains earth by robbery and makes a brick of it, he does not acquire title to it, for if the brick is crushed, it becomes earth again. If one obtains a bar of metal by robbery and makes a coin, he does not acquire title to it, for if the coin is melted, it becomes a bar again. And so, too, in all similar cases.

12. But if one obtains timber by robbery and planes it smooth and cuts it into shape, or hollows it out and makes it into utensils; or if he obtains wool by robbery and dyes it, or combs it and bleaches it; or if he obtains yarn by robbery and makes it into cloth, or obtains a brick by robbery and turns it into earth, or obtains stones and crushes them, or money and melts it, this is deemed an alteration while in his possession, for even if he makes other coins, they are considered to be something essentially new. The same rule applies in all similar cases.

13. If one obtains old money by robbery and polishes it like new, he does not acquire title to it, for it will age and become as it was. But if he obtains new money by robbery and ages it, he does acquire title to it, for even if he were then to renovate it, it would be regarded as something essentially new. If one obtains a growing palm by robbery and cuts it down, he does not acquire title to it

even if he cuts it into logs. But if he makes it into rafters, he does acquire title to it.

14. If one obtains large rafters by robbery and makes them into small ones, he does not acquire title to them. But if he makes them into boards so that their designation is changed, he does acquire title to them. If he obtains a palm branch by robbery and separates its leaves, he acquires title to the leaves. If he obtains the leaves by robbery and makes a broom, he acquires title to it. If he obtains a lamb by robbery and it becomes a ram, or a calf and it becomes an ox, this is considered an alteration while in his possession, and he acquires title to the animal and need repay only its value as of the time of the theft, even if the owner does not abandon hope of recovery.

15. If one obtains a vessel by robbery and breaks it, we do not assess the depreciation for him, rather he must pay the full value, and the broken vessel belongs to him. But if the owner wishes to take the broken vessel, he may do so, and the robber must then pay the depreciation. For the above rule was made for the benefit of the owner, and if he does not wish to take advantage of it, he need not do so. The same rule applies in all similar cases.

16. A robbed article which has not changed but has appreciated in value must be returned to its owner even if he has abandoned hope of recovering it, and the robber is not entitled to any part of it. For the enactment of the Sages, whereby a robber acquires the right to an improvement occurring after the owner has abandoned hope of recovery, applies only to improvements such as fleece and offspring, but where an improvement in value occurs, then if the robbed article is itself returned, the robber is not entitled to any share of it.

CHAPTER III

1. If one robs another of a cask of wine worth a denar at the time of the robbery, and its value goes up to four while it is in his

possession, the rule is as follows: If the robber breaks the cask, or drinks the wine, or sells it or gives it away as a present after it has increased in value, he must pay four, its value as of the time it vanished, since the wine itself would have had to be restored if he had let it alone. If, however, the cask breaks through no fault of his, or is lost, the robber need pay only a denar, its value as of the time of the robbery.

2. If the wine is worth four at the time of the robbery, and a denar at the time it vanishes, the robber must pay four, its value as of the time of the robbery, no matter whether he breaks the cask or drinks the wine or whether the cask is broken or the wine lost accidentally. The same rule applies in all similar cases.

3. If one obtains by robbery a packet containing fifty dates which sells for nine if sold together but would fetch ten if sold one by one, he need pay only nine, and the person robbed cannot say to him, "I would have sold them one by one." The same rule applies to one who causes damage or the like to any private property. But this is not the case with dedicated property, where he must pay ten.

4. If one obtains an animal by robbery and it becomes old or grows lean beyond hope of improvement—for example, through a disease for which there is no proper cure—or if one obtains a coin by robbery and it cracks or is made obsolete by the government, or if one obtains produce by robbery and all of it rots, or if one obtains wine by robbery and it sours: in any such instance it is regarded as if he had obtained a utensil by robbery and broken it, and he must pay the value as of the time of the robbery. But if one obtains animals by robbery and they grow lean but are able to be fattened, or if he obtains slaves by robbery and they grow old, or if he obtains a coin by robbery and it falls out of use in one country but is still current in another, or if he obtains produce by robbery and only part of it rots, or priestly heave offering and it becomes ritually unclean, or if he obtains leavened food by robbery and it outlasts the Passover week, or an animal and it is abused or

is rendered unfit for sacrifice or is being taken to be stoned: in any such instance, he may say to the owner, "Here is your own property before you," and he may give back the object itself.

5. The above rule applies only if one restores the robbed property itself, but if this is burned or lost after its use has become forbidden, he must repay its value as of the time of the robbery. Consequently, if, after its use has become forbidden, he denies having it on oath, he is liable for payment of its value plus a fifth part and must bring a guilt-offering.

6. If one obtains an animal by robbery and uses it to carry a burden, or rides on it, or ploughs or threshes with it, or does anything similar, and then restores it to its owner, he need pay nothing, although he has transgressed a negative commandment. For he has done it no damage, nor has he made it any leaner. But if this person is known to rob, or to withhold money illegally, or to do these things time after time, we may impose a fine on him, even outside the Land of Israel. The hire of the animal or the advantage that he has obtained from it should be evaluated, and he must pay this amount to the person robbed.

7. If one seizes another's slave and makes him labor but without causing him to neglect other work, he need not pay, for it is to a person's advantage that his slave does not become idle. If, however, one takes another's slave from other work, he must pay the owner the rate for a laborer.

8. If one seizes another's ship and makes use of it, the rule is that if it is not usually hired out, we assess the amount it has depreciated, and he must pay this amount. If, however, the ship is usually hired out and the intruder enters it with the intention of hiring it, the owner may demand payment for its hire if he so desires or for its depreciation if he prefers, inasmuch as the intruder enters the ship without permission. But if he enters it with the intention to commit robbery, he need pay only for the depreciation. The same rule applies in all similar cases.

9. If one takes residence in another's courtyard without his knowledge, the rule is that if the courtyard is not usually rented, the tenant need not pay the owner any rent even though he does usually rent a place for himself. For one has benefited without the other having lost anything. But if the courtyard is usually rented, the tenant must pay the owner rent even if it is not usual for him to rent a place, seeing that he has deprived the owner of money.

10. If one has wool and ready-mixed dyes, and another comes and dyes the wool in the dye without the owner's knowledge, the dyer must pay the owner the amount by which he has depreciated the wool, but the owner cannot call him to account for the improvement of the dye on the wool. But if the owner seizes the value of the dye that he has lost, it may not be reclaimed from him.

11. If one makes unauthorized use of an object bailed to him, either himself or through his son or a slave or an agent, he is deemed a robber and is held responsible for all accidental damage, and the robbed object is deemed to be in his care as is the rule for all other robbers. If he intends to make unauthorized use of the object, he is not held responsible for it until he has actually used it. Once he does make use of it, however, he is held responsible for it. Even if his action does not depreciate the value of the object at all, but he merely moves it on his premises from one place to another in order to make use of it, he is held responsible for it, seeing that unauthorized use need not involve depreciation.

12. If one lifts up a cask to take from it a quarter loḡ of wine, he is held responsible for accidental damage even if he does not actually take the wine. But if one picks up a purse to take a denar from it—or some similar object which does not form part of a connected substance—the rule remains a matter of doubt whether he is responsible for the whole purse or whether he is responsible only for the denar.

13. If produce is deposited with a bailee and he takes some of it, he is held responsible only for the produce that he takes. The remainder of the bailment, left in its place, is still the responsibility of its owner. If, however, the remainder suffers damage because

of what is taken, the bailee is responsible for all of it. Thus, if a bailee tips a cask where it rests and takes from it a quarter log̅ of wine or more, the rule is as follows: If the cask breaks after he takes wine without moving it from its place, he is held responsible only for the wine he takes, since he has not lifted up the cask. However, if the rest of the wine sours, he must pay the value of the entire cask as of the time of the robbery. The same rule applies in all similar cases.

14. If one denies before the court that he has received a bailment, the rule is as follows: If it is in his possession at the time that he denies it, he is deemed a robber with respect to it and is held responsible for accidental damage.

15. If one borrows an article without its owner's knowledge, he is deemed a robber. If a vessel is in the hand of its owner's son or in the hand of his slave, and one takes it from him and makes use of it, he is regarded as is one who borrows an article without its owner's knowledge, and it is deemed to be in his care, so that he is held responsible for accidental damage until he returns it to the owner. Consequently, if he returns it to the minor in whose hand it was, or to the slave, and it is lost by them or broken, he must pay for it. The same rule applies in all similar cases.

16. If one snatches a pledge from a debtor's hand without the permission of the court, he is deemed a robber, even though the other is in his debt. It is needless to say that if one goes into another's house and takes a pledge, he is deemed a robber, for Scripture says, *Thou shalt stand outside* (Deut. 24: 11).

CHAPTER IV

1. The Sages have penalized robbers by allowing the person robbed to confirm his claim by taking an oath that the object in question is his and then recover it from the robber, provided that there is a presumption supported by two witnesses that the defendant has robbed him.

2. Thus if one has nothing under his coat when he enters another's house in the presence of witnesses to seize a pledge, but when he comes out he does have articles under his coat, and the witnesses do not know what they are and the householder says, "You have robbed me of such-and-such," the rule is as follows: No matter whether the robber says, "I did not go in, and I took nothing," or "I went in to take a pledge, as the witnesses saw, but I did not take anything of yours, and I had only things of my own under my coat," or "I took such and such a thing," while the householder pleads that the person has taken the article admitted and something else as well, the householder takes an oath while holding a sacred object and may then recover whatever he claims.

3. The above rule applies only if one claims articles he can be expected to own, or if there is a likelihood that persons may have deposited with him the articles that he claims, and if he claims articles that can be carried under a coat in the manner testified to by the witnesses.

4. If witnesses see a person enter another's house to take a pledge but do not see him when he comes out; or if, when he comes out, nothing is seen under his coat, and the householder brings a charge and says, "He took this and this," the rule is that the defendant goes free even if he replies, "I never went in at all," and thus contradicts the witnesses. For if he were to say, "I went in but did not take anything," he would only have to take an oath of inducement confirming that he took nothing and he would go free, since it is possible that he could enter with the intention to rob without actually robbing.

5. If one witness testifies that a person has entered another's house and has carried things out under his coat, but the witness does not know what they were, and the accused replies that he robbed the other of nothing, or says, "I took it for a debt," the rule is that since the witness does not know what was under the coat, the accused may take an oath, holding a sacred object, affirming that he did not commit robbery. For one is not presumed guilty of robbery unless two witnesses testify against him.

6. Just as a householder himself may take an oath and exact his claim from a robber, so may the caretaker of a householder, or even the caretaker's wife, take an oath affirming that the accused took such-and-such, and the accused must pay.

7. If a retainer or an employee of the householder was there, he may not take an oath to reclaim what was robbed. Nor may the person robbed take an oath in this instance, seeing that he was not at home when he was robbed; nor, inasmuch as the witnesses do not know what he took out under his coat, may they render the robber liable for restoring it; nor may an oath be administered to the robber, inasmuch as he is suspected of being apt to swear falsely.

8. What then is to be done in such an instance? The householder may pronounce a general ban against anyone who has taken something from his house and who does not confess in court. Even if the robber confesses that he took a part, he need return only the part that he confesses to have taken, for the householder does not bring a definite charge against him.

9. If a person robs one of five people, and it is not known which is robbed, but each sues the robber, saying, "You robbed me," the rule is that even if there are no witnesses to the robbery, each one of the five may swear that the accused robbed him, and the accused must pay to each one the amount taken. This decision, too, is a penalty imposed on a robber by the Sages because he commits a sin and robs. But, according to the law of Scripture, a person is not obliged to pay if there is doubt.

10. If one says to two people, "I robbed one of you—or the father of one of you—and I do not know which," the rule is that if he wishes to fulfill his moral obligation, he must repay to each one what was taken. But legally he need provide only once the amount taken by robbery, and the two people share it between them, since neither of them knows that he was robbed apart from what the robber tells them. Nor did the Sages impose a penalty in this case, seeing that there is no claimant.

11. If one accuses another, saying to him, "You robbed me of a hundred," the rule is as follows: If the other replies, "I did not rob you," he takes an oath of inducement, as does everyone against whom a claim is made. But if he confesses that he took fifty by robbery, he must pay this amount and must also take a scriptural oath concerning the remainder, as is the rule for everyone who admits part of a claim, inasmuch as there is no presumption supported by witnesses that he is a robber. Similarly, if one accuses another of having entered his house and robbed him of certain articles, but the accused says, "I took them as a pledge for a debt you owe me," to which the householder replies, "I owe you nothing," the rule is as follows: Although the accused admits that he took a pledge from the other without permission, he may take an oath and collect his debt from the pledge, seeing that there are no witnesses to testify that he committed a robbery. For "the mouth that forbids is the same mouth that permits." Since, however, the claimant swears and takes his claim, he must take the oath holding a sacred object, as will be explained in the Laws Concerning Pleading.

12. If witnesses see a person enter another's house in the owner's absence and take things from it—even if he carries them out openly, and even if the owner does frequently sell articles of his own—the rule is that if the owner claims that they were taken by robbery, while the other replies, "I came with your permission, for you sold—or gave—them to me," or "I seized them in payment of a debt you owe me," he is not believed. For if one enters another's house in the owner's absence and takes things from it in the presence of witnesses, he is presumed to be a robber. Consequently, he must return the robbed articles to the owner, an oath being unnecessary inasmuch as the witnesses saw what he took by robbery. After he has returned the articles, he may in turn sue the owner for whatever he claims, and the law will adjudicate between them.

13. Similarly, if there is only one witness present, and the owner pleads that the article in another's possession was obtained by

robbery while the accused says, "I have it by purchase," or "I collected it for a debt," or "It was mine and was deposited with you," he must return the article to its owner without an oath being taken. For if two witnesses had been present, he would be condemned to pay, and inasmuch as only one witness was present, he should by law be required to take an oath. However, he is unable to take an oath, for he does not contradict the witness. Now the rule is that if one is by law required to take an oath but cannot do so, he must pay. Consequently, if he denies it, saying, "I did not enter his house or take anything," he must swear a scriptural oath that he took nothing from the house and he then goes free, seeing that there is only one witness whom he contradicts.

14. It once happened that a person snatched a bar of silver from another in the presence of one witness and later came and said, "I did snatch, but what I snatched was mine," and the Sages condemned him to return it since he was obliged to swear, because of the testimony of the witness, but he could not do so because he admitted what the witness said. If, however, there had been no witness present, he would have taken an oath of inducement confirming that what he snatched was his. Again, if he had contradicted the witness, saying, "I did not snatch anything at all," he would have taken a scriptural oath confirming that he did not snatch anything. This is how any similar case should be adjudicated, no matter where it occurs.

15. If one snatches gold coins from another in the presence of one witness, and then says, "I snatched my own property and there were twenty of them," he must repay the twenty even though the witness does not know how many were snatched. For the witness knew definitely that gold coins were snatched, and if there had been two witnesses, the accused would have been obliged to pay. Thus, seeing that only one witness testifies against him, it follows that he is obliged to take an oath; but he cannot, as we have explained.

16. If the accused says, "I snatched twenty that were mine," and the accuser claims that he snatched a hundred, and the witness does

not know the number involved, the accused must pay the twenty that he admits snatching and take a scriptural oath concerning the remainder, inasmuch as he was deemed liable for part of the claim. My own opinion, however, inclines to the view that in this case he need take only an oath of inducement, since he admits nothing but says, "What I snatched was my own."

17. If one enters another's house in the owner's absence and takes articles from it in the presence of a witness, but the witness does not know how much he has taken, and the owner says, "There were twenty articles in my house," while the robber says, "I took only ten and they were my own," then he must restore these ten because he is liable for an oath but cannot take one. However, he need not take even an oath of inducement concerning the remainder, since the owner cannot bring a definite charge against him.

CHAPTER V

1. It is forbidden to buy from a robber property obtained by robbery, and it is also forbidden to assist him in making alterations to enable him to acquire title to it. For if one does this or anything similar to it, he encourages transgressors and himself transgresses the commandment, *Thou shalt not put a stumbling block in front of the blind* (Lev. 19:14).

2. It is forbidden to derive any benefit from property obtained by robbery even after hope of recovery has been abandoned, provided that one knows for certain that this is the very property obtained by robbery. Thus, if it is known for certain that a specific animal was obtained by robbery, it is forbidden to ride it or plough with it.

3. If one obtains a house or a field by robbery, it is forbidden to pass through it or to enter it in the summer to keep out of the sun or in the rainy season to get out of the rain. If one lives in it, he must pay rent to the owner as must any one who lives in another's

courtyard without the latter's knowledge. If one takes palm trees by robbery and makes a bridge out of them, it is forbidden to cross it. And the same rule applies in all similar cases.

4. If one transgresses and consumes things obtained by robbery, after hope of recovery has been abandoned, he need not pay for them. But if one consumes them before hope of recovery has been abandoned, and the owner wishes to collect from the consumer, he may do so, for the property still belongs to the owner. But if he prefers, he may collect from the robber.

5. If one commits robbery and then dies, the rule is that if he leaves real property, his heirs must pay indemnity, whether he had allowed the robbed article to be consumed by them after hope of recovery was abandoned, or whether he had not given it to them but sold it or lost it instead. They are not, however, obliged to pay from inherited movable property. For the value of what is obtained by robbery is regarded as a debt owed by the robber, and movable property is not under lien to a creditor.

6. The Geonim, however, have long since made a rule that a creditor may collect his debt from movable property even if his loan was made only by word of mouth, and so the heirs of a robber are now obliged to repay what was robbed, whether they have consumed it or not, whether hope of recovery has been abandoned or not, and whether the robber bequeathed real property or movable property.

7. The law regarding the purchase of movable property from a robber is the same as that regarding purchase from a thief: If the seller was a notorious robber, the Sages did not apply the principle of market overt for the purchaser, but if he was not notorious, they did apply this principle and the one robbed had to repay the money given by the purchaser to get back the property of which he was robbed. The one robbed could then sue the robber for the value of the robbed property. If, however, the owner had already abandoned hope of recovery, the purchaser acquired title to the property obtained by robbery and did not have to return it.

8. It is forbidden to receive any benefit from a robber, but if a small share of his possessions is his own, even though most of them were obtained by robbery, it is permissible to benefit from him, unless one knows for certain that the article in question is robbed property.

9. When persons are presumably robbers and all their property is presumably obtained by robbery, because they are robbers by occupation, such as tax collectors and bandits, it is forbidden to benefit from them since the presumption is that their occupation involves robbery. Nor may small coins be changed into denar from their till, since everything there is presumed to have been obtained by robbery.

10. If tax collectors take away one's coat and give him another instead, or if they take away his ass and give him another instead, he may keep the one given him because this is regarded as a transaction of sale and the presumption is that the owner has already abandoned hope of recovery. Nor does the recipient know for certain that it is property obtained by robbery. But if he is a conscientiously pious person who is particularly strict with himself, he should return it to its original owner.

11. This rule, namely that a tax collector is regarded as is a brigand, applies only if the collector is a heathen, or is self-appointed, or was appointed by the king but is not required to collect a fixed amount, and may take what he likes and leave what he likes. But if the king fixes a tax of, say, a third or a quarter (denar) or another fixed sum, and appoints to collect it on his behalf an Israelite known to be a trustworthy person who would not add to what was ordered by the king, this collector is not presumed to be a robber, for the king's decree has the force of law. Moreover, if one avoids paying such a tax, he is a transgressor, for he steals the king's property, whether the king be a heathen or an Israelite.

12. The same rule applies to cases where a king imposes as a tax on the citizenry, or on each person individually, a fixed annual amount, or imposes a fixed amount on each field, or decrees that

if one breaks a specified law, he shall forfeit all his property to the palace, or decrees that if one is found in a field at harvest time, he shall pay the tax due on it whether he is the owner of the field or not, or makes some similar regulation. None of these cases is deemed robbery, nor is an Israelite who collects these levies on behalf of the king presumed to be a thief; rather he may well be a worthy person, provided only that he does not add, alter, or take anything for himself.

13. Similarly, if a king becomes angry with one of his servants or ministers among his subjects and confiscates his field or his courtyard, this is not deemed robbery and one is permitted to benefit from it. If one buys it from the king, he becomes its owner and the original owner cannot take it away from him. For the law of all kings permits them to confiscate all the property of those ministers with whom they are displeased, and the king has therefore canceled the owner's original right to it, so that the courtyard or field in question is regarded as ownerless, and if one buys it from the king, he becomes its lawful owner. But if a king takes the courtyard or field of one of the citizens, contrary to the laws he has promulgated, he is deemed a robber, and the original owner may recover it from anyone who buys it from the king.

14. The general rule is: any law promulgated by the king to apply to everyone and not to one person alone is not deemed robbery. But whatever he takes from one particular person only, not in accordance with a law known to everyone but by doing violence to this person, is deemed robbery. Consequently, when the king's treasurers or officers sell fields for the fixed tax due on such fields, their sale is valid. But the tax imposed on each individual may not be collected except from the person himself, and so, if they sell his field to recover the poll tax, it is not a legal sale unless the king's law permits such action.

15. If the king's law provides that if one fails to pay the tax on his field the field shall belong to whoever pays the tax, and the owner of the field runs away because of the tax, and another comes and pays the king the tax due on it and consumes its produce, this

is not deemed robbery; rather he may consume the produce and pay the tax until the owner returns. For, as we have explained, the king's law is binding.

16. Similarly, if a king decrees that whoever pays the fixed tax due from any individual may compel the one delinquent to work for him, and then an Israelite comes and pays the tax due from some other impoverished Israelite, he may make him work more than would be usual, for the king's law is binding. But he must not make him work like a slave.

17. If a king cuts down trees belonging to a private individual and makes them into a bridge, it may be crossed. Similarly, if he demolishes houses and makes from the material a road or a wall, one is permitted to benefit from it. The same rule applies in all similar cases, for the king's law is binding.

18. All the above rules apply only to a king whose coins circulate in the localities concerned, for then the inhabitants of the country have accepted him and definitely regard him as their master and themselves as his servants. But if his coins do not circulate in the localities in question, he is regarded as a robber who uses force, and as a troop of armed bandits, whose laws are not binding. Moreover, such a king and all his servants are deemed robbers in every respect.

CHAPTER VI

1. Rafters, masonry, timber, and the like floated away by a river are deemed permissible if the owner has abandoned hope of recovery, and they then belong to the one who retrieves them. But if one does not know whether the owner has abandoned hope of recovery or not, he must return them, and it is needless to say that this is the rule if the owner is striving to recover his property.

2. Consequently, if one rescues anything from a stream, or from the ebb of the sea, or the flotsam of a river, or from a heathen, or

from a fire, or from a lion or a bear or a leopard or a panther, it becomes his if he knows for certain that the owner has abandoned hope of recovery. But if he does not know this, he must return it.

3. If one rescues anything from an Israelite brigand, it becomes his since it is generally assumed that the owner has abandoned hope of recovery; but if one knows the owner has not abandoned hope of recovery, he must return it. On the other hand, if one rescues anything from a heathen brigand or a heathen tax collector, he must return it, since it is generally assumed that the owner did not abandon hope of recovery; but if one knows for certain that the owner has abandoned hope of recovery, it becomes his. Why is it that it is generally assumed that the owner abandons hope of recovery in the case of an Israelite brigand but not in the case of a heathen? Because the owner knows that heathen courts reclaim property from a robber on the basis of circumstantial evidence and conjecture, even though there are no witnesses that he committed robbery.

4. If cress growing in (a field of) flax is picked while fresh, this is not deemed robbery because the cress spoils the flax of the owner of the field. But if it has dried, taking it is deemed robbery, since it has already done all the harm it will do. And if it is on the edge of the field, it is forbidden even while it is fresh.

5. We have already explained in Laws Concerning Damage by Chattels that if straw or stubble is put in the public domain, taking it is not deemed robbery. On the other hand, if dung has been put in the public domain, whether at the customary time for putting out dung or not, taking it is forbidden and is deemed robbery.

6. If one's clothes have become exchanged with another's at a house of mourning or at a festivity, he may not use them before the owner comes, whereupon he must return them and then take back his own. If, however, they become exchanged at the tailor's the rule is as follows: If the wife or children of the tailor gave the owner the wrong clothes, or if the tailor himself gave them to

him, saying, "Here are your clothes," he may not use them before the owner comes, whereupon he must return them and then take back his own. But if the tailor says to him, "Take this garment," he may use it until the owner comes, whereupon he must return it and then take back his own. For it may be the tailor's own garment or the owner may have instructed the tailor to sell it for him. The same rule applies in all similar instances.

7. Many actions have been prohibited by the Sages as being robbery. If one transgresses these prohibitions, he is deemed a robber on the authority of the Scribes, as are pigeon fliers and dice players, for example. The rule concerning pigeon fliers may be illustrated as follows: No one may fly a pigeon in an inhabited region because he will be taking other people's property illegally, since if he sends out a male it will bring a female from some other dovecote, or if a female, it will bring a male. Moreover, not only one who flies pigeons, but also one who behaves similarly with any other bird or wild or domestic animal is deemed a robber on the authority of the Scribes.

8. Similarly, the Sages have forbidden the catching of pigeons in an inhabited region because they belong to someone else. Snares for pigeons may therefore not be set except at a distance of four miles from any inhabited region. If, however, the region is one where vines are cultivated, snares may not be set even within a hundred miles, for the pigeons belong to the owners of the vineyards. Again, one may not set a snare among dovecotes, even if they be his own, or belong to a heathen, or are ownerless and are a hundred miles away from any inhabited region, since other doves are apt to come to any collection of dovecotes.

9. A dovecote must be kept at least fifty cubits away from a town. Nor may one set up a dovecote in his own field unless he has fifty cubits on each side, so that the young birds will not be drawn to do damage in the fields and eat from another's property. If, however, one buys a dovecote from someone else, its position is deemed legitimate by prescriptive right and he is not obliged to

move it away, even if there is no more land between it and the beginning of the neighboring field than is needed to sow a quarter ḳab̲ of seed.

10. What is meant by dice players? If persons play with blocks of wood or stone or bone or the like and stipulate among themselves that the winner of the game receives a certain amount from the other, this is deemed robbery on the authority of the Scribes, even though the winner gets his winnings with the consent of the owner. He is committing robbery, seeing that he takes another's money for nothing by means of a game or sport. Similarly, if persons play with domestic or wild animals or birds and stipulate that the one whose animal wins or runs faster should receive an agreed amount from the other, or make any similar wager, this is forbidden and is deemed robbery on the authority of the Scribes.

11. Playing dice with a heathen does not involve robbery but entails the prohibition of wasting time on useless pursuits, for it is not fitting for a person to spend any part of his life other than on gaining knowledge and furthering civilization.

12. If traps laid for wild animals, birds, or fish have caught prey and a stranger takes them, he is liable for robbery on the authority of the Scribes only, because they had not yet reached the possession of one entitled to acquire them.

13. A flowing river and a gushing spring belong to everyone. If a poor person is lopping forgotten olives from the top of an olive tree and another poor person comes and picks them up from the ground, this is deemed robbery on the authority of the Scribes. However, if the poor person at the top of the tree collects them by hand and throws them to the ground, the other commits robbery on the authority of Scripture, for they have already been in the possession of one entitled to acquire them.

14. Bees are not under human control in the same way as are poultry or geese, yet one can acquire title to them on the authority of the Scribes. If one obtains a swarm of bees by robbery and keeps

it away from its owner when it enters his premises, this is deemed robbery on the authority of the Scribes. Consequently, if a swarm of bees has left one person's domain and come to rest in his neighbor's domain, the owner of the swarm has the right to walk across his neighbor's field until he has recovered his swarm. If he does any damage, he must pay for the damage done, but he may not cut off a branch even though he intends to pay for it.

15. A woman or a minor is considered trustworthy if either of them says that a particular swarm came from a certain place, provided that they are speaking without premeditation and provided that the owner is pursuing the swarm and asks where it has alighted. For although a woman or a minor is not qualified to give evidence, the Sages accepted their word in this case, seeing that the ownership of bees rests only on the authority of the Scribes.

16. If one has in his possession anything obtained by what is considered robbery on the authority of the Scribes, it cannot be exacted from him by a court of law. Also, if he denies (falsely) on oath that it is in his possession, he need not add a fifth part as he would have to do in the case of actual robbery.

CHAPTER VII

1. If one is obligated to pay money to a fellow Israelite and denies it and swears falsely, he must repay him the capital value denied plus a fifth part. He must also bring a sacrifice, known as the guilt offering for robbery.

2. The same rule applies whether one robs or withholds money illegally or steals, or whether the money was lent him or deposited with him, or whether he finds lost property and denies it, or whether he and another are in partnership and he retains some of the joint property, or whether work is done for him and he does not pay the amount due. The general rule in such cases is as follows: Wherever one would have been legally liable for payment if

he had confessed, he must repay the capital amount plus a fifth part if he denies on oath, for Scripture says, *And deal falsely with his neighbor in a matter of deposit* . . . (Lev. 5:21).

3. The above rule applies only where it is one's obligation to pay on his own account, but if it is his obligation to pay on his father's account, he need not pay the fifth part. Thus, if one's father has robbed or stolen or owes money to others, and the son knows of this and yet denies it on oath and then later admits it, he need repay only the capital amount, for Scripture says, *Which he took by robbery* (Lev. 5:23), thus implying that he must add a fifth part to what he obtains by robbery himself, but not to what his father obtained by robbery.

4. The above rule applies only if the property obtained by robbery is no longer in existence. If, however, the father robbed and died and the property he obtained by robbery is still in existence, and the heir first denies it on oath and afterwards confesses, he must pay the capital plus a fifth part.

5. If the father robbed and denied it on oath, then confessed and later died, the heir must pay the capital plus a fifth part.

6. If one robs, denies it on oath, and then dies, and his heir confesses, the heir need repay only the capital amount. In either case, the heir is exempt from bringing a guilt offering.

7. If one swears to a heathen, he must repay the capital but not the fifth part, for Scripture says, *And deal falsely with his neighbor* (Lev. 5:21). Similarly, if one takes by robbery property worth less than a pĕruṭah and denies it on oath, he need not pay the fifth part, because property worth less than a pĕruṭah is not deemed property. How much is the fifth part? One fourth part of the capital; so that if one robs another of an article worth four and denies it on oath, he must repay five. However, if the robbed property is still in existence, he must return it and also pay one fourth of its value.

8. If one takes an oath denying money that is due, he need not pay the fifth part unless he confesses himself. But if witnesses come

while he is maintaining his denial, he need pay only the capital, on the testimony of the witnesses, and he need not pay the fifth part. For the fifth part and the offering are intended as an atonement, and one need not provide them unless he confesses of his own accord.

9. If one robs another, even if he denies it, seeing that he did not take an oath, he need not, upon subsequent confession of guilt, chase after the owner to return to him the money in his possession. The money may remain in the possession of the robber until the owner comes to take what is his. If, however, one has denied on oath a robbery of a pĕruṭah worth or more, he is obligated to pursue the owner to make restitution to him even if the latter be on oceanic islands. For the owner will long since have abandoned hope of recovery and will not come again to sue the robber, seeing that the latter has already denied the robbery on oath.

10. Even if one has restored the entire property obtained by robbery with the exception of a pĕruṭah worth, he is obligated to take it also to the person robbed. He may give it neither to the son of the person robbed nor to his agent, unless the person robbed made him his agent in the presence of witnesses. If, however, one brings property obtained by robbery plus the fifth part to the local court of law, he may offer the guilt offering and atonement is effected for him, and the court must arrange for its care until it reaches its owner. Similarly, he may give it to an agent of the court. If one gives property obtained by robbery or a similar act to the court, he has fulfilled his obligation.

11. If one has restored the capital but not the fifth part, or if the capital was remitted but not the fifth part, or if both were remitted with the exception of less than a pĕruṭah worth of the capital, he need not go with it after the person robbed; rather the latter must come and get the remainder. Even if the property obtained by robbery is in existence, the possibility that the remainder might increase in value and be worth a pĕruṭah is ignored. If, however, one has restored the fifth part but not the capital, or the fifth part has

been remitted but not the capital, or both have been remitted with the exception of a pĕruṭah worth of the capital, he must take this to the owner or give it to the local court, as we have explained.

12. If one restores the capital to the owner and denies the fifth part a second time on oath, the fifth part then assumes the status of capital in every respect, and he must repay an additional fifth part on its account, as it is said, *And shall add the fifth part more thereto* (Lev. 5:24), meaning that he must add fifth to fifth until the fifth part which he last denies on oath is worth less than a pĕruṭah.

13. If one taking care of a deposit pleads on oath that it is lost and then admits that he still has it, and then again pleads on oath that it is lost and again admits that he has it, he must pay a fifth part for each oath, together with one capital amount, for Scripture says, *And shall add the fifth part more thereto* (*ibid.*), meaning that one may pay several fifth parts on the same capital.

CHAPTER VIII

1. If one robs another and the person robbed dies, the property obtained by robbery—or its value, if it has been lost or altered—must be restored to the heirs. If the robber took an oath and the person robbed died afterward, he must give the heirs the capital value and the additional fifth part.

2. If one robs his father and denies it on oath and then the father dies, the rule is that if the property obtained by robbery no longer exists or has been altered, he must account to his brothers for their share of the capital value and the additional fifth part. However, if the property obtained by robbery is still in existence, it is his duty to divest himself of this property. He should therefore give the property obtained by robbery and the additional fifth part to his brothers and render them an account for his share.

3. If the robber has no brothers but is himself the sole heir, he may hand the property obtained by robbery to his sons. If he has

no sons, he may give the property to his creditor in payment of a loan or donate it to charity. For once the property itself has left his possession, he is cleared, even if he gives it away as a present or in settlement of a debt, provided however that he tells the recipient, "This is what was taken by robbery from my father."

4. Similarly, if one robs a proselyte and denies it on oath but then confesses, and the proselyte agrees to convert the robbery into a loan and he subsequently dies, the rule is that the robber must divest himself of the property concerned, although he did acquire title to it.

5. The above rule applies only if he confesses in the meantime. However, if one robs an heirless proselyte and denies it on oath and then the proselyte dies, he must pay the capital value and the additional fifth part to the priests of the current watch and bring his guilt offering, and only then will he have made atonement thereby.

6. It is known from tradition that when Scripture says, *But if the man have no kinsman to whom restitution may be made for the guilt, the restitution for guilt which is made shall be the Lord's, even the priest's* (Num. 5:8), this refers to a proselyte who has died and is heirless, and the *guilt* spoken of here refers to the property obtained by robbery, or its value. For this reason, if one restores at nighttime property obtained by robbery from a proselyte, he has not fulfilled his obligation, since Scripture terms the restitution a *guilt,* and a guilt sacrifice cannot be offered at night. Nor may the priests divide unevenly one restitution for robbery from an heirless proselyte and compensate by a proportionate division of another such restitution, just as they may not divide unevenly the flesh of one guilt offering and compensate by a proportionate division of the flesh of another.

7. If property robbed of a proselyte does not, after its return, provide each priest of the watch with the value of a pĕruṭah, the duty to restore it has not been discharged, for Scripture says, *The restitution for guilt which is made shall be the Lord's, even the*

priest's (Num. 5:8), implying that there must be a restitution to each priest.

Why does Scripture when referring to robbery from a proselyte say, *if the* MAN *have no kinsman* (Num. 5:8)? To teach us that if the proselyte is an adult, we must make inquiry and investigate to discover whether he has heirs or not; but if he is a minor we need make neither inquiry nor investigation concerning him but can assume that he has no heirs.

8. In relation to property robbed from a proselyte, the priests are regarded as the recipients of a gift. Consequently, if one robs an heirless proselyte of leavened food and keeps it until the Passover week is over, he must pay the priests the value of the leavened food as of the time of the robbery. For were he to give them the food itself now, it would not be deemed a gift, since its use would be prohibited. However, if the proselyte were still alive, the robber could say to him, "Here is your own property before you," as we have explained.

9. If a priest robs an heirless proselyte and denies it on oath and then the proselyte dies, the priest does not acquire title to the robbed property in his possession but must give it up to be shared by his fellow priests of the current watch.

10. If one robs a proselyte and denies it on oath and then the proselyte dies, and the robber then puts aside a guilt offering and the robbed property to take them to the priests but dies before atonement has been made, the rule is as follows: The robber's heirs inherit the money put aside in lieu of the robbed property, or the robbed property itself, and the guilt-offering must be allowed to pasture until it becomes unfit, as we have explained in the appropriate passage.

11. If the robber has already given the money to the members of the watch but dies before atonement has been made, his heirs cannot reclaim anything from the priests, for Scripture says, *Whatsoever any man giveth the priest, it shall be his* (Num. 5:10). Even

if the robber was a minor, whose gift is not valid, his heirs cannot reclaim anything from the priests.

12. If the robber gives the money to any one of the watches and the guilt offering to the watch that is on duty that week, the money should be handed over, as was the guilt offering, to the proper current watch. For a watch which receives money at any time other than its own week of duty must hand it to the current watch. It does not acquire title to the money, which must be reclaimed from it.

13. The guilt sacrifice may not be offered until the robber has restored the amount robbed to its owner or, in the case of robbery of an heirless proselyte, to the priests.

If the robber has paid the amount robbed and offered his guilt sacrifice, his atonement is complete and is not hindered by non-payment of the added fifth part. He is, however, still under an obligation to pay the added fifth part after the atonement.

14. There is no added fifth part in the case of slaves, documents, or land. For Scripture says, *And deal falsely with his neighbor in a matter of deposit . . .* (Lev. 5:21). Everything mentioned in this context is movable property with an intrinsic value, thus excluding land, slaves—who are legally regarded in the same way as land—and documents, seeing that the latter have no intrinsic value. Similarly, if any of these is robbed of an heirless proselyte, it need not be restored to the priests.

Again, title to land can never be acquired by a robber; rather it is always deemed to be in the possession of its owner. Even if the land is sold to a thousand people, one after another, and the owner has abandoned hope of recovery, it must be restored to its owner without payment. The buyer who gives it up may make claim from the one who sold it to him, and he in turn may make claim from the next seller, and so on until the one who bought it from the robber makes claim and exacts payment from the robber, as will be explained.

CHAPTER IX

1. If one robs another of land and damages it, such as by digging pits or ditches or caves in it, or by cutting down trees, or destroying springs, or demolishing a building, the robber must replace the house or the field as it was at the time of the robbery, or pay for whatever damage he has done. If, however, the land is spoiled through natural causes, such as if a river floods it or a lightning bolt burns it, the robber may say to the other, "Your property is here before you." For land remains in the possession of its owner, and the robber is held responsible only for that damage wrought by his own hand. This is not the rule in the case of movable property, as we have explained.

2. If one takes a field by robbery and he is then robbed of it by oppressive officials acting with royal warrant, the rule is as follows: If the whole country suffers, for example if the king takes fields or houses from everybody in the province, the robber may say to the owner, "Your property is here before you." But if it is taken from the robber on his own account, he must provide the owner with another field.

3. If the king brings pressure upon the robber, saying to him, "Show us all you have," and the robber shows him the field obtained by robbery among his other fields, and the king takes it, he must provide the owner with a field like it or pay him its value.

4. If one obtains a field by robbery and damages it himself, the rule is as follows: When the owner of the field collects the value of the damage done by the robber, he may collect it only from the robber's free property, since the obligation is regarded as a verbal loan. But if the robber has already appeared in court and has been adjudged to pay and then sells property, the owner may collect his due even from the property sold.

5. If one obtains a field by robbery and consumes its produce, he must pay from his free property for all produce consumed. If

he obtains it by robbery and improves it, the improvement is evaluated for him, but he is at a disadvantage, for if the value of the improvement exceeds what he has spent on it, he may recover only his expenditure from the person robbed; but if his expenditure exceeds the value of the improvement, he may recover only the equivalent of the improvement.

6. If one obtains a field by robbery and sells it, and the buyer improves it, the rule is as follows: If the value of the improvement exceeds the expenditure, the buyer may recover the expenditure from the owner of the field, and the capital sum, together with the remainder of the improvement, from the robber.

7. The capital sum may be taken from property sold previously, but the remainder of the improvement only from free property. A buyer who is aware that he is buying a field obtained by robbery may recover from the robber the capital sum only and loses the remainder of the improvement in excess of the expenditure. If, however, the expenditure exceeds the value of the improvement—whether the buyer knows that the field was obtained by robbery or not—he may recover of his expenditure only the equivalent of the improvement, receiving this from the owner of the field. He may also exact the capital sum from the robber, if necessary from property already sold.

8. If one obtains a field by robbery and sells it, and the buyer consumes the produce, an accounting must be made of all the produce he has consumed and he must make restitution for this to the owner of the field, and then he may collect it from the robber's free property. However, if he knows that the field was obtained by robbery, he may not recover the value of the produce but may collect from the robber only the capital sum.

9. If one sells a field that is not his, the sale is invalid and the buyer acquires nothing, as we have explained. If, after selling it, the robber buys it from its owner, the one who bought it from the robber acquires title to it. Even if the robber gives it away while he still has it by robbery, the recipient acquires title to it as soon

as the robber buys it from the owner. For the robber's reason for bothering to buy it is to preserve his reputation.

10. Consequently, if the buyer sues the robber for having sold him a field that is not his and the robber is required to pay, and the court begins to advertise the robber's own property in order to collect from it on behalf of the buyer, and, after the advertisement has begun, the robber buys the field from its true owner, then the buyer does not acquire title to it. For as soon as the court advertises the robber's property, it is known that the robber is not honest and his reason for buying the field from the owner was not in order to gain title to it for the buyer.

11. If, after selling a field obtained by robbery, the robber buys it from the true owner and then sells it to another buyer, or gives it away or bequeaths it, he thereby shows that his intention when purchasing it was not to gain title for the first buyer, who bought it from him while it was still property obtained by robbery.

Similarly, if the robber inherits it, the buyer does not acquire title to it.

12. If the robber receives the field (from the true owner) in settlement of a debt, the rule is as follows: If the person robbed has other real property and the robber says to him, "This is what I wish to collect for my debt," he intends to gain title to it for the buyer. But if the person robbed has no land other than this, the robber intends only to collect his debt.

13. If the original owner makes the robber a present of the field, the buyer acquires title to it. For if the robber had not endeavored to please the owner, the latter would not have given it to him, and he was thus careful to please in order to acquire title to it legally and keep his reputation for honesty by gaining title to it for the buyer.

14. If one obtains a field by robbery and then, after becoming known as the robber of the field, buys it from the original owner, who afterward pleads, "I acted under duress when I sold it to

him, and sold it not of my own free will but because of his robbery," the robber does not acquire title to the field even if witnesses testify he bought it. The field must revert to its owner, who must repay the robber the money received for it.

15. The above rule applies only if witnesses testify that the robber counted out the money in their presence. But if their testimony is that the owner of the land sold it to the robber and admitted in their presence that the robber had given him a specified sum of money, and the owner now pleads that the other gave him no money and that he only made his original statement out of fear, then inasmuch as he is known to have obtained the field by robbery, the robber gets nothing, the field being taken away from him without payment because the owner admitted the sale only out of fear.

16. The owner of the field need not issue a prior declaration invalidating the sale. Inasmuch as the buyer is known to have obtained the field by robbery, and his proof of purchase is not regarded as proof, no prior declaration is necessary. The rule in the case of a robber is not the same as that of one who compels another to sell him something under duress, for one who merely uses duress has no wish to rob and has in fact robbed the owner of nothing. Therefore, a sale to him is valid unless the owner thus under duress issues a prior declaration (invalidating the sale).

CHAPTER X

1. If a heathen man of violence forcibly seizes the property of an Israelite and enters a field because its owner owes him a debt or because the Israelite owes him compensation for damage or because the Israelite has caused him monetary loss, the rule is that if, after seizing the field, the heathen sells it to another Israelite, the owner cannot recover it from the purchaser.

2. This rule applies only if the owner admits that the heathen seller's claim is true, or if Israelite witnesses testify that the claim

is true. Similarly, if at the place in question there is a king or prince who could compel the heathen seller to submit to judgment, but the owner does not sue, he cannot then recover anything from the buyer, even if he does not admit that the heathen's claim is true and even if witnesses do not testify to the truth of the claim. For the buyer can say to the owner, "If that heathen is a robber, why did you not sue him under heathen law?"

3. If a heathen oppresses and seeks to kill an Israelite who saves himself by giving up his field or house to the oppressor, who then lets him alone, the rule is as follows: If, when the oppressor wishes to sell the property in question, the original owner has enough money to buy it, he has precedence over anyone else. But if the owner cannot afford to buy it, or if the oppressor has kept the land for more than twelve months, whoever buys it first acquires title to it. He must, however, give the original owner either a quarter of the land or a third of the purchase price, since an oppressor sells cheaply. He will sell for approximately a quarter less, since the land he is selling is not his own, and this quarter belongs to the original owner, since the oppressor's reason for selling cheaply is that the land belongs to another. Consequently, if one buys from the oppressor for thirty, he must give the owner ten or a quarter of the land, and he then acquires title to the rest. If, however, he does not do this, one quarter of the land is regarded as robbed property in his possession.

4. If one enters another's field without permission and plants trees in it, the rule is as follows: If the field would normally have been planted with trees, we estimate how much one would be prepared to pay to have such a field planted, and this amount may be recovered from the owner of the field by the trespasser. But if it would not normally have been planted with trees, the improvement is assessed for him, the planter always having the disadvantage.

5. If the owner of the field says to the planter, "Pull up your trees and go away," his demand must be complied with. But if the planter says, "I will pull up my trees," he is not permitted to do so, because he would impoverish the soil.

6. Courtyards are suitable places for construction and for adding new houses or upper stories. Consequently, the Geonim have ruled that if one builds in another's courtyard without the owner's knowledge, he is deemed as one who plants in a field that would normally be planted. We therefore assess for him how much one would give to have such a building constructed, provided that the building is useful and suitable for that courtyard in accordance with local custom.

7. If one enters his neighbor's field with permission, an evaluation is made to his advantage even if he plants trees in a field where they would not usually be planted. If the expenditure is greater than the improvement, he recovers the expenditure, and if the improvement is worth more than the expenditure, he recovers the improvement.

A husband, with regard to his wife's property, and a partner, with regard to a field in which he has a share, are deemed as one who has entered with permission, and an evaluation is made to their advantage.

8. If one enters another's field without permission and plants trees or builds, and the owner afterward finishes the building or cultivates the saplings, or gives any similar indication that he is inclined to approve of the action of the first person and that it has his consent, an evaluation is made to the advantage of the trespasser.

9. If one enters another's ruins and rebuilds them without permission, an evaluation is made to his disadvantage.

If the builder says, "I would rather take my timber and my masonry," the rule is as follows: In the case of a house, the request is granted, but in the case of a field the request is not granted because it would impoverish the soil. If, however, the owner of the land says to him, "Remove what you have built," the demand must be complied with.

10. One for whom an evaluation is made, whether to his advantage or disadvantage, may not receive payment until he has

sworn, while holding a sacred object, how much he spent. However, if he says, "Let craftsmen come and make an evaluation of the expenditure, which is entirely visible, and let them evaluate the timber and the masonry and the mortar and the laborers' wages at the lowest market rates," his request is complied with and he may receive the amount due without an oath. Similarly, if one seeks to receive payment for the improvement alone when he has the advantage, he need not swear.

11. In every case where an evaluation must be made before payment is exacted, if the owner of the field says, "I have paid," while the trespasser says, "I have not been paid," the trespasser is held trustworthy but must take an oath that the other gave him nothing, and then he may recover his money. For we say to the owner of the field, "No evaluation has yet been made for you and you do not know how much you must pay. How then could you have paid?"

If, however, the evaluation has already been made and the court has said to the owner of the field, "Pay him," and he later says, "I have paid," the rule is that even though the trespasser has not yet taken an oath, the owner of the field is heeded but must take an oath of inducement confirming his claim and then is exempt. For land is presumed to be in the possession of its owner.

12. If a husband engages tenants for his wife's real property and then divorces her, the rule is as follows: If the husband is himself a farmer, then when he departs, his tenants must also leave, for they came only on the authority of the husband. An evaluation must be made for them, but to their disadvantage. However, if the husband is not a farmer, the tenants came there because of the land, and an evaluation must be made for them as for any tenant farmer.

CHAPTER XI

1. The return of lost property to an Israelite is a positive commandment, for Scripture says, *Ye shall surely return them to your*

brother (Deut. 22:1). Moreover, if one sees the lost property of an Israelite and ignores it and leaves it, he transgresses a negative commandment in addition to disregarding a positive commandment, for Scripture says, *Thou shalt not see thy brother's ox (or his sheep go astray) and hide thyself from them (ibid.)*. If he returns it, however, he has fulfilled a positive commandment.

2. If one takes lost property and does not return it, he disregards a positive commandment and transgresses two negative ones, namely, *Thou mayest not hide thyself* (Deut. 22:3), and *Thou shalt not rob* (Lev. 19:13). Even if the owner of the lost property is wicked and would eat improperly slaughtered meat to gratify his appetite, or do anything similar, to return his lost property to him is still a commandment. But if one eats improperly slaughtered meat defiantly, he is deemed a heretic, and it is forbidden to return lost property to heretics, idol-worshiping Israelites, or Israelites who publicly profane the Sabbath, just as it is to (return lost property) to heathen.

3. The lost property of a heathen may be kept, for Scripture says, *Lost thing of thy brother's* (Deut. 22:3). Furthermore, if one returns it, he commits a transgression, for he is supporting the wicked of the world. But if one returns it in order to sanctify God's name, thereby causing persons to praise the Israelites and realize that they are honest, he is deemed praiseworthy.

In cases involving a profanation of God's name, it is forbidden to keep a heathen's lost property, and it must be returned. In all cases, however, their belongings must be taken into safekeeping to save them from thieves, as is the rule for Israelite belongings, this being necessary for the sake of peace.

4. A heathen's error is regarded as is his lost property and one may take advantage of it, provided the heathen makes the mistake himself. But it is forbidden to cheat him.

5. Thus if a heathen makes an error in calculation, for example, the Israelite must say to him, "Observe that I rely on your calculation and do not know (whether it is correct) but give you what

you tell me," and he may then take advantage of the mistake. But if the Israelite does not say this to the heathen, it is forbidden to take advantage of the mistake, lest the heathen intend to test him, and profanation of the name of God result.

6. If a town contains both Israelites and heathen, each forming half the inhabitants, and one finds lost property there, he must take it and advertise it. If an Israelite then comes and gives marks of identification, the finder is obliged to return it.

7. If the majority of the inhabitants are heathen, the rule is that if one finds lost property in a part of town which is chiefly frequented by Israelites, he must advertise it. But if he finds it in a public highway or a large square, or in assembly halls or lecture halls frequented regularly by heathen or in any other place frequented by the general public, whatever he finds belongs to him, even if an Israelite comes along and identifies it. For the owner will abandon hope of its recovery as soon as he loses the property, since he thinks that a heathen will find it. Yet even though it belongs to the finder, if he wishes to follow the good and upright path and do more than the strict letter of the law requires, he must return the lost property to an Israelite who identifies it.

8. If one finds a cask of wine in a town containing a majority of heathen, any benefit from the wine is forbidden, but the cask may be retained as lost property. Furthermore, if an Israelite comes and identifies it, the finder may drink the wine.

9. If a bird seizes meat and drops it into another courtyard, it may be retained as lost property, even if the majority of the town's inhabitants are Israelites, because its owner will have abandoned hope of its recovery.

10. If one finds lost property among that which is washed up by the sea, or deposited by a river in its uninterrupted flow, it belongs to the finder, even if it has a mark of identification. For Scripture says, *Which he hath lost and thou hast found* (Deut. 22:3), meaning that the property is lost to the owner but is available to other

persons. This excludes the present case, where the property was lost both to the owner and to all other persons, seeing that the owner will certainly have abandoned hope of its recovery.

11. If one willfully causes his property to become lost, we do not concern ourselves with him. Thus, if one leaves his cow untied in a shed that has no door and goes away, or throws down his purse in a public domain and goes away, or does something similar, he has willfully lost his property, and although a spectator may not take the property for himself, he is not obliged to return it, for Scripture says, *Which he hath lost* (*ibid.*), excluding cases where one willfully causes property to become lost.

12. One is not obliged to care for or return lost property not worth a pĕruṭah.

13. If one finds a sack or a basket, the rule is as follows: If he is a scholar or a respected elder who is not accustomed to taking such things in his hand, he need not concern himself with them. He must, however, examine his own conscience. If he would have taken these things back for himself had they belonged to him, he must also return them when they belong to another. But if he would not have overlooked his dignity even had they belonged to him, he need not return them when they belong to another.

If it is his custom to return similar articles in the country but not in town, and he finds them in town, he need not return them. If he finds them in the country, however, he must return them and see that they come into their owner's hands, even though he must enter into town with them and he is not accustomed to do this.

14. Similarly, if one finds a lost animal and slaps it, he has thereby become obligated to care for it and to return it to its owner, even if it is below his dignity, seeing that he has already begun to perform the laudable act. If, after he returns it, it runs away again, even a hundred times, he is still obligated to return it, for Scripture says, *Thou shalt surely bring them back* (Deut. 22:1), implying that he should return it even a hundred times.

He must continue to care for it until he has returned it to a safe place on its owner's premises. But if he returns it to an unsafe place, such as a garden or a waste plot of ground, and it strays from there, he is obligated to replace it.

15. If one returns lost property in the morning to a place that the owner normally goes in and out of mornings, he need not concern himself with it any longer, even if the place is unsafe, for the owner will see it. This rule applies only to inanimate property. In the case of a living creature, however, he must continue to care for it until he brings it into a safe place belonging to the owner. He need not, however, notify the owner.

16. If one sees an animal run out of a pen and returns it to its place, he has thereby fulfilled the commandment and need not notify the owner.

17. If one follows the good and upright path and does more than the strict letter of the law requires, he will return lost property in all cases, even if it is not in keeping with his dignity.

18. If a priest sees lost property in a cemetery, he may not defile himself in order to return it, for to perform the commandment to return lost property he will have to disregard a positive commandment, namely, *They shall be holy* (Lev. 21:6) and transgress a negative commandment, namely, *He shall not defile himself, being a chief man amongst his people* (*ibid.* 21:4). Now a positive commandment cannot supersede both a positive and a negative commandment.

19. If one sees lost property and his father says to him, "Do not return it," he must nevertheless return it and need not obey his father. For if he obeys his father, then in fulfilling the positive commandment, *Honor thy father* (Exod. 20:12), he at the same time disregards the positive commandment, *Thou shalt surely bring them back* (Deut. 22:1), and transgresses the prohibition, *Thou mayest not hide thyself* (Deut. 22:3).

20. If one sees water flooding and threatening to destroy another's building or land, he must place a barrier in its way to stop

it, for Scripture says, *With every lost thing of thy brother's* (Deut. 22:3), including also loss of his land.

CHAPTER XII

1. If one loses property and finds his own lost property and the lost property of another, the rule is as follows: If he can return both of them, he is obligated to do so, but if he can return only one of them, his own lost property takes precedence; it takes precedence over that of any other person, even over the lost property of his father or his teacher.

2. If one finds his teacher's lost property and his father's lost property, the rule is as follows: If his father is the equal of his teacher, his father's property takes precedence; if not, his teacher's property takes precedence, provided that he is his pre-eminent teacher, from whom he learned most of his knowledge of the Law.

3. If one leaves his own lost property and returns the lost property of another, he may receive only the usual fee. Thus, if a river sweeps away his ass and another's ass, his own being worth a hundred and the other's two hundred, the rule is as follows: If he leaves his own and rescues that of the other person, he receives only the usual fee. But if he says to the other, "I will rescue yours, but you must give me the value of mine," or if he makes this stipulation before a court, the other must pay him the value of his ass. Even if his own ass saves itself without help, the rescuer is still entitled to whatever he stipulated with the other, inasmuch as he himself did not attend to it.

4. If one goes forth to rescue another's lost property but does not succeed, he receives only the usual fee. Similarly, if one is working at his trade and deprives himself of a denar's worth of work to return lost property worth a hundred denar, he may not say to the owner, "Give me the denar I have thus lost." Rather the other need pay him only the rate payable to any laborer to refrain from following the occupation in which the rescuer was employed. If, however,

he stipulates with the owner or before a court that he should receive what he has to give up and they grant him permission, he receives this amount. If neither the owner nor a court is there, his own (occupation) takes precedence.

5. Similarly, if two persons are traveling on a road, one with a cask of wine and the other with a jar of honey, and the jar of honey cracks, the rule is as follows: If before the honey begins to trickle onto the ground the first person pours out his wine and catches the honey in the cask, he is entitled only to the usual fee; but if he says, "I will rescue your property if you pay me the value of mine," or if he makes such a stipulation before a court, the other must give him the sum agreed upon.

If, however, the honey trickles onto the ground, it is regarded as ownerless property, and whoever rescues it may keep it for himself.

6. If one travels with a jar of honey and the other with empty bottles, and the jar of honey cracks and the owner of the bottles says to the other, "I will not catch your honey in my bottles unless you give me half of it—or a third of it—or so many denar," and the owner of the honey agrees to this and says, "Very well," the rule is that he is regarded as having spoken in jest and need not give him more than the usual fee, for he has caused the other no loss at all.

7. Similarly, if one escaping from prison comes to a ferry and says to the ferryman, "Take me across and I will give you a denar," and he is taken across, the ferryman receives only the usual fee. If, however, there is a fisherman there to whom he says, "Leave your net and take me across," he must give the fisherman whatever he stipulates. The same rule applies in all similar cases.

8. If a caravan is crossing a desert and bandits fall on it and plunder it, the rule is as follows: If the travelers are unable to save their goods from the bandits, but one person does manage to rescue some articles, he may keep whatever he rescues. However, if the travelers could have saved their goods themselves, but one of them

rescues some articles first, whatever he rescues belongs to all, even if he has said, "I am going to rescue this for myself."

9. If the travelers are able to rescue the goods only with great difficulty, the rule is that if one rescues anything, he rescues it for all, unless he says, "I am going to rescue it for myself," in which case he may keep for himself whatever he rescues. For when the others hear him say, "I am going to rescue it for myself," they ought to exert themselves to rescue the goods, and seeing that they sit still without attempting to rescue (the plundered property), they are regarded as having abandoned hope of recovering any of it.

10. If two partners are in the caravan and one of them rescues some property, the rule is that he has rescued it for both in common. If, however, one says, "I am going to rescue it for myself alone," he becomes dissociated from the other and may keep what he rescues.

Similarly, if one hires a laborer for rescue work, the rule is that whatever he rescues belongs to the hirer. But if the laborer says, "What I rescue is for myself," he cancels his contract thereby, and whatever he rescues after making this statement belongs to him.

11. If a caravan is encamped in the desert and a robber band threatens to attack it but the travelers buy off the band with a stipulated sum of money, the contribution of each must be fixed in proportion to his wealth and not per capita. But if they hire a guide to show them the way, his wage must be computed on the basis of both the value of the property and the number of persons traveling. They may not, however, vary the usual custom of ass drivers.

12. Ass drivers have the right to stipulate among themselves that if any one of the drivers in a caravan loses an ass, the others must replace it with another ass. If, however, it is lost through his negligence, they need not provide him with another.

13. If an ass driver loses his ass and says, "Give me its value, for I do not wish to buy another ass, but will keep guard with you,"

they need not comply with his request, but they should provide him with another ass in order that he may be more alert and take care of his own animal. This rule applies even if he has another animal in the caravan, seeing that there is no comparison between a person taking care of one animal and a person taking care of two.

14. If a ship is sailing on the sea, and a high gale springs up and threatens to sink it, and its load is lightened, the rule is that the contribution of each passenger must be apportioned according to the weight of his load, not according to its value. The passengers may not, however, vary the usual custom of sailors.

15. Sailors have the right to stipulate among themselves that if any one of them loses his boat, another will be provided for him. However, if one was negligent and loses his boat, or if he sets out for a place where boats are not sailed at that time of year, they need not provide him with another.

CHAPTER XIII

1. If one finds lost property which he is obligated to return, he must advertise and let it be known, saying, "Let anyone who has lost property of such a kind come and identify it and take it." He must advertise it even if, although worth a pĕruṭah at the time it is found, it becomes worth less. There was a high rock outside Jerusalem on which such announcements were made.

2. How should the announcement be made? If one finds money, he should announce, "Let anyone who has lost a coin"—or, similarly, "Let anyone who has lost a garment or an animal or documents"—"come and identify it and take it." The finder need not be apprehensive for making known the kind of lost property, seeing that he need not return it unless he is given unmistakable marks of identification.

3. If the owner of lost property comes and gives marks of identification that are not unmistakable, the finder may not return it to

him until he does give marks of identification that are unmistakable. As for a notorious cheat, even if he gives unmistakable marks of identification, the property may not be returned to him until he produces witnesses who testify that it is his. For when Scripture says, *And it shall be with thee until the inquiring of thy brother* (Deut. 22:2), the Sages interpret it as meaning, "until thou hast investigated him to ascertain whether or not he is a deceiver."

4. Formerly, if one lost property and came and identified it, it was returned to him unless he was a proven deceiver. But when deceivers became numerous, the court decreed that one seeking to retrieve lost property should be told, "Bring witnesses that you are not a deceiver and you may take it."

5. That unmistakable identification marks may be relied upon and that they may serve as proper basis for adjudication in all cases is a law of Scripture. Size, weight, number, or the place where the property was lost is each deemed an unmistakable mark of identification.

6. If two persons come and each one gives the same identification marks of the lost property, the finder may not give it to either of them, but it must be kept intact until one defers to the other or until they reach a settlement.

If one of them gives identification marks and the other brings witnesses, it must be given to the one with witnesses. If one gives identification marks and the other gives identification marks and has one witness, the witness is regarded as nonexistent and the property must be kept intact.

7. If one finds a garment or a similar article, and a person produces witnesses who had woven it for him, and another produces witnesses who testify that he had dropped it, the finder must give it to the person who produces witnesses to the fact that he had dropped it.

If one person specifies the length of the garment, and the other its width, the finder must give it to the one who specifies its length, for a deceiver could have guessed the width, having seen the owner wearing it.

If one person specifies the length and the width of the garment, and the other its correct weight, the finder must give it to the one who specifies its correct weight. If one person specifies its length and width and the other its perimeter, the finder must give it to the one who specifies its length and width.

8. Formerly, if one found lost property, he would advertise it on three festivals. On the first festival the finder would say, "This is the first," on the second he would say, "This is the second," but on the third festival he would advertise it without mentioning the festival, so that no one would confuse the second with the third. Seven days after the last festival, he would advertise it a fourth time, to enable a listener to take a three-days' journey home, search among his belongings, return in three days, and find the advertiser proclaiming it on the seventh day.

9. After the Temple was destroyed, however, the Sages decreed that if one finds lost property, he should advertise in synagogues and lecture rooms. However, when men of violence increased and went about saying that anything found belonged to the king, the Sages decreed that a finder of lost property should tell his neighbors and friends, and that this would suffice.

10. If after the finder advertises the lost property or lets it be known that he has found lost property the owner does not come forward, he is obligated to keep it with him until Elijah shall come.

As long as the lost property is in his possession, the finder must replace it if it is stolen or again lost, but if it is accidentally destroyed, he is exempt. For one taking care of lost property is regarded as a paid bailee, seeing that he is engaged in fulfilling a scriptural commandment as long as he continues to be occupied with its care, and is therefore exempt for many positive commandments.

11. The finder must inspect and examine lost property to ensure that it does not spoil or waste away of itself, for Scripture says, *And*

thou shalt restore it to him again (Deut. 22:2), meaning that thou shalt be careful how thou returnest it to him. Thus, if one finds a woolen garment, he must shake it out once every thirty days. He may not beat it with a stick, nor may two people shake it. He may spread it on a couch for its own benefit alone, but not both for its benefit and his own. If he has visitors, he may not spread it out in their presence even for its own benefit, lest it be stolen.

12. If one finds wooden utensils, he must use them to prevent their rotting. Copper vessels may be used with hot water but not over a fire, as this wears them out. Silverware may be used with cold water but not with hot, as this tarnishes them.

If one finds trowels or mattocks he may use them on soft ground but not on hard, as this damages them. If one finds articles of gold or glass, or a linen garment, he may not touch them until Elijah shall come.

These rules that the Sages decreed concerning lost property apply equally to a bailment whose owner has gone abroad.

13. If one finds scrolls, he must read in them once every thirty days. If he is unable to read, he should roll them up every thirty days. He should never learn anything from them for the first time, nor read any section and repeat it, nor read a section and translate it, nor open it at more than three columns, nor should two persons read in it at two different places, lest each one pull it and the scroll become torn; but two may read at the same place. Three persons, however, may not read in a scroll even at the same place.

14. If one finds phylacteries, he may assess their value and put them on, because these are readily obtainable and are made only for the fulfillment of the commandment enjoined concerning them.

15. If one finds a living creature that he must feed, the rule is as follows: If it is a creature that works and eats, such as a cow or an ass, he must take care of it for twelve months from the day of finding it and should hire it out, take the wage, and feed it. If the wage is more than is needed to feed the animal, the excess belongs to the owner. Similarly, in the case of hens, the finder must sell their eggs

and feed them for a full twelve months. After this, he may assess their value and they belong to him and to the owner jointly, in accord with the rule applicable to anyone who takes an animal on evaluation from another.

16. If one finds calves or foals, he must care for them for three months if they can be grazed, and for thirty days if they must be fed. He must take care of large geese or hens for thirty days. If he finds small ones, or anything else which costs more to care for than they can earn, he must take care of them for three days. Thereafter, he may sell them with the permission of the court. Similarly, fruit that has begun to spoil, or anything similar, may be sold with the permission of the court.

17. What is to be done with the money (from the sale)? It is to be given to the finder of the property, who then has the right to use it. Therefore, if it is lost unavoidably—for example, if bandits seize it or if it is lost at sea—he must repay it even if he has not made use of it. For inasmuch as he has the right to make use of it, it is regarded as borrowed money.

18. The above rule applies to the proceeds of lost property, seeing that the finder has taken care of the property. But if one finds money, he may not make use of it, and consequently if it is lost unavoidably, he is exempt from liability, for he is deemed a paid bailee, as we have explained.

19. If the finder feeds the animal from his own funds during the entire period that he must care for lost property before selling it with the permission of the court, he can recover his expenditure from the owner. It appears to me that, in the public interest, he may recover this expenditure without taking an oath.

20. If one finds property, he need not take an oath, this rule being in the public interest. For if the finder were obliged to take an oath, he would ignore any property he might find and go away in order to avoid taking an oath. Even if one finds a purse and the owner of the property pleads that there were two purses tied to-

gether and it would have been impossible to find one without finding the other, the finder still need not take an oath.

CHAPTER XIV

1. The loss of a garment is properly included in *Every lost thing of thy brother's* (Deut. 22:3), as is also an ox, a sheep, and an ass. Why then does Scripture mention an ass especially? To enjoin that the ass must be returned if the saddle is identified. Although the identification mark is only on an accessory, the animal must be restored.

Why are an ox and a sheep mentioned especially? To require the return of even the shearings of a sheep or the shearings of the tail of an ox, although this is but a trifle.

And why is a garment specifically mentioned? In order that we infer as follows: Just as a garment distinctive in possessing marks of identification is apt to be claimed and must be returned by the finder, so all things which have marks of identification are apt to be claimed and must therefore be returned. But anything that has no one to claim it belongs to the finder, even if it has marks of identification, because its owner has abandoned hope of its recovery.

2. The following rule applies to lost property: As soon as any article with no mark of identification—such as a single nail or a single needle or a coin—is lost and its owner becomes aware that it is lost, it is presumed that the owner has abandoned hope of its recovery, for he cannot identify it to retrieve it, and it therefore belongs to the finder.

3. If, however, any property has a mark of identification, such as a garment or an animal, it is presumed that the owner has not abandoned hope of its recovery, for he expects to retrieve it by stating its identification marks. The finder must therefore advertise it unless he knows that the owner has abandoned hope of its recovery. Thus, if he hears the owner say, "What a misfortune that

I've suffered a loss of money," or use a similar expression which indicates that the owner has abandoned hope of its recovery, the lost property in question belongs to the finder.

4. Similarly, if one finds identifiable property in the sea or in a river or in some similar location, or in a place where the majority of the inhabitants are heathen, it is presumed that the owner abandoned hope of its recovery the moment it fell, and consequently it belongs to the finder even if he has not heard the owner actually abandon hope of its recovery.

5. Potential abandonment of hope of recovery, even if the lost property has no mark of identification, is not deemed abandonment. Thus, if one drops a denar but is not aware that he has dropped it, although when he discovers that he has dropped it he will abandon hope of its recovery, it is not regarded as though hope has been abandoned until the owner becomes aware that he has dropped it. If, however, the owner still says, "Perhaps I gave it to So-and-So," or "Perhaps it is in my cupboard," or "Perhaps I made a mistake in calculation," or the like, this is not deemed abandonment of hope of recovery.

6. If one sees another drop a denar on the ground without being aware of it, and he takes the denar before hope of its recovery is abandoned, he transgresses one positive and two negative commandments, as we have explained. Even if he returns the denar after hope of its recovery is abandoned, it is deemed merely a gift, but he has already transgressed the commandments.

7. If one takes a denar before hope of its recovery is abandoned but with the idea of returning it, and then decides to steal it after hope of its recovery is abandoned, he transgresses the commandment, *Thou shalt surely bring them back* (Deut. 22:1).

If the finder waits, without either informing the owner or taking the denar, until the owner discovers that he has dropped it and thus abandons hope of its recovery, as explained above, and then picks up the denar from the ground, he has transgressed only

Thou mayest not hide thyself (Deut. 22:3). The same rule applies in all similar cases.

8. If one sees a sela' or other coin fall even from among three people, he must return it even if there is not in it a pĕruṭah worth for each, for they may be partners, one of whom has given up his share to another, so that the loss of the latter will be found to be worth a pĕruṭah.

9. If one sees another drop a denar into sand or dirt and lose sight of it, it is regarded as though it had fallen into the sea or into a river, and it belongs to the finder. For the loser abandons hope of its recovery because it is unidentifiable. Even if one sees the other bring a sieve and search for it, the other does so with but faint hope; for just as other searchers, even if they have dropped nothing, delve in dirt hoping perchance to find something someone else has dropped, so does the loser search in this case, not because he has not abandoned hope of recovery.

10. If one finds a sela' in the street and another person meets him and says to him, "It is mine—a new one of such-and-such a country and of such-and-such a king," or even, "My name is written on it," his words are not heeded and the finder need not return it. For identification marks on a coin are not valid criteria since the presumption is that a coin will be spent. We say that the coin was once the claimant's, but he spent it and it was dropped by another who abandoned hope of its recovery as soon as it fell, inasmuch as the mark of identification is not one that can be relied on. It therefore belongs to the finder.

11. If one finds unidentifiable property alongside identifiable property, he must advertise his find. If the owner of the identifiable property comes and takes what belongs to him and says that he lost only this, the finder acquires title to the unidentifiable article.

12. If one finds earthenware vessels or the like, all of which are identical in form, the rule is as follows: If they are new, they belong to him, for they are regarded as one denar among other denars, unidentifiable and unrecognizable by the owner, who can-

not know whether this jar or this flask belongs to him or to another. But if they are old utensils which have become familiar to the owner's eye, the finder must advertise them. For if a scholar comes and says, "Although I am unable to give an identification mark on a vessel of this type, I can tell it at sight," the finder must show the article to him. If the scholar recognizes it and says, "It is mine," the finder must return it.

13. The above rule applies only to a scholar of repute who never tells an untruth except to promote peace, or about a treatise of the Talmud, a bed, or the house where he is a guest. Thus if, when studying the treatise *Niddah* (*Menstruant*), he says that he is studying *Miḵwa'oṯ* (*Immersion Pools*) in order not to be asked questions concerning menstruation; or, having slept in one bed, he says that he slept in another lest signs of noctural emission be found there; or, when staying with Simeon, he says that he is staying with Reuben in order that people should not annoy his host; or, when making peace between one person and another, he embellishes or conceals the facts in order to make them more friendly to one another—the misrepresentation is permissible. But if witnesses come and testify that he has told an untruth in a matter other than one of these, lost property need not be returned to him merely on the strength of his recognition of the article.

CHAPTER XV

1. If one finds property, identifiable or unidentifiable, that appears to have been deliberately placed where it is found, he is forbidden to touch it, for it is possible that its owner placed it there until he might return for it. If the finder should decide to take it and it is unidentifiable, he thereby causes the loss of another's property, for the loser cannot identify it to retrieve it. If it is identifiable, he causes the owner the bother of going after it and identifying it. He is therefore forbidden to touch it unless he finds it lying as though it had fallen. Even if he is in doubt about the matter and

does not know whether the property was lost or was placed there, he may not touch it. But if he transgresses and takes it, he may not put it back, and if it is unidentifiable property, he acquires title to it and need not return it.

2. Anything identifiable, however, must be advertised by the finder, whether it appears to have been deliberately placed where it is found or whether it appears as though it had fallen or whether it is found on a private or a public domain.

What is meant by "appears to have been deliberately placed where it is found"? If one finds an ass or a cow grazing at the roadside by day, or finds a vessel concealed in a rubbish heap, he may not touch it, for Scripture says, *Going astray* (Deut. 22:1). But if he finds an ass with its trappings in disorder, or a cow running among vineyards, or a vessel exposed on a rubbish heap, it is deemed lost property and he must take it and advertise it.

3. If one sees an ass or a cow grazing in a meadow at night in its usual manner, it is deemed lost property. Also if he sees it towards evening or at dawn on three successive days, it is deemed lost property and he must take it and advertise it.

If one sees a cow running along the road, the rule is as follows: If it is going towards town, it is not considered lost property, but if it is going towards fields, it is then regarded as lost property.

4. If one finds a cow grazing among vineyards, he must return it because of the damage it might do to the land. Therefore, if the vineyards belong to a heathen, the cow is not deemed lost property and he need not return it. But if he suspects that the heathen might kill it, if he finds it, because it has damaged the vineyard, it is deemed lost property and he must take it and advertise it.

5. If one finds a cow in a public domain, the rule is as follows: If it is standing outside the Sabbath limit, he must return it. If it is grazing in the grass or is in a shed which is not guarded but which would not necessarily cause it to stray, he may not touch it, for it is not deemed lost property.

If one finds a garment or an axe alongside a fence, he may not touch it, but if it is on a public highway, he must take it and advertise it. The same rule applies in all similar cases.

6. If one finds young doves with their wings tied hopping behind a fence or behind a stone wall or on field paths, he may not touch them, for it is possible that their owner deliberately put them there. But if he takes them, they belong to him. If the wings are tied with an identifiable knot, he must advertise the doves because the knot is a mark of identification. Similarly if he finds them attached to a certain place, he must advertise them because the place is a means of identification.

7. If one finds a vessel concealed in a rubbish heap, he may not touch it, as we have explained. However, if the rubbish heap is one that is not usually cleared away and he decides to clear it away, he must take the vessel and advertise it, even if he finds it concealed. Similarly, if the article is small, such as a knife or a spit or the like, the finder must take it and advertise it even if it is concealed in a permanent rubbish heap.

8. If one finds scattered produce that appears to have been deliberately put down, he may not touch it; if it appears as though it had been dropped, it belongs to him.

Similarly, if one finds in a public domain small sheaves of ears of corn, which are, of course, not identifiable, or if he finds round cakes of pressed figs or baker's loaves or strings of fish or slices of meat or wool fleeces in the state in which they arrive from the country, or stalks of flax or skeins of purple, any of these belong to him because they are unidentifiable. If, however, they happen to have a mark of identification, the finder must take them and advertise them, for an identification mark that is likely to be effaced is still regarded as a mark of identification.

9. If, however, one finds a householder's loaves, or wool fleeces as bought from a wool worker's shop, or jars of wine, or jars of oil, he must advertise them, for all these articles have unquestionable marks of identification. However, if the jars of wine or oil have already been opened, they belong to the finder even if they

are marked. For since all the jars are marked similarly, they have the status of baker's loaves, all of which look alike and weigh alike.

10. If one finds loaves in a private domain, the rule is as follows: If they appear as though they had been dropped, they belong to the finder, but if they appear as though they had been deliberately placed there, he must advertise them, for although they themselves are unidentifiable, the place is deemed a mark of identification.

If one finds large sheaves, whether in a private or in a public domain, he must take them and advertise them.

11. If one finds a cake of figs with a potsherd in it, or a loaf of bread with money in it, or a slice of meat of an unusual cut, or a coiled fish, or the like, the rule is that inasmuch as there is an unusual feature about them, the finder must advertise his find, for the owner has devised these features only as marks of identification.

12. If one finds produce scattered about in the neighborhood of threshing floors, the rule is that if there is as much as a ḳaḇ in four cubits square or more, it belongs to the finder, because the owner will not bother to collect it. However, if it is scattered in less than four cubits square, he may not touch it, for it is possible that the owner deliberately put it there. If there is as much as half a ḳaḇ in two cubits, or two ḳaḇ in eight cubits, or a ḳaḇ consisting of two or three species, such as dates, sesame, and pomegranates, the rule in these cases is a matter of doubt and consequently the finder may not take it. If, however, he does take it, he need not advertise it.

13. If one finds heaps of produce, or produce in a vessel, or a vessel by itself, he must advertise it. If one finds a vessel with produce in front of it, the produce belongs to the finder, but he must take the vessel and advertise it. For we assume that the vessel belongs to one person and the produce to another, and the produce is not identifiable. However, if circumstances suggest that both belong to the same person, he must advertise both.

14. Thus, if the back of a vessel faces produce, the produce belongs to the finder. If the front of the vessel faces produce, we

consider it possible that this has spilled from the vessel. However, if there are rims on the vessel, the produce belongs to the finder, even if the front of the vessel is turned towards it. For if the produce had spilled from the vessel, some of it would have remained inside because of the rims. If part of the produce is in the vessel and part on the ground, the finder must advertise both.

15. If one finds dried figs on a road, they belong to him, even if they are alongside a field of dried figs. Similarly, if a fig tree leans over the roadside and figs are found underneath it, they are permissible and taking them does not constitute robbery, because a fig or a similar fruit is spoiled by falling. They are also exempt from tithes. Olives or carobs or the like, however, are forbidden.

16. Dates blown down by the wind are permissible because the owner renounces them to everyone, and this is their presumed status. However, if the dates belong to orphan minors, who are not competent to renounce them, they are forbidden. Similarly, if the owner of the field carefully fences off the part occupied by the trees, or prepares a place on which the unripe dates should fall until he can gather them, then they are forbidden, for he has shown clearly that he has not renounced them.

17. A vicious cat that kills infants may not be kept, and the laws of robbery and of returning lost property do not apply to it, in spite of the fact that its pelt is of some value. If one finds it, he acquires title to it, and when he has killed it the pelt is his.

18. A young dove found within fifty cubits of a dovecote belongs to the owner of the dovecote. If it is found beyond fifty cubits, it belongs to the finder, because a young dove does not hop more than fifty cubits. If it is found between two dovecotes, it belongs to the owner of the nearer one. If it is exactly halfway, the respective owners may share it. This rule applies only if the doves in both cotes are exactly equal in number. But if the doves of one are more numerous, the majority is decisive even if this dovecote is more distant from the young dove than the other.

CHAPTER XVI

1. If one finds needles or hooks or nails or the like, the rule is as follows: If he finds them one at a time, they belong to him; but if two or more are found at a time, he must advertise them, because number is deemed a mark of identification.

2. Similarly, if one finds money scattered about, it belongs to him. Coins are regarded as scattered about even if some of them are on top of others. If, however, he finds a heap of money, he must advertise it.

If one finds three coins, one on top of the other in the shape of a turret, or two side by side and one on top of them, or part of one on part of the other in such a way that if a splinter of wood were placed under them they could be picked up together, he must advertise them. If they are placed in a circle or in a row or in a triangle or like a ladder, the rule is a matter of doubt and the finder may not take them.

3. If one finds money in a purse, or a purse without money, he must advertise it. If one finds a purse with money scattered in front of it, the money belongs to him. But if appearances suggest that the money and the purse belong to the same person and that it fell from the purse, the finder must advertise it.

4. If one finds money in a shop, the rule is as follows: If it is between the counter and the shopkeeper, it belongs to the shopkeeper, but if one finds it on the counter and, needless to say, if one finds it on the outer side of the counter, it belongs to him. Now why is it that the shop does not acquire the money for its owner? Because it is not deemed a guarded courtyard, and thus even if its owner is in it, he must declare, "I want my shop to acquire it for me," as will be explained.

5. If money is found in a money-changer's shop between the stool and the money changer, it belongs to the money changer. If it is found on the stool in front of the money changer, even if it

is tied up and lying on the table, it belongs to the finder, provided that the majority of customers are heathen, as we have explained. But if the majority are Israelites, the finder must advertise it, for inasmuch as it is tied up, it is identifiable.

6. If one buys produce from someone, or if someone sends him produce, and he finds tied-up money in it, he must take it and advertise it. If he finds the money scattered, it belongs to him. This rule applies only if the produce comes from a merchant or from a private individual who has bought it from a merchant. But if the private individual has threshed the produce himself, or with the help of his Canaanite slaves or bondwomen, the finder must return it.

7. If one finds a treasure in a heap of stones or in an old wall, it belongs to him, for we assume that it belonged to the ancient Amorites; provided, that is, that he finds it deep down, as is usual with ancient treasures. But if appearances suggest that it was concealed recently, or even if he is in doubt about it, he may not touch it, for it might have been put there deliberately.

8. Now, seeing that one's courtyard can acquire title to property for its owner without his knowledge, as will be explained, why should not the owner of the courtyard acquire the treasure in the old wall even if it did belong to the Amorites, and why should not this find belong to the owner of the courtyard? Inasmuch as its existence is not known, either to him or to anyone else, this treasure is deemed lost for him and for everyone else, and consequently it belongs to the finder. For if, concerning property lost by its owner, Scripture says, *Which he hath lost and thou hast found* (Deut. 22:3)—meaning (it must be returned only if) *he* has lost it but it is available to all other persons, thereby excluding that which has fallen into the sea and is lost for the owner and for all other persons too—how much more should this rule apply to an ancient treasure that never belonged to the owner of the courtyard and was lost for him and for all other persons too. Therefore it belongs to the finder.

9. If one finds a treasure in a wall built recently, the rule is as follows: If the treasure has an indication that it belongs to the householder, it is his, but if there is an indication that it belongs to some outsider, it belongs to the finder. For example, the handle is an indication in the case of a knife, and the mouth in the case of a purse. If the interior of the wall is fully occupied by the treasure, the rule is that the householder and the finder may share it.

10. If a wall contains money or bars of gold which give no indication (as to ownership), the rule is as follows: If they are in the outer half, they belong to the finder, but if they are in the inner half, they belong to the householder.

11. It is my opinion that the above rules apply only if the householder claims the treasure is his, or if he has inherited the house, in which casc wc advancc on his behalf the plea that the treasure might have belonged to his father. But if he admits that it is a find, it belongs to the finder. Consequently, if he rents his house to others, the treasure belongs to the most recent tenant. But if he rents it to three heathen at one time, he converts the house into an inn, and whatever is found even inside the house belongs to the finder, for no one can claim that it is his or that he hid it, seeing that the householder has converted the house into an inn.

CHAPTER XVII

1. Wherever we have said that property found belongs to the finder, he does not acquire title to it until it reaches his hand or his premises. However, if one sees lost property, or even throws himself on it, and another comes and takes possession of it, the rule is that the one who takes possession of it is entitled to it.

2. If one is riding an animal and sees lost property and says to a friend, "Acquire title to it on my behalf," the rule is that as soon as the friend picks it up for him, the rider acquires title to it, even though it has not yet reached his hand. But if the rider says

to his friend, "Give it to me," and the friend takes it and says, "I myself have acquired title to it," the one who has taken it acquires title to it. However, if after having given it to the rider he says, "I acquired it first," his words are of no avail.

3. If A picks up lost property for B, then B acquires title to it even if he has not said anything at all to A. If two persons pick up lost property, both acquire title to it.

4. If a deaf-mute or an imbecile or a minor picks up lost property for a normal person, the latter does not acquire title to it, seeing that the former are legally incompetent. If a deaf-mute and a normal person pick it up together, the rule is that inasmuch as the normal person does not acquire any of it, the deaf-mute does not acquire any of it either. If both are deaf-mutes, however, both do acquire title to it; the Sages decreed that they should acquire title to it, in order that they should not quarrel.

5. If two persons see a camel or a donkey which is deemed a find, and drive it or lead it at the same time, or if one drives and the other leads, then both acquire title to it. This last rule applies only to a donkey, but in the case of a camel, if one drives and the other leads, the one who leads acquires title to it, not the one who drives.

6. If one seizes the rein of an animal deemed a find—or, similarly, of an animal from the estate of an heirless proselyte—he does not acquire title to the animal until he leads it or drives it, but he does acquire the rein itself.

7. If one mounts the animal and another holds the rein, the rule is that the rider acquires title to the animal, together with only that part of the rein which is on its jaw, whereas the one holding the rein acquires title to as much of it as he is holding, and the rest of the rein is acquired by neither of them.

8. One's courtyard can legally acquire property for its owner without his knowledge. Therefore, if an article deemed a find is dropped in a courtyard, it belongs to the owner of the courtyard. This rule applies only in the case of a guarded courtyard. In the

case of a field or a market garden or the like, the rule is as follows: If the owner is standing alongside the field and says, "My field has acquired it for me," he becomes entitled to it. But if he is not standing there, or if he is standing there but does not say, "My field has acquired it for me," the rule is that whoever takes it up first is entitled to it.

Similarly, the four cubits of ground in the vicinity of which a person stands can legally acquire property for him. Hence if a lost article is within one's four cubits, he gains title to it.

9. The Sages decreed the above rule to prevent finders from quarreling with each other. This rule applies only in a back street, or at the sides of a public domain where there is no pressure of people, or in an ownerless field. But if one stands in a public domain or in another's field, the four cubits do not acquire title for him, nor can one acquire lost property there unless he holds it in his hand.

10. A female minor can legally acquire title by means of her courtyard and by means of four cubits, but a male minor can acquire property neither by means of his courtyard nor by means of four cubits. This is because the legal efficacy of the courtyard of a female minor derives from the legal efficacy of *her hand* (cf. Deut. 24:1, 3), the argument being that just as she becomes divorced when a document of divorce reaches her hand, so does she become divorced if it enters her courtyard; and just as she can acquire title by means of a courtyard with respect to a bill of divorcement, so can she acquire title by the same means with respect to lost property. As for the four cubits in the immediate vicinity of a person, they are deemed his courtyard with respect to lost property. That the courtyard of a male can legally acquire title for him, however, derives from the principle of agency, the argument being that just as his agent can legally acquire title for him, so can his courtyard. Now, seeing that a male minor is not competent to appoint an agent, he is also unable to acquire title by means of his courtyard or his four cubits, but only when he holds the lost property in his hand.

11. If one sees others running after a find, such as an injured hart or young birds as yet unable to fly, the rule is as follows: If the find is in one's field and he is standing beside the field, and if he can overtake the find by running, and he says, "My field has acquired it for me," the field does acquire the find for him. But if he cannot overtake the find, it is considered the same as the case of a hart able to run normally or of birds able to fly, and his words are of no avail, and whoever gets the find first is entitled to it.

If one acquires the above creatures as a gift, the field does acquire title to them for him, seeing that another person transfers to him title to them and they are moving about in his field. If, however, the hart is running normally, or the birds are flying, his field does not acquire title to them for him.

12. The Sages extended the commandment prohibiting robbery to property found by a deaf-mute, an imbecile, or a minor, in order to safeguard peace. Consequently, if one transgresses and robs one of these of a find, it cannot be recovered by the court; and if one denies on oath having taken it, he need not pay a fifth part.

13. The finds of one's son and daughter who are still at his table, even if they are already adult; the find of a maiden daughter, even if she is not supported at his table and even if she has been sold as a maid-servant; the find of his Canaanite male and female slaves; and the find of his wife—all these belong to him. But the find of a son who is not supported at his table, even if the son is a minor; the find of his Israelite male and female servants; and the find of a wife whose divorce from him is of doubtful status—these do not belong to him.

CHAPTER XVIII

1. If one finds a note of indebtedness, he should not return it to the creditor even if no lien on property is specified in it, and

even if the debtor admits liability and the note is certified. For the note may have in truth already been remitted, after which the debtor and the creditor may have entered a conspiracy (to use the note) to make unlawful seizure of property sold by the debtor, and this is why the debtor now admits liability. For although the note does not stipulate a lien, the creditor is nevertheless entitled to make seizure on the strength of such a note, seeing that lack of such stipulation is presumed to be an oversight on the part of the scribe, both in notes of indebtedness and in deeds of sale. Accordingly, if it is explicitly stated in the found note that the creditor is to have no lien, the rule is as follows: If the debtor admits liability, the finder should return the note to the creditor. But if he does not so admit, the note should not be returned, since the debtor may have paid the debt.

2. Similarly, if one finds a certified document dated that same day and the debtor admits liability, the finder must return it. If, however, it is not certified, the finder may not return it, for the note might have been drawn up for a loan which has as yet not been transacted.

3. If one finds a document inside a leather bottle or in a wooden utensil or the like, he must return it to the one who identifies it. If one finds three documents tied together in a single roll or lying one on top of the other and tied into one bundle, he must return them to the one who identifies them.

4. If the debtor is in each case the same individual but the creditors are three different persons, the rule is as follows: If the documents are certified, they must be returned to the debtor. If not, they must be returned to the one who identifies them, for the creditors might have given their documents to a scribe for certification and they may have been lost by the scribe.

If the creditor is the same individual and the debtors are three (different persons), the documents must be returned to the creditor. If, however, all are in the handwriting of the same scribe, they must be returned to the one who identifies them, for it is possible that all three creditors took their documents to be written by the same scribe, and they may have been lost by the scribe.

5. If one finds torn-up documents and among them is an untorn note of indebtedness, he may not return them. However, if there is a receipt among them, even one unsigned by witnesses, he must give the note of indebtedness to the borrower. For if this note had not been paid, the lender would not have thrown it among torn documents, and there is also a written statement saying that it has been paid.

6. If one finds a bill of divorcement and the husband admits its validity, the finder must return it to the wife. However, if the husband does not admit its validity, the rule is as follows: If the wife identifies it unmistakably, it must be returned to her, but if she does not, it may be returned to neither of them. If the husband says, "I lost it," and identifies it, and the wife also says, "I lost it," and identifies it, it must be given to her, provided that her identification mark is unmistakable, for example when she says, "There is a little hole at the side of such-and-such a letter." For if it had not been in her possession, she would not have known of this.

7. If the husband identifies the string with which the bill of divorcement is tied, and the wife also identifies the string, it must be given to her, provided that she identifies it unmistakably, for example by stating the length of the string. However, if she says, "It is red," or "It is black," this is not considered an unmistakable mark of identification.

If the husband says, "It was in a leather bottle," and the wife also says, "It was in a leather bottle," it must be given to him, because this is not considered an unmistakable mark of identification.

8. If one finds a deed of manumission, the rule is as follows: If the master admits its validity, it must be returned to the slave. But if the master does not admit its validity, it should be returned to neither of them.

9. If one finds a deed of gift, the rule is as follows: If the donor made the gift while in normal health, the finder may return the

deed neither to the donor nor to the donee, even if both admit its validity. For it is possible that the donor wrote the deed intending to make the gift to the named donee A but did not do so and, instead, sold the field or presented it to B after writing the deed, but has now changed his mind, and therefore admits the validity of the lost deed to enable him to swindle B to whom he gave or sold the field.

However, if the gift was made while the donor was seriously ill, the rule is as follows: If he admits its validity, it must be returned to the donee, but if not, it may not be returned. For if one who is seriously ill gives property to two people, one after the other, the rule is that the second one acquires it, as will be explained.

10. If the one who was seriously ill when he made the gift dies, the deed may not be returned to either the heir or the donee, even if the heir admits that the testator made the gift. For the deed might have been drawn up for delivery to the donee A, but was not given to him, and the heir might have sold the property or given it to B, but has now changed his mind and is plotting jointly with A to get it away from B.

11. If a receipt (of payment of a debt) is found, the rule is as follows: If the creditor admits that his note of indebtedness has been receipted because it was paid or waived, the receipt must be given to its addressee. But if neither of them so admits, the receipt should be returned to neither.

12. If a marriage contract is found, it may not be returned either to the husband or to the wife even if both admit its validity. For this marriage contract might have been paid or waived, and then the husband might have sold his property and now wants to swindle the purchaser.

13. If one finds documents of evaluation or of maintenance, documents certifying *ḥăliṣah* or "refusal," records of pleas, in which the judges note the pleas of each of the litigants, documents of selection, that is, documents recording the parties' choice of

judges to try the suit and their agreement to a trial by the persons named, or any document issued by a court, it must be returned.

The general rule is as follows: Any document recording a debt that might have been paid must not be given back, for possibly the debt has in truth been paid. If liability is admitted by the debtor but it is possible that the object of this admission is to perpetrate a swindle and deprive a purchaser or a donee of property received after the date of the document, by seizing the property illegally, the document may not be returned even if both persons named in it admit its validity. But wherever there is no fear that payment has been made or that a swindle might be perpetrated, the document must be returned to its owner.

14. If a lost document that should not have been returned is returned, it is deemed valid and enforceable and may not be taken away from its possessor, for it is presumed to have its original validity and is not subject to suspicion.

TREATISE IV

LAWS CONCERNING WOUNDING AND DAMAGING

Involving One Positive Commandment

To Wit

To administer the law of one who wounds another or damages another's property.

An exposition of this commandment is contained in the following chapters.

CHAPTER I

1. If one wounds another, he must pay compensation to him for five effects of the injury, namely, damages, pain, medical treatment, enforced idleness, and humiliation. These five effects are all payable from the injurer's best property, as is the law for all who do wrongful damage.

2. How are the damages determined? If one cuts off another's hand or foot, we determine—as if he were a slave being sold in the market—how much the injured man was worth previously and how much he is worth now. The offender must then pay the amount by which he has diminished the other's value, for when Scripture says, *An eye for an eye* (Exod. 21:24; Lev. 24:20), it is known from tradition that the word translated *for* signifies payment of monetary compensation.

3. When Scripture says, *As he hath maimed a man so shall it be rendered unto him* (Lev. *ibid.*), it does not mean that the injurer himself is to be wounded in the manner he wounded the other, but only that the injurer deserves to be deprived of a limb or to be wounded to the same extent, and consequently that he need only pay for the injury he inflicted. Moreover, Scripture says, *Ye shall take no ransom for the life of a murderer* (Num. 25:31), meaning that it is for the slayer alone that ransom may not be taken, but ransom may be taken for causing the loss of limbs or for inflicting wounds.

4. Similarly, when Scripture says of one who wounds another and causes him injury, *Thine eye shall not pity him* (Deut. 19:21), it means that we shall have no pity when exacting payment; that is, to prevent us from saying, "Since he is a poor man and wounded the other unintentionally, we will be merciful to him," Scripture says, *Thine eye shall not pity him.*

5. How then do we know that when Scripture says, concerning limbs, *An eye for an eye,* etc. (Exod. 21:24), it means compensa-

tion? It says in the context, *Stripe for stripe* (Exod. 21:25), and also says explicitly, *And if a man smite another with a stone or with his fist . . . he shall only pay for the loss of his time and shall cause him to be thoroughly healed* (Exod. 21:18–19). We thus learn that the word *for* (*taḥaṯ*) in the case of a *stripe* signifies compensation. The same conclusion applies to *for* in the case of the eye and the other limbs.

6. Although these rules appear plausible from the context of the Written Law, and were all made clear by Moses, our Teacher, from Mount Sinai, they have all come down to us as practical rules of law. For thus did our forebears see the law administered in the court of Joshua and in the court of Samuel, the Ramathite, and in every court ever set up from the time of Moses, our Teacher, until the present day.

7. How do we know that if one wounds another, he is liable separately for the pain caused? Because Scripture says, concerning a man guilty of rape, *Because he hath afflicted her* (Deut. 22:29), and the same rule applies to anyone who causes bodily pain to another: he must pay compensation for the pain caused.

8. How do we know that the injurer is liable separately for the enforced idleness and for the medical treatment? Scripture says, *He shall only pay for the loss of his time and shall cause him to be thoroughly healed* (Exod. 21:19).

9. How do we know that the injurer is liable separately for resultant humiliation? Because Scripture says, *And putteth forth her hand and taketh him by the secrets; then thou shalt cut off her hand* (Deut. 25:11–12). Included in this law is anyone who causes humiliation.

10. If one causes humiliation, he is not obligated to pay compensation unless he acts with intent, for Scripture says, *And putteth forth her hand* (*ibid.*). However, if one unintentionally puts another to shame, he is exempt. Consequently, if one who is asleep or in a similar state causes humiliation, he is exempt.

11. A person is always deemed forewarned whether he acts inadvertently or deliberately, whether he is awake, asleep, or intoxicated, and if he wounds another person or causes damage to another's property, he must pay compensation from the best of his own property.

The rule that one who does injury while asleep must pay compensation applies only when two lie down at the same time to sleep and one turns over in his sleep and injures the other or tears his clothing. However, if one is asleep and another comes and lies beside him, the one who comes last is deemed the forewarned one, and if the sleeper injures him, he is exempt. Similarly, if one places an article alongside a person who is asleep and the latter breaks it, he is exempt, seeing that the one who put it down is deemed forewarned and commits an act of negligence.

12. If one is blown from a roof by an ordinary wind and causes damage, he must pay for four effects but is exempt from paying for humiliation. If, however, he is blown off by an unusual wind, he is liable for damage only and is exempt from payment for the four other effects. If he turns over to break his fall, he is liable for all five effects, including humiliation, because if one has intent to do damage, he is deemed liable for the humiliation caused even though he does not intend to humiliate.

13. If two persons wound a third at the same time, they are both held liable and the liability is apportioned between them. If one acts with intent and the other without intent, the one who acts without intent is exempt from paying compensation for the humiliation.

14. If one intends to humiliate a minor and instead humiliates an adult, he must pay the adult the compensation due for the humiliation of a minor. If one intends to humiliate a slave and instead humiliates a freeman, he must give the freeman the compensation due for the humiliation of a slave.

15. If one has a stone in his lap—no matter whether he was never aware of it or whether he once knew of it but subsequently

forgot—and when he gets up it falls and causes damage, he is held liable for the damage alone but is exempt from the remaining four effects. Similarly, if one intends to throw a stone two cubits and instead throws it four and causes damage, or if one causes damage while asleep, he is liable for the damage but is exempt from (paying compensation for) the remaining four effects.

16. If one intentionally injures another, he is liable for the five effects wherever the injury occurs. Even if one enters another's premises without permission and the owner injures him, the latter is held liable, for although he has the right to expel a trespasser, he has no right to injure him. If, however, the trespasser suffers accidental injury due to the owner, the owner is exempt. If the owner suffers accidental injury due to the trespasser, the trespasser is held liable because he entered without permission. If both have authority to enter the premises or neither has, and each is accidentally injured by the other, both are exempt.

17. If one is chopping wood in a public domain and a piece of wood flies off and causes injury in a private domain, or if one is chopping in a private domain and causes injury in a public domain, or if one is chopping in a private domain and causes injury in another private domain, or if one enters a carpenter's shop, with or without permission, and a chip of wood flies up and strikes him in the face, the rule in each of these cases is that the one causing the injury is liable for four effects but is exempt from paying compensation for humiliation.

18. Just as an appraisal of the capacity to harm must be made in the case of death, so must such an appraisal be made in cases of injury. Thus, if one strikes another with a small pebble not large enough to cause injury, or with a small splinter of wood, and it inflicts a wound that an object of this kind would not be expected to inflict, he is exempt. For when Scripture says, *With a stone or with his fist* (Exod. 21:28), it refers to an object that is apt to cause injury. He is, however, liable for the humiliation caused, for even if one merely spits upon another's person, he is held liable for humiliation.

The witnesses must therefore know by what means the injury was caused, and the object with which the injury was inflicted must be brought before the court for the court to appraise it and adjudicate upon it. If the object is lost and the offender says, "It was not large enough to cause injury and it is as if I were party to a mishap," while the wounded man says, "It was large enough to inflict injury," the latter may take an oath and then receive compensation, as will be explained.

19. In the case of iron, no appraisal is necessary, for even a small needle can potentially kill, let alone injure a person.

If one throws a stone, and after it leaves his hand someone puts his head out of a window and is struck by the stone, the thrower is completely exempt. For when Scripture says, *And it lighteth upon his neighbor* (Deut. 19:5), it excludes any case where the neighbor subsequently places himself within range.

CHAPTER II

1. If one inflicts on another a wound for which compensation for all five effects is due, he must pay for the five. If one causes another an injury with only four effects, he must pay for the four; if there are three, he must pay three; if two, he must pay two; if one, he must pay one.

2. Thus, if one cuts off another's hand or his foot, or a finger or a toe, or blinds his eye, he must pay for five effects, namely, damages, pain, medical treatment, enforced idleness, and humiliation. If, however, one strikes another on the hand so that it swells but will eventually return to normal size, or on his eye so that it becomes inflamed but will eventually heal, he must pay for four effects, namely, pain, medical treatment, enforced idleness, and humiliation. If one strikes another on the head so that it swells, he must pay for three effects, namely, pain, medical treatment, and humiliation. If one strikes another on a spot that is not exposed—for example, if he strikes him on the knee or on the back—he must

pay for two effects, namely, pain and medical treatment. If one strikes another with his handkerchief or with a document or the like, in such a case he must pay for only one effect, namely, humiliation.

3. If one burns another on the fingernail with a spit or a nail at a spot where he neither causes a bruise nor interferes with his employment, he must pay for the pain alone. If one gives another a drug to drink, or smears him with an ointment and changes the color of his skin, he must pay him for medical treatment alone until such time as its appearance returns to normal. If one imprisons another in a room, he must give him compensation for his enforced idleness alone. The same rules apply in all similar cases.

4. If one shaves off the hair of another's head, he must compensate him for his humiliation alone, since the hair will eventually grow again. However, if he shaves him with a depilatory or burns him in such a way that the hair will not grow again, he is liable for all five effects: for damages, pain, and medical treatment, because the burning or the depilatory will have caused his head to be inflamed and give him a headache; for the enforced idleness, because he was previously able to dance and toss the locks of his head during the dance and is now barred from this employment; and for humiliation, because there can be no humiliation greater than this.

5. We thus learn that if one deprives another of any part of the body that will not grow again, he is liable for all five effects. Even if one knocks out another's tooth, he is liable for all five effects, since the mouth is certain to be sore for a time, and although the tooth itself is beyond treatment, the gums do require treatment.

6. Even if one deprives another of skin no larger than a grain of barley, he is liable for all five effects since the skin does not grow again but leaves a scar. Consequently, if one wounds another and tears the skin so that blood flows, he is liable for all five effects.

7. If one frightens another, he is legally exempt, although morally liable, even if the other is made ill by the fright, provided

that he does not touch him, as for example, if he shouts behind him or suddenly confronts him in the dark, or does something similar. Also, if one shouts into another's ear and deafens him, he is legally exempt but morally liable. If, however, one grabs another and blows into his ear and deafens him, or if he touches and pushes him when he frightens him, or if he takes hold of his clothes, or does something similar, he is liable and must pay compensation.

8. It appears to me that if the person assaulted says, "I have become deaf and cannot hear" or "My eye is blinded and I cannot see," he is not believed immediately, since we do not know the facts and he may be pretending. Thus, he may not receive compensation for damages until he has been examined over a long period of time and it is confirmed that he has lost the sight of his eyes or has become deaf. Only then need the injurer pay him compensation.

9. How much is the payment for pain? It depends upon the person injured. One person may be extremely delicate and pampered and rich, so that even if given a large sum of money, he would not voluntarily submit to even a little pain. Another person may be hardened and robust, but poor, so that he would voluntarily submit to great pain even for a single zuz. These are the principles on which compensation for pain is evaluated and determined.

10. How is pain assessed in a case where one has deprived another of a limb? If one cuts off another's hand or his finger, we estimate how much more a person of his status would be willing to pay for having his limb removed by means of a drug than for having it cut off with a sword, should the king decree that his hand or his foot be cut off. The difference thus estimated is what the offender must pay for the pain.

11. How is enforced idleness estimated? If one is not deprived of a limb but becomes ill and bedridden due to injury, or if his hand becomes swollen but will eventually return to normal size,

the offender must pay the amount of each day's enforced idleness at the rate that would be paid a laborer in his particular trade to refrain from work. However, if one is deprived of a limb or has his hand cut off, the offender must pay the compensation (1) for his hand, this being the damages, and (2) for the enforced idleness, that is, the amount he would receive if he were a cucumber watchman. That is to say, we find out what the daily wage of a cucumber watchman is and calculate the total for all the days that he is ill, and the offender must give him this amount. Similarly, if one's leg is cut off, we determine the amount as if he were a doorkeeper; if his eye is blinded, we determine the amount as if he were a mill grinder. These rules apply in all similar cases.

12. If one boxes another's ear, or seizes him and blows into his ear, and thereby deafens him, he must pay him his whole value, seeing that he is now unfit for any work whatsoever.

13. If one blinds another's eye and no assessment is made, then cuts off his hand and no assessment is made, then cuts off his leg and no assessment is made, and then deafens him, the rule is that inasmuch as no assessment was made for each injury separately, the offender need pay him only his whole value. If an assessment is first made for each injury separately, and then an assessment is made of his whole value, only the whole value may be collected from the offender. If, however, the injured person seizes the damages for each limb, together with his whole value, this cannot be reclaimed from him.

14. How is the payment for medical treatment determined? We estimate the number of days it will take the injured person to recover from his illness and the amount of money he will require. The offender may pay this to him forthwith and is not compelled to pay in daily installments. This method of payment was instituted for the benefit of the injurer.

15. Enforced idleness is estimated in the same manner, and the total amount is paid at once. If one is slow to recover from his illness and it is protracted beyond the estimated time, the injurer

need add nothing. Similarly, if one recovers immediately, nothing may be subtracted from the estimated sum.

16. The above rule applies only if the injurer agrees, seeing that it is intended for his benefit. If, however, he says that he does not desire this advantage but that he would rather provide the daily medical expenses, his request must be granted.

17. If the injured person says to the offender, "Fix a definite sum in agreement with me and give it to me and I will see to my own cure," his request is not granted, for the offender can reply, "Possibly you will not cure yourself and I shall be looked upon as a wrongdoer." He must therefore either give him the amount required daily or settle for a lump sum and give him the cost of the medical treatment through the court.

18. If the injurer says, "I will cure you myself," or "I have a doctor who will cure you free of charge," his suggestion is not heeded; rather he must bring a skilled physician to effect a cure for a fee.

19. If the total amount is not fixed in advance but medical expense is provided daily, and ulcers appear as a result of the wound or the wound re-opens after it has healed, the rule is that the injurer is obliged to pay for further medical treatment and for continued enforced idleness. If ulcers do appear but not as a result of the wound, he must pay for the medical treatment but need not pay for continued enforced idleness. If the patient disobeys the physician and his illness worsens, the injurer need not pay for further medical treatment.

20. When the court fixes a definite sum to be paid by the injurer and requires him to pay it, the court must collect the whole sum from him immediately and may not set a time during which he shall pay. If, however, he is required to pay for humiliation only, the court must give him time to pay, seeing that he did not deprive the other of money.

CHAPTER III

1. How is humiliation assessed? It depends upon the relative status of the one who causes the humiliation and the one who is humiliated. Humiliation caused by an insignificant person cannot be compared with humiliation caused by a great and eminent person. The humiliation caused by the lesser individual is greater.

2. If one humiliates another who is naked or is in a bath, he is exempt. If the wind blows up the hem of one's garment over his face so that he becomes exposed, and another uncovers him still more, the offender is liable for humiliation. But one who humiliates another who is already exposed cannot be compared with one who humiliates another who is not exposed at all. Similarly, if one lifts up his clothes to go down into a river, or is coming up from a river, and another humiliates him, the offender is liable. But one who humiliates such a person cannot be compared with one who humiliates another who is properly clothed.

3. If one humiliates another who is sleeping, he is liable for humiliation. If the person dies without waking up from his sleep and without feeling that the other humiliated him, we may not exact compensation for this humiliation from the offender. If, however, there is seizure by the heirs, it cannot be reclaimed from them.

4. If one humiliates an imbecile, he is exempt, but if one humiliates a deaf-mute, he is liable. If one humiliates a proselyte or a slave, he is liable. If one humiliates a minor, the rule is as follows: If the minor feels ashamed when insulted, the offender is liable; if not, he is exempt. Nevertheless, there is no comparison between one who humiliates a minor and one who humiliates an adult, or between one who humiliates a slave and one who humiliates a freeman, or between one who humiliates a deaf-mute and one who humiliates a normal person.

5. If one insults another in speech or spits on another's clothes, he is exempt from paying compensation, but the court should institute preventive measures in this matter everywhere and at all times, as it sees fit. If one humiliates a scholar, the offender must pay him full compensation for humiliation, even if he humiliates him merely in speech. There is already a well-established decision that if one humiliates a scholar, even in speech, he is to be fined and made to pay thirty-five denar in gold, which is equal in weight to nine sela' less a quarter; and we have a tradition that this fine may be enforced everywhere, both inside and outside the Land of Israel.

6. Cases of this kind occurred regularly in Spain. Some scholars used to forgo their right to claim, which was commendable of them, but at times one would claim and a compromise would be reached. The judges, however, used to say to the offender, "You are really obliged to give him a pound of gold."

7. Although if one humiliates ordinary persons by using derogatory speech he need not pay compensation, such action is considered a grave sin. Only a foolish scoundrel blasphemes and curses people, and the Sages of old have said, "If one makes an honorable Israelite blanch by his words, he will have no share in the world to come."

8. There are many types of blows which cause humiliation and a little pain but no permanent damage, and the Sages have long since fixed definite amounts of compensation for them. If one strikes another a blow of this kind, he must pay the corresponding fixed sum. All are regarded as fines; and the fixed sum covers the pain, the humiliation, the medical treatment, and the enforced idleness. This is the amount the offender must pay, whether or not medical treatment and enforced idleness are necessary.

9. How much need he pay? For kicking another, the offender must pay five sela'; for knocking him with his knee, he must pay three sela'; for tightening his fingers as though into a bunch and striking the other person with his fist tight, he must pay thirteen

sela'; for slapping another with the palm of his hand, he must pay one sela'; for slapping the other's face, he must pay fifty sela'; for slapping him with the back of his hand, he must pay one hundred sela'. Similarly, if he gives another a stinging blow on the ear, or pulls his hair, or spits so that the spittle reaches another's body, or pulls off another's cloak, or uncovers a woman's head, he must pay a hundred sela'.

This is the amount one must pay for each act. Thus, if one kicks another four times, even one after the other, he must pay twenty sela'; if he slaps his face twice, he must pay a hundred sela'. The same rule applies in the case of the other offensive acts.

10. The sela' mentioned is a coin of the Land of Israel current at the time when each sela' contained half a denar of silver and three and a half denar of bronze. Therefore, if one is required to pay a hundred sela' for inflicting blows of this kind, he must pay twelve and a half sela' of pure silver.

11. The above amounts apply only in the case of a respectable person, but a common person who remains indifferent to these and similar insults may receive only an amount commensurate with his status, as the court might deem proper for him to take. For there do exist contemptible individuals who are indifferent to humiliation and degrade themselves all day long in every possible way out of mere sport and frivolity or to earn a copper from low persons seeking amusement.

CHAPTER IV

1. If one assaults a woman even unintentionally, and her child is born prematurely, he must pay the value of the child to the husband and the compensation for injury and pain to the woman.

2. How is the value of the child determined? We estimate how much the woman was worth before she gave birth and how much she is worth after giving birth, and the difference is given to the husband. If the husband dies, it is given to his heirs. If, how-

ever, one assaults a woman after the husband's death, the woman is given the value of the child as well.

3. If the woman is married to a proselyte and one injures her during the proselyte's lifetime, the offender must give the value of the child to the husband. If the proselyte dies, the offender is exempt. If, however, one injures her after the proselyte's death, she herself becomes entitled to the value of the child.

4. If the woman was a bondwoman or a heathen at the time of conception but had been set free or had become a proselyte at the time of the assault, the value of the child belongs to her.

5. If one assaults a woman so that her child is born prematurely and she herself dies, he is exempt from paying compensation even if he acted inadvertently, and he need pay nothing at all. For Scripture says, *And yet no harm follow he shall be surely fined* (Exod. 21:22). Thus Scripture does not distinguish between one acting inadvertently and one acting deliberately in a case in which the death penalty is incurred, in so far as exemption from the payment of compensation is in question.

6. The above rule applies only if one intended to assault the woman. If, however, one intends to assault another man but assaults the woman, then even if she dies it is regarded as a case to which the death penalty is not applicable, seeing that the death was not intended, and the offender must pay the value of the child.

7. If one strikes his father or his mother without bruising, he must pay for the five effects. If, however, he does bruise, or if one wounds another on the Sabbath, even though inadvertently, he is exempt from paying compensation. For this is a crime to which the penalty of death is applicable, and we have already explained that Scripture does not distinguish between one acting inadvertently and one acting deliberately in a case where the death penalty is applicable, in so far as exemption from the payment of compensation is in question.

8. Now if one inflicts a wound on another, he is doing a destructive act, and anyone who performs a destructive act on the Sab-

bath is exempt from the death penalty. Why then should we consider the person who wounds another as committing a crime for which the death penalty is applicable? Because it is deemed a constructive act, since he affords his evil inclination satisfaction at the moment that he is wounding the other person. The crime is thus one for which the death penalty is applicable, and so he is exempt from paying compensation.

9. If one wounds another on the Day of Atonement, even deliberately, he must pay compensation even though he transgresses a prohibition for which he is liable to a flogging. But should not one who is liable to both a flogging and monetary penalty be flogged only and be exempt from the monetary penalty on the grounds that no one who is condemned to a flogging need pay a monetary penalty? This principle is indeed true in every case except that of one who wounds another, in which case he must pay compensation, because Scripture explicitly includes one who wounds another among those who must pay compensation, saying, *Only he shall pay for the loss of his time* (Exod. 21:19).

10. If one wounds his Canaanite slave, he is exempt. If one wounds his Hebrew slave, he is liable for all the effects except enforced idleness.

If one wounds another's Canaanite slave, the slave's master may take compensation for the five effects. Even if the slave is treated with a (special) painful drug so that he recovers quickly, the full compensation for (normal) medical treatment belongs to the master.

11. A fine is not payable with respect to any slave who has been set free but has not yet received his document of manumission. If others wound him, he himself cannot exact compensation from them because his manumission has not yet been completed, while his master cannot exact compensation from them because he has no ownership in the slave remaining. Consequently, if one knocks out his slave's tooth and then blinds his eye, the slave goes free because of the tooth but the master need not pay him the value

of his eye. However, if the slave seizes its value, it cannot be reclaimed from him.

12. If one insults another who is half slave and half free, or causes him pain, or if an ox gores him, or something similar happens, the rule is as follows: If it occurs on his master's day, the compensation belongs to the master; if, however, it happens on his own day, the compensation belongs to him.

13. If one wounds another's Hebrew slave, he must pay for all five effects, but land must be bought with the money and the master may consume its fruits. When the slave goes free, the field is removed from the master's control.

If one causes this slave an injury which does not interfere with his work at all—for example, if one cuts off the tip of his ear or his nose—all the effects belong to the slave, and the master has no claim to the fruits deriving from the compensation.

14. If one wounds another's minor daughter, the compensation for an injury which diminishes her value belongs to her father, and similarly compensation for her enforced idleness belongs to her father, seeing that the work of her hands and her sale value both belong to her father. Compensation for pain, humiliation, and medical treatment, however, belong to her. Similarly, compensation for an injury which does not diminish her value belongs to her. So, too, if one wounds his own daughter, he must pay for the pain, the medical treatment, and the humiliation.

15. If one wounds a married woman, compensation for enforced idleness and medical treatment belongs to her husband, and compensation for the pain belongs to her. With regard to compensation for humiliation and injury, the rule is as follows: If this is visible—for example, if one strikes her on the face or neck or hands or arms—one third belongs to her and two thirds to her husband; if, however, the injury is concealed, one third belongs to her husband and two thirds to the woman. The husband's share must be given to him at once. With regard to the wife's share, land must be bought and the husband may enjoy its fruits.

16. The above rule applies only if others wound her. If, however, a husband wounds his wife, he must pay her immediately for the whole of the injury, and the whole of the humiliation and the pain. The entire compensation belongs to her, and her husband has no right to the fruits. If she wishes to give the money away to another, she may do so. The Geonim, also, have ruled in this manner. The husband must also pay for medical treatment in the same manner he pays for treatment of any of her ailments.

17. If one injures his wife during marital intercourse, he is liable for the injury done to her.

18. If a woman wounds her husband, the rule is as follows: If there is a supplement to her marriage settlement and the husband is willing, we compel her to sell the supplement to her husband at its present market value, and he may then collect the compensation from her. If he wishes to divorce her and collect the compensation from the entire marriage settlement, he may do so.

However, if she has no supplement, she cannot sell him the principle item in the marriage settlement—for a man is forbidden to keep his wife with him for a single hour without a marriage settlement, lest it be an easy matter to divorce her. But if the husband is willing, he may draw up a document recording the compensation for his wound due him from her, or else he may divorce her and take the amount due him from the marriage settlement.

19. If one wounds his grown sons, the rule is as follows: If they do not receive support at his table, he must pay them immediately. And if they are minors, land must be bought with the compensation for their injuries and they may enjoy its fruits. The same rule applies if others wound them.

However, if they do receive support at their father's table and he wounds them, he is exempt whether they are adult or minors. If others wound them, the rule is as follows: If the injured are adult, the offender must pay them the compensation immediately, but if they are minors, land must be bought with the compensation and they may enjoy the fruits until they reach the age of majority.

20. To clash with a deaf-mute, an imbecile, or a minor is bad, seeing that if one wounds one of these, he is liable, whereas if they wound others, they are exempt. Even if a deaf-mute becomes normal, or an imbecile becomes sane, or a minor reaches majority, they are not liable for payment inasmuch as they were legally irresponsible when they caused the wound.

21. To clash with a slave or a married woman is bad, seeing that if one wounds one of these, he is liable, whereas if they wound others, they are exempt. They must, however, pay at a later date—the woman must pay if she is divorced, or if her husband dies, and the slave must pay if he is freed—for they are legally responsible and their status is deemed that of a debtor who has no means but who must pay when he acquires property.

22. One's slave is regarded as his own person, but his animal is regarded as his inanimate property. Thus, if one places a burning coal on the breast of another's slave so that he dies, or if one pushes a slave into the sea or into a fire from which he can escape but he does not escape and dies, the injurer is exempt from paying compensation. If, however, one does the same to another's animal, it is regarded as if he had placed a burning coal on another's clothing and burned it, in which case he is liable for payment. The same rule applies in all similar cases.

CHAPTER V

1. One is forbidden to wound either himself or another. Not only one who wounds another but even one who strikes a law-observing Israelite in the course of a quarrel, whether an adult or a minor, whether a man or a woman, transgresses a negative commandment contained in the verse, *He shall not exceed . . . to smite him* (Deut. 25:3). For if Scripture here warns against

excess in lashing an offender, how much more does this warning apply to smiting an innocent person.

2. It is forbidden even to lift a hand against another, and if one does lift a hand against another, he is deemed wicked even if he does not actually strike him.

3. If one gives another a blow which does not injure him to the extent of a pĕruṭah, he incurs flogging, for there is no compensation in this case (to exempt him on the grounds) that the negative commandment is rectified by monetary compensation. Even if one inflicts a blow on another's slave which does not result in injury valued at a pĕruṭah, he must be flogged, for a slave is subject to certain commandments.

If a heathen strikes an Israelite, he is liable for the penalty of death, for Scripture says, *And he looked this way and that and . . . he smote the Egyptian* (Exod. 2: 12).

4. The Sages have penalized strong-armed fools by ruling that the injured person should be held trustworthy and should swear holding a sacred object that the person in question did inflict a specific wound upon him and then receive the compensation due to him, provided that witnesses were present. Thus, if two witnesses testify concerning one that he came into another's hands unwounded and emerged wounded, but they did not see him being wounded, and the accused says, "I did not wound you," while the injured person replies, "You did wound me," the latter takes an oath and then receives compensation.

5. The above rule applies only if the wound is so located that it could be self-inflicted, or if there was present a third individual whom the wounded person could have asked to inflict a wound on him so that he could accuse the other. But if no one else was present, and the wound is so located that it could not be self-inflicted, such as a bite between the shoulder blades or the like, the wounded person may exact compensation without an oath.

6. If the offender admits that he inflicted the wound, he must pay for all five effects, since witnesses were present and testify that

the plaintiff was unwounded when he came into the offender's hands at the time of the quarrel and wounded when he emerged. However, if there were no witnesses present, and the plaintiff says, "You wounded me," and the offender admits this of his own accord, he is exempt from paying for the injury and the pain, but he must pay, because of his own confession, for enforced idleness, humiliation, and medical treatment. Consequently, if the accused says, "I did not inflict a wound," he must take an oath of inducement.

7. Why is it that one must pay for these three effects on his own confession? Because compensation for enforced idleness and medical treatment is deemed a monetary payment and not a fine—for if the offender does not pay them, he deprives the other of the money that his medical treatment and unemployment costs him—and because humiliation is suffered only when the defendant confesses in our presence that he wounded the other. For if one is wounded without others being present, he does not suffer humiliation. It is the defendant's confession in court that humiliates the plaintiff.

8. We thus learn that there is no difference between the humiliation one suffers if he is wounded in the presence of others and the humiliation he suffers if the defendant confesses in the presence of others that he wounded him. For this reason one must pay compensation for humiliation on his own confession.

9. If one inflicts a personal injury on another, he may not be compared to one who damages another's property. For if one damages another's property, atonement is effected for him as soon as he pays whatever is required. But if one wounds another, atonement is not effected for him even if he has paid for all the five effects, or even if he has sacrificed all the rams of Nebaioth, for his sin is not forgiven until he begs forgiveness of the injured person and is pardoned.

10. The injured person, however, is forbidden to be harsh and to withhold forgiveness, for such behavior does not become a descendant of Israel. But once the offender has asked forgiveness and

has entreated him a first and a second time, and he knows that the offender has repented of his sin and regrets his evil deed, he should forgive him. Whoever forgives quickly is praiseworthy and his behavior meets with the approval of the Sages.

11. There is another difference between personal injury and damage to property. If one says to another, "Blind my eye, or cut off my hand, with the understanding that you are to be exempt," he is nevertheless liable for the five effects since it is quite certain that a person does not really consent to such treatment. But if one says to another, "Tear my coat, or break my jar, with the understanding that you are to be exempt," he is exempt.

If one fails to say, "With the understanding that you are to be exempt," the offender is deemed liable even though the injured person permits him to be destructive.

12. The above rule applies only if the article in question originally came into the offender's possession as a bailment, having been either loaned to or deposited with him. If the owner then says to him, "Break, or tear, them," and he does so, he is liable unless the other adds, "With the understanding that you are to be exempt." But if one says to another, "Take this article and break it, or this garment and tear it," and he does so, he is exempt.

13. If one says to another, "Break So-and-So's articles, with the understanding that you are to be exempt," the offender is nevertheless liable for payment, just as if the first person had said to him, "Blind So-and-So's eye with the understanding that you are to be exempt." Yet even though it is the agent who must pay, the person who prompts him is his partner in wrongdoing and is an evildoer, since he has in a way caused the blind to stumble and has encouraged a law breaker.

CHAPTER VI

1. If one damages another's property, he must pay full compensation; for whether one acts inadvertently or accidentally, he is

regarded as one who acted deliberately. Thus, if one falls from a roof and breaks articles, or if one stumbles while walking and falls on an article and breaks it, he must pay full compensation. For when Scripture says, *And he that killeth a beast shall make it good* (Lev. 24:21), no distinction is made between one acting inadvertently and one acting deliberately.

2. There is no difference between killing another's animal, breaking his utensils, tearing his clothes, or cutting down his saplings. One rule applies in all these cases.

3. The above rule applies only if one causes damage on the premises of the injured party. On his own premises, the offender is liable for payment of compensation only if he causes damage deliberately; he is exempt, however, from paying for damage he causes inadvertently or accidentally.

Similarly, if two persons have the right to be in a place, or if neither of them has this right, and one of them unintentionally causes damage to the other's property, he is exempt.

4. If one is climbing a ladder and a rung slips from under him and it falls and causes damage, the rule is as follows: If the rung was not strong and firmly fixed, he is liable. But if it was strong and firmly fixed and yet it slipped, or if it was rotted, he is exempt, for this damage is a blow from Heaven. The same rule applies in all similar cases.

The aforesaid applies only if the damage occurs on the premises of the injured party, but on his own premises the offender is exempt unless, as we have explained, he causes damage intentionally.

5. If one fills another's courtyard with jars of wine and oil, the rule is as follows: Even if one takes them in with the permission of the owner of the courtyard, the latter, seeing that he does not agree to guard them, may pass in and out in the usual manner and is exempt from responsibility for whatever jars are broken as he does so. If, however, he breaks them intentionally, he is obliged to pay compensation even if the owner of the jars brings them in without permission. The same rule applies in all similar cases.

6. If one's ox clambers onto another ox to kill it, on the premises of the owner of the ox attacked, the rule is as follows: If the owner of the ox attacked comes and pulls his ox out of the way in order to save it and the attacking ox falls and dies, he is exempt, whether the attacking ox is innocuous or forewarned.

7. However, if the owner of the ox attacked pushes the attacking ox over and it dies, the rule is as follows: If he could have pulled the ox attacked out of the way but did not do so, he is deemed liable; but if he could not have pulled it out of the way, he is exempt.

8. If two persons meet one another on a public domain, one carrying a jar and the other a wooden beam, and the jar is broken by the beam, the one carrying the beam is exempt, because each of them has the right to be walking there.

If the one with the beam is in front and the one with the jar is behind, and the jar is broken by the beam, the one with the beam is exempt. If, however, the one with the beam has stopped to rest because of the weight of his burden, he is held liable; but if he warns the one with the jar and tells him to halt, he is exempt. If the one with the beam stops to adjust his burden, he is regarded as if he were still walking and he is exempt even if he does not warn the other, seeing that his mind is occupied with the path in front of him.

If the one with the jar is in front and the one with the beam is behind, and the jar is broken by the beam, the owner of the beam is held liable because it is as though he broke the jar intentionally with his own hand. However, if the one with the jar has stopped to rest, the other is exempt; but if he warns the one with the beam and tells him to halt, the one with the beam is held liable. If the one with the jar stops to adjust his burden, the one with the beam is liable even if the other does not warn him.

The same rule applies if one carries a lamp and the other flax, and also in all similar cases.

9. If two persons proceed along a public domain, one walking and the other running, and one suffers unintentional damage from

the other, the one running is liable inasmuch as he was acting unusually. If, however, it is near dusk on the Sabbath eve, he is exempt, because he has the right to run then lest the Sabbath begin before he has finished his business.

If both are running and they injure each other, both are exempt, even on other days of the week.

10. It is immaterial whether one causes damage with his own hand, or if one throws a stone or shoots an arrow and causes damage thereby, or if one pours water onto another or onto articles and so damages them, or if one expectorates mucus or phlegm and causes damage with the mucus or the phlegm while these are still moving under his impetus. In each case one is regarded as if he caused damage with his own hand, these being deemed subspecies of damage by persons. However, if the mucus or the phlegm falls to the ground and another skids on them, the offender is liable due to damage caused by his "pit." For, as we have explained, every obstacle is regarded as a subspecies of damage by "pit."

11. If a smith strikes a blow with a hammer and a spark flies from under the hammer and causes damage, he is as liable as one who throws a stone or shoots an arrow. Similarly, if a builder undertakes to demolish a wall and breaks the stones or causes damage, he is liable. If masonry collapses at one end while he is demolishing the other, the builder is exempt; but if the collapse is a result of his blow, he is liable, for this is deemed similar to shooting an arrow and causing damage thereby.

12. If one forces another's animal under water, or if it falls into water and he prevents it from getting out so that it dies there, or if he leaves it in the sun and pens it in so that it is unable to find shade and the sun kills it, he is obliged to pay compensation. The same rule applies in all similar cases.

13. If two persons kill an animal or break an object together, the liability is divided between them proportionately.

14. If five persons put five bundles on an animal and it does not die, but when another person comes and puts his bundle on

it, it dies, the rule is as follows: If it walked with the original bundles but after the last person added his bundle it stopped and did not walk, the last person is liable. However, if it did not walk from the outset, the last person is exempt. If the matter is uncertain, all must pay equally.

15. Similarly, if five persons sit on a bench and it does not break, but when another person comes and sits on it, it breaks, the last person is liable even if it could have been expected to break because of its occupants before he sat down, seeing that he hastened its collapse. For the others can say to him, "If you had not added your weight to ours, we would have risen before it broke." If, however, they sit down simultaneously and it breaks, all are liable. The same rule applies in all similar cases.

16. If a person and an ox together push into a pit an animal or a person or articles or a dedicated animal that has become disqualified for sacrifice, and the living victim is injured or dies, or the articles are broken, the rule is as follows: For injury to the person or damage to the animal, all three are liable, namely, the one who pushed, the owner of the ox and the owner of the pit, and the liability must be shared proportionately between them. For compensation for a child born prematurely and for the other four effects (of wounding), the one who pushes is liable and the owner of the ox and the owner of the pit are exempt. For ransom and the thirty shekels payable for killing a slave, the owner of the ox is liable and the one who pushed and the owner of the pit are exempt. For damage to the articles and to the dedicated animal that is disqualified for sacrifice, the one who pushed and the owner of the ox are liable and the owner of the pit is exempt.

CHAPTER VII

1. If one causes, to another's property, damage that is not discernible, he is exempt from paying compensation according to scriptural law, seeing that the property has not been altered and

its form has not been adversely affected. But the Sages, on the authority of the Scribes, declared him liable inasmuch as he has reduced the value of the property, and he must pay the amount by which he has reduced its value.

2. Thus, if one defiles another's ritually clean food, or if one mixes heave offering with another's produce, or mixes a drop of forbidden libation wine with another's wine thereby causing it all to become forbidden, or if one does any similar thing, the depreciation is estimated and the offender must pay full compensation from his best property, as do all who cause damage.

3. This payment is a penalty imposed by the Sages on the offender to prevent mischievous persons from defiling another's ritually clean food and saying, "I am exempt." Consequently, if one who has caused damage which is not discernible dies, the compensation may not be collected from his estate. For the Sages penalized only the person who transgressed and caused the damage, but they did not penalize the heir, who committed no such act. Similarly, if one inadvertently or accidentally causes damage which is not discernible, he is exempt, because the Sages penalized only that person who knowingly intended to inflict damage.

4. Priests who deliberately render a sacrifice invalid must pay compensation; if they do so inadvertently, they are exempt. Similarly, if one deliberately does work with a Heifer of Purification or with Water of Purification, he must pay compensation; if he does so inadvertently, he is exempt.

5. If one takes the Heifer into a cattle stall in order that it may suckle, and it threshes some grain, or if he diverts his attention from Water of Purification, he is legally exempt but morally liable.

6. If one pours out another's wine as a libation to an idol, the wine does not become forbidden, because no Israelite can render forbidden that which does not belong to him. If, however, he owns a share of the wine, or if he is an apostate—who is deemed a heathen—or if he was warned and accepted the warning—so that

he is regarded as an apostate—he does render the wine forbidden and must pay compensation. But, seeing that he has incurred the penalty of death, why should he be held liable for compensation? Because he becomes liable for compensation from the moment he lifts up the wine, whereas his life does not become forfeit until he pours it out as a libation.

7. If one causes damage to another's property indirectly, he must pay full compensation from his best property as must others who do damage. Although it may not be he himself who ultimately inflicts this damage, he is nevertheless held liable, seeing that he is the original cause of it. Thus, if one throws an article of his own from a rooftop onto pillows or cushions and another hurries and removes the pillows so that the article strikes the ground and breaks, the latter must pay full compensation as if he had broken it with his own hand, for the removal of the pillows or the cushions caused it to break. The same rule applies in all similar cases.

8. If one throws another's article from a rooftop onto pillows or cushions belonging to the owner of the article, and the owner removes the pillows or the cushions before the article reaches them, the thrower is liable because his throwing of the article is the original cause of its breaking. If a third person removes them, both the thrower and the remover are liable, for both caused the loss of another's property.

9. Similarly, if one burns a creditor's bonds, he must pay the full debt recorded in the bond—for although the bond itself is not intrinsically money, he has caused the loss of money—provided that the offender admits the bond was one confirmed in court, that it recorded the specific amount claimed, and that the creditor cannot collect the debt because the offender burned the bond. However, if he does not believe the creditor, the offender need pay only the value of the paper.

10. Similarly, if A, to whom B owes a debt, sells the bond to C and then, after having sold it, forgives B the debt, B is released from the debt, as will be explained in its proper place; but A must

pay C whatever sum is recorded in the bond. For A caused C to lose the content of the bond, and it is regarded as if A had burned it.

Similarly, if A's heir forgives the debt, the heir must pay compensation from his best property.

11. Similarly, if one mortgages his slave and then sets him free, he must pay the creditor compensation, seeing that he has nullified the creditor's lien on the slave and caused him a loss of money. We also compel the creditor himself to manumit the slave in order that he should not, on chancing to meet the slave, say to him, "You are my slave."

Similarly, if one pushes another's coin so that it rolls down into the sea, he must pay compensation.

Likewise, if one nicks the ear of a heifer, he must pay compensation because he causes its value to be reduced.

So, too, if one flattens another's coins and removes the design on them, he must pay compensation due to his causing a loss to another. The same rule applies in all cases similar to these.

12. If one throws an object from a rooftop to the ground where there is no clothing underneath it, and another breaks it with a stick while it is still in the air, the rule is that the latter is exempt because he does no more than break an object which is certain to be broken immediately. He is thus regarded as one who breaks a broken object and is not deemed one who causes damage indirectly. In any case similar to this, one is exempt.

13. If an ox is to be killed because it inflicts injury upon persons, or if a tree is to be felled because it causes public damage, and one slaughters the ox or fells the tree without the owner's knowledge, the rule is that he must pay the owner whatever sum the judges consider appropriate, seeing that he has prevented the owner from performing a religious duty. If, however, he pleads that the owner told him to kill the ox or to fell the tree, he is exempt, inasmuch as this was to be done in any case.

14. Similarly, if one slaughters a wild animal or a bird, and another person comes and covers the blood without the slaughterer's

consent, he must pay whatever the judges consider appropriate. Some authorities have ruled that he must pay a fixed fine, namely, ten gold pieces. Similarly, they have ruled that whenever one prevents another from performing a positive commandment which he is qualified to perform, and the one who prevents performs it first, he must pay the other ten gold pieces.

15. An evaluation must be made for one who inflicts damage with his own hand in the same way as an evaluation must be made for him if his property causes damage. Thus, if one kills another's animal or breaks another's article, we determine how much the animal was worth and how much the carcass is worth, or how much the article was worth whole and how much it is worth now, and the offender must pay the difference to the plaintiff, together with the carcass or the broken article, exactly as we have explained in the case where one's ox inflicts damage, for the law is the same.

If one treads another's grapes, we must evaluate for him the damage he has inflicted. The same rule applies in all similar cases.

16. When the depreciation is collected from the offender, it should be collected from his movable property. If he possesses no movable property, it may be collected from his best real property. Similarly, the fine of one guilty of rape, seduction, or postmarital slander (cf. Deut. 22:13 ff.) may be collected from his best real property.

17. If one inflicts damage on another's property and does not know what damage he has caused, the plaintiff must swear, under a regulation of the Sages, and may then receive what he claims as does one robbed, provided that he claims objects that he is likely to have possessed, as we have explained in the case of one robbed.

18. Thus, if one takes another's purse and throws it into the sea or into a fire, or hands it to a villainous person so that it is lost, and the owner of the purse says, "It was full of gold pieces," while the offender says, "I do not know, it might have been full of earth or straw," the rule is that the plaintiff must take an oath, holding a sacred object, and then receive what he claims, provided that he

claims objects which he is considered likely to possess or likely to hold on deposit, and which are usually kept in a purse or the like. If, however, the objects claimed are not usually kept in a receptacle of this kind, the plaintiff has himself committed an act of negligence. Thus, if one snatches a filled and covered water-skin or basket and throws it into the sea or burns it, and the plaintiff says it contained pearls, he is not heeded and may not take an oath to this effect. For persons do not usually keep pearls in baskets or water-skins. However, if the plaintiff seizes property belonging to the defendant, it may not be taken away from him, but he must swear that the receptacle contained pearls and may then take what he claims from the property he has seized. The same rule applies in all similar cases.

19. If the defendant knows that the purse contained gold pieces but does not know how many, and the plaintiff says that the number was a thousand, he is entitled to collect a thousand without taking an oath, provided that his claim is considered to be a reasonable one. For in reality it is the defendant who should take an oath, except that he is unable to swear, as will be explained in connection with the laws of bailment.

CHAPTER VIII

1. If one, acting as an informer, delivers another's property into the hands of a villainous person, he must pay compensation from his best property. If he dies, the compensation may be collected from his heirs as is the rule in the case of all others who inflict damage. Whether the villainous person is a heathen or an Israelite, the informer must pay for whatever the villainous person takes, even if the informer does not take the money with his own hand and surrender it but merely supplies information.

2. The above rule applies only when the informer points out the property voluntarily. If, however, he was compelled to do so by a heathen or a villainous Israelite, he is exempt from paying

compensation. But if he takes the property with his own hand and surrenders it, he must pay even though he acts under constraint, for one who saves himself by appropriating another's money must repay it.

3. Thus, if a king decrees that wine or fodder or the like must be brought to him, and an informer comes forward and says that a certain person has a store of wine or fodder at a specified place and the king's men go and take it, he must pay compensation. If, however, the king applies constraint to the informer, compelling him to reveal stores of wine or fodder or to reveal the money of another who has fled from the king, and he does reveal it under such constraint, he is exempt. For if he did not reveal the property, the king would have beaten him or killed him.

4. If one takes another's money and gives it to a villainous person with his own hand, he must pay under any circumstances, even if the king compels him to secure it.

This rule—namely, that if one is compelled to secure something and he does so, he is liable—applies only when the money has not yet come under the control of the villainous person. If, however, a villainous person compels an Israelite to reveal property and stands beside the property so that it comes under his control and he then compels an Israelite to take it for him to another place, even if the informer who reveals the property is also the one who takes it, he is exempt from paying compensation. For as soon as the villainous person stands beside the store of property, everything in it is deemed already lost, and it is regarded as if it had been burned.

5. If litigants are quarreling over real or movable property, each one claiming it as his, and one of them gives it to a heathen, we place him under a ban with orders that he must restore the property and remove any threat of intervention by a villainous person, so that the litigants may bring their case to an Israelite court.

6. If A is seized for B, and heathens take money from A on B's account, B need not repay A. The only cases in which, when A is seized for B, B need repay A are the following: If A is seized on

account of a fixed tax payable annually by each individual or if he is seized on account of a requisition payable by each individual when the king or his army passes through. In each of these cases, B is obliged to repay A, provided that the money is taken from A specifically on account of B, in the presence of witnesses.

7. If there are witnesses that one has informed against another's property, either by pointing it out voluntarily or by taking it under constraint and surrendering it, but the witnesses do not know how much loss he has caused the other by acting as an informer, and the plaintiff says, "He caused me such-and-such a loss," but the informer denies this claim, the rule is as follows: If the plaintiff seizes property from the informer, it may not be taken away from him, but he must take an oath, holding a sacred object, and then becomes entitled to whatever he has seized. But if he does not seize property, nothing may be exacted from the informer without clear proof.

8. We do not administer either a stringent oath or an oath of inducement to an informer who has informed voluntarily, because he is deemed wicked and one can have no greater disqualification than this. But if an informer is compelled to inform or to secure, and he takes the property with his own hand and surrenders it, then even though he is under obligation to pay, he is not deemed wicked but is merely one subject to a monetary penalty, and an oath may be administered to him as to any other law-observing person.

9. It is forbidden to give either another's person or his property into the hand of a heathen, even if the other is wicked and a sinner and even if he causes one distress and pain. If one gives another's person or his property into the hand of a heathen, he has no share in the world to come.

10. An informer may be killed anywhere, even at the present time when we do not try cases involving capital punishment, and it is permissible to kill him before he has informed. As soon as one says that he is about to inform against So-and-So's person or prop-

erty, even a trivial amount of property, he surrenders himself to death. He must be warned and told, "Do not inform," and then if he is impudent and replies, "Not so! I shall inform against So-and-So," it is a religious duty to kill him, and he who hastens to kill him acquires merit.

11. If the informer has carried out his intention and given information, it is my opinion that we are not allowed to kill him unless he is a confirmed informer, in which case he must be killed lest he inform against others. There are frequently cases in the cities of the Maghrib where informers who are known to reveal people's money are killed or are handed over to the heathen authorities to be executed, beaten, or imprisoned, as befits their crime.

Similarly, if one oppresses the community and troubles them, it is permissible to hand him over to the heathen authorities to be beaten, imprisoned, and fined. But if one merely distresses an individual, he must not be handed over.

Although the punishment of an informer is permitted, it is forbidden to destroy his property, for it belongs to his heirs.

12. If one pursues another to kill him or for an immoral purpose, and he breaks objects belonging to the person pursued or to another, he is exempt from paying compensation because his life is forfeit. For as soon as one pursues another, he surrenders himself to be killed.

13. If the one pursued breaks articles belonging to the pursuer, he is exempt, for the pursuer's property is not regarded as more precious than his own person. If, however, he breaks articles belonging to other people, he is liable; for if one saves himself by appropriating another's property, he is liable.

14. If one chases after the pursuer in order to rescue the pursued, and he breaks objects belonging to the pursuer or to anyone else, he is exempt. This rule is not strict law but is an enactment made in order that one should not refrain from rescuing another or lose time through being too careful when chasing a pursuer.

15. If a ship threatens to break up because of the weight of its load, and one of those on board lightens the load by throwing some of the objects overboard, he is exempt because the load carried is regarded as pursuing the passengers to kill them. He fulfills an important religious duty in throwing some of the load overboard and saving the passengers.

TREATISE V

LAWS CONCERNING MURDER AND THE PRESERVATION OF LIFE

Involving Seventeen Commandments,
Seven Positive and Ten Negative

To Wit

1. Not to commit murder;
2. Not to accept ransom for the life of a murderer, rather to put him to death;
3. To exile the inadvertent slayer;
4. Not to accept ransom from one liable for exile;
5. Not to kill one who has committed murder before he has been tried;
6. To rescue the pursued (even) at the cost of the life of the pursuer;
7. Not to spare the pursuer;
8. Not to stand idly by the blood of another;
9. To set apart cities of refuge and to make direct roads leading to them;
10. To behead the heifer in a *valley;* *
11. Not to till or sow the land of that *valley;* *
12. Not to bring blood upon one's house;
13. To make a parapet;
14. Not to mislead the innocent in any matter;

* Cf. Deut. 21: 4, 6.

15. To help unload with one who is in trouble by the roadside;
16. To help him load;
17. Not to leave him confused over his burden and depart.

An exposition of these commandments
is contained in the following chapters.

CHAPTER I

1. If one slays a human being, he transgresses a negative commandment, for Scripture says, *Thou shalt not murder* (Exod. 20:13). If one murders willfully in the presence of witnesses, he is put to death by the sword, for when Scripture says, *He shall surely be punished* (Exod. 21:20), we have learned from tradition that this means death by the sword. Whether one slays another with an iron weapon or burns him in fire, he is put to death by the sword.

2. The avenger of blood is commanded to slay the murderer, for Scripture says, *The avenger of blood shall himself put the murderer to death* (Num. 35:19). Whoever is eligible to inherit from another is deemed the avenger of blood. If the avenger of blood is unwilling or unable to put the murderer to death, or if the victim has no avenger of blood, the court must put the murderer to death by the sword.

3. If a father kills his son, the rule is as follows: If the murdered son has a son of his own, the latter must slay his own grandfather, because he is the avenger; but if there is no son, none of the brothers may become the avenger of blood with the duty of killing the father, rather the court must put him to death. The law of the avenger of blood applies to men and to women alike.

4. The court is warned against accepting ransom from a murderer, even if he offers all the money in the world and even if the avenger of blood agrees to let him go free. For the life of the murdered person is not the property of the avenger of blood but the property of God, and Scripture says, *Moreover ye shall take no ransom for the life of a murderer* (Num. 35:31). There is no offense about which the Law is so strict as it is about bloodshed, as it is said, *So shall ye not pollute the land wherein ye are; for blood, it polluteth the land* . . . (Num. 35:33).

5. If a murderer kills willfully, he may not be put to death by the witnesses or the spectators before he is brought to court and

condemned to death, for Scripture says, *That the manslayer die not until he stand before the congregation for judgment* (Num. 35: 12). The same rule applies to anyone who is liable for death at the hands of the court because he has transgressed and committed a crime. He may not be put to death until he is sentenced by the court.

6. The above rule applies when the offender has already transgressed and committed the crime for which he is liable for the death penalty at the hands of the court. But if one person is pursuing another with the intention of killing him, even if the pursuer is a minor, it is the duty of every Israelite to save the pursued, even at the cost of the pursuer's life.

7. Thus, if one has been warned but still pursues the other person, he may be killed even if he does not accept the warning, seeing that he continues to pursue. If it is possible to rescue the pursued at the cost of one of the pursuer's limbs, such as by striking him with an arrow or a stone or a sword and cutting off his hand or breaking his leg or blinding his eye, this should be done. If, however, it is impossible to judge exactly and the pursued can be rescued only if the pursuer is killed, he may be killed even though he has not yet killed anyone, for Scripture says, *Then thou shalt cut off her hand, thine eye shall have no pity* (Deut. 25: 12).

8. Concerning this rule there is no difference either between the private parts (cf. Deut. 25: 11) and any other part of the body (injury to which) may endanger one's life, or between a man and a woman. The intent of the above scriptural passage is that if one intends to deal another a death-blow, the pursued should be saved at the cost of the pursuer's hand. If this is impossible, he must be saved even at the cost of the pursuer's life, for Scripture says, *Thine eye shall have no pity* (*ibid.*).

9. This is, moreover, a negative commandment, that we have no pity on the life of the pursuer. Consequently, the Sages have ruled that if a woman with child is having difficulty in giving birth, the child inside her may be taken out, either by drugs or by sur-

gery, because it is regarded as one pursuing her and trying to kill her. But once its head has appeared, it must not be touched, for we may not set aside one human life to save another human life, and what is happening is the course of nature.

10. The rule is the same whether one is pursuing another to kill him, or whether he is pursuing a betrothed girl to ravish her. For Scripture says, *For as when a man ariseth against his neighbor and slayeth him, even so is this matter* (Deut. 22:26), and says further, *The betrothed damsel cried and there was none to save her* (*ibid.*, 22:27), intimating that if there is someone to save her, he should save her by any possible method, even by killing the pursuer.

11. The same rule applies to all other forbidden sexual contacts, apart from offenses with animals. In the case of homosexuality, however, the one pursued should be saved (even) at the cost of the pursuer's life, as is the rule concerning all other sexual offenses.

If, however, one pursues an animal to lie with it, or is bent on doing prohibited work on the Sabbath, or on committing an act of idolatry—although the laws concerning the Sabbath and those concerning idolatry involve basic principles in the religion of Israel—he may not be killed until he has committed the transgression, whereupon he must be brought to court and duly tried and then put to death.

12. If one pursues a woman forbidden to him, seizes her, lies down with her, and commences coition, he may not be killed until after his trial, even though he has not completed the act. If one is pursuing a woman forbidden to him, and others are pursuing him to save her, and she says to them, "Let him alone so that he will not kill me," they may not grant her request but should confound him and prevent him from coition by injuring his limbs, or, if they cannot do this at the cost of his limbs, then even at the cost of his life, as we have explained.

13. If one is able to save the victim at the cost of only a limb of the pursuer, and does not take the trouble to do so, but saves the victim at the cost of the pursuer's life by killing him, he is deemed

a shedder of blood, and he deserves to be put to death. He may not, however, be put to death by the court.

14. If one person is able to save another and does not save him, he transgresses the commandment, *Neither shalt thou stand idly by the blood of thy neighbor* (Lev. 19:16). Similarly, if one person sees another drowning in the sea, or being attacked by bandits, or being attacked by wild animals, and although able to rescue him either alone or by hiring others, does not rescue him; or if one hears heathen or informers plotting evil against another or laying a trap for him and he does not call it to the other's attention and let him know; or if one knows that a heathen or a violent person is going to attack another and although able to appease him on behalf of the other and make him change his mind, he does not do so; or if one acts in any similar way—he transgresses in each case the injunction, *Neither shalt thou stand idly by the blood of thy neighbor* (*ibid.*).

15. If one sees someone pursuing another in order to kill him, or sees someone pursuing a woman forbidden to him in order to ravish her, and although able to save them does not do so, he thereby disregards the positive commandment, *Then thou shalt cut off her hand* (Deut. 25:12), and transgresses two negative commandments, *Thine eye shall have no pity* (*ibid.*), and *Neither shalt thou stand idly by the blood of thy neighbor* (Lev. 19:16).

16. Although there is no flogging for these prohibitions, because breach of them involves no action, the offense is most serious, for if one destroys the life of a single Israelite, it is regarded as though he destroyed the whole world, and if one preserves the life of a single Israelite, it is regarded as though he preserved the whole world.

CHAPTER II

1. If one person kills another himself, such as by striking him with a sword or with a deadly stone, or by strangling him, or by

thrusting him into a fire, he must be put to death by the court, seeing that he himself killed another in some manner.

2. If, however, one hires an assassin to kill another, or sends his slaves to kill him, or ties another up and leaves him in front of a lion or another animal and the animal kills him, and, similarly, if one commits suicide, the rule in each of these cases is that he is a shedder of blood, has committed the crime of murder, and is liable for death at the hand of Heaven; but there is no capital punishment at the hands of the court.

3. How do we know that this is the rule? Because Scripture says, *Whoso sheddeth man's blood by man shall his blood be shed* (Gen. 9:6), referring to one who commits the murder himself and not through an agent; *And surely your blood of your lives will I require* (Gen. 9:5), referring to suicide; *At the hand of every beast will I require it* (*ibid.*), referring to one who places another before a wild animal for it to devour; *And at the hand of man, even at the hand of every man's brother, will I require the life of man* (*ibid.*), referring to one who hires others to kill someone. In these last three cases, the verb *require* is explicitly used to show that the judgment is reserved for Heaven.

4. Regarding any of these or similar murderers who are not subject to being condemned to die by verdict of the court, if a king of Israel wishes to put them to death by royal decree for the benefit of society, he has a right to do so. Similarly, if the court deems it proper to put them to death as an emergency measure, it has the authority to do as it deems fit, provided that circumstances warrant such action.

5. If the king does not kill them, and the needs of the time do not demand their death as a preventive measure, it is nevertheless the duty of the court to flog them almost to the point of death, to imprison them in a fortress or a prison for many years, and to inflict severe punishment on them in order to frighten and terrify other wicked persons, lest such a case become a pitfall and a snare,

enticing one to say, "I will arrange to kill my enemy in a roundabout way, as did So-and-So; then I will be acquitted."

6. Whether one kills an adult or a day-old child, a male or a female, he must be put to death if he kills deliberately or exiled if he slays inadvertently, provided that the child is born after a full-time pregnancy. But if it is born before the end of nine months, it is regarded as an abortion until it has lived for thirty days, and if one kills it during the period of thirty days, he may not be put to death on its account.

7. Whether one kills a healthy person or a dying invalid or even a person in his death throes, he must be put to death on this account. But if the death throes are humanly caused, for example, if one who has been beaten to the point of death is in his throes, the court may not put his slayer to death.

8. If one kills another who suffers from a fatal organic disease, he is legally exempt even though the victim ate and drank and walked about the streets. But every human being is presumed to be healthy, and his murderer must be put to death unless it is known for certain that he had a fatal organic defect and physicians say that his disease is incurable by human agency and that he would have died of it even if he had not been killed in other ways.

9. If such an organically defective individual kills a person, he must be put to death, for Scripture says, *So shalt thou put away the evil from the midst of thee* (Deut. 19: 19), provided that he kills in the presence of a court. However, if he kills before witnesses, he is exempt, for the witnesses might possibly be proved to be conspirators, in which case they could not be put to death since they would have plotted to kill someone afflicted with a fatal organic disease. Now evidence that cannot possibly be subject to the law concerning conspiracy is not deemed valid in capital cases.

10. Whether one kills an Israelite or a Canaanite slave, he must be put to death on his account, or—if he slays inadvertently—he must go into exile.

11. If an Israelite kills a resident alien, he does not suffer capital punishment at the hands of the court, because Scripture says, *And if a man come presumptuously upon his neighbor* (Exod. 21:12). Needless to say, one is not put to death if he kills a heathen. Whether one kills another's slave or his own, he must be put to death on the slave's account, seeing that a slave has taken upon himself the yoke of the commandments and is added to God's people.

12. The difference between one's own slave and another's slave is that one has the right to flog his own slave. Consequently, if one deals his slave blows sufficient to kill him, and the slave is dying but lives for twenty-four hours and then dies, he should not be put to death on the slave's account even though the latter dies as a result of the flogging. For Scripture says, *He shall not be punished, for he is his property* (Exod. 21:21). By *a day or two* in the same verse is meant a day that is like two, namely, twenty-four hours.

13. But if one strikes a slave not his own, then since he has dealt the slave a blow sufficient to kill him he is condemned to die on the slave's account as he would be in the case of a freeman, even if the slave dies as a result of the blow several days later.

14. In my opinion, if one strikes his slave with a knife or a sword or a stone or his fist or in any similar manner, and the slave's injuries are declared to be fatal and he does die, the law of survival for *a day or two* does not apply; rather the master must be put to death on his slave's account even if the slave dies after a year. For Scripture says, *With a rod* (Exod. 21:20), because the Law grants him authority merely to strike his slave with a rod or a stick or a strap or the like, but not to deal him murderous blows.

15. If one sells his slave and stipulates with the buyer that the slave should serve him for another thirty days, and one of them strikes the slave during the thirty days and kills him, the slayer is put to death on the slave's account, and the law of survival for *a day or two* does not apply to the first master because the slave is not

entirely *his property,* nor to the second because the slave is not yet owned by him.

16. Similarly, if one who is half slave and half free is killed by his master, or if a slave owned by two persons is killed by one of them, the law of survival for *a day or two* does not apply, seeing that in neither instance was the slave entirely *his property*. Accordingly, in these cases, the master is put to death for killing this slave, just as any other person would be.

CHAPTER III

1. If one deliberately strikes another with a stone or a piece of wood and kills him, a careful appraisal should be made of the object used for striking and the place on which the blow struck, to see whether or not that object was likely to deal a death blow when struck on that part of the body. For when Scripture says, *If he smote him with a stone in the hand whereby a man may die . . . or if he smote him with a weapon of wood in the hand whereby a man may die* (Num. 35:17–18), it teaches that the blow must be sufficient to kill, and there is no comparison between striking another on the heart and striking him on the thigh.

2. From the scriptural utterance, *Whereby a man may die,* it is deduced that an appraisal should be made of the location of the blow. Moreover, just as an appraisal should be made of the weapon used in striking and the location of the blow, so should an appraisal be made of the force of the blow, for Scripture says, *With a stone in the hand,* which implies that the hand must be appraised. There is no comparison between one throwing a stone at another at a distance of two cubits and throwing it at him at a distance of ten, for at a distance of ten the force will be greater. There is also no comparison between throwing it a distance of ten and throwing it a distance of a hundred, for at a very great distance the force of the blow is lessened.

3. Similarly, the blow itself should be appraised, and likewise the strength of the slayer and of the slain should be appraised, it being noted whether one is tall or short, strong or weak, healthy or sick, and so on. For Scripture says, *Whereby a man may die,* indicating that all the circumstances of this person's death must be taken into account.

4. The Law states no minimum size for a metal instrument, for the verse merely says, *And if he smote him with an instrument of iron so that he die, he is a murderer* (Num. 35:16), indicating that it may be even a needle, provided that the instrument has a sharp point as has a needle, or a spike or a knife or the like. If, however, one strikes another with a slab of metal or the like, the weapon must be appraised exactly as is done in the case of wood or stone.

5. If one strikes another without an instrument and kills him—for example, if one strikes another with his hand or his foot, or if one butts another with his head and kills him—an appraisal must be made of the force of the assailant's blow, the strength of the murdered person, and the location of the blow. There is no comparison between pushing another with a finger and kicking him with all one's might, or between striking another on the heart and striking him on the hip, or between a weak person who strikes one strong and healthy and a strong and healthy person who strikes one who is weak or sick.

6. How do we know that all these things must be appraised? Because Scripture says, *Or in enmity smote him with his hand that he died, he that smote him shall surely be put to death* (Num. 35:21). Now, although it says *with his hand,* Scripture still requires that the blow be dealt *in enmity,* implying that the force of the blow must be appraised.

7. Similarly, if one pushes another from a rooftop so that he falls and dies, an appraisal should be made of the height of the roof, of the place onto which he was made to fall and of the strength of the victim, for there is no comparison between a day-old infant falling and an adult falling. How do we know that the

height should be appraised? Because Scripture says, *And if he thrust him of hatred* (Num. 35:20). In my opinion, no place less than ten handbreadths high can be deemed sufficient to kill, as the Sages have stated in the case of a pit with regard to animals.

8. It makes no difference whether one strikes another with a stone or wood or with a clod of earth or a lump of salt or sulphur or with a basketful of earth or stones or even with a slice of pressed figs. For when Scripture says, *Whereby a man may die,* it means anything able to kill, since it is the impact of the weight which kills.

9. If one thrusts another into water or into fire, an appraisal should be made. If the victim was able to escape, the other is exempt from the penalty of death by the court; otherwise he is liable. Similarly, if one holds another down under water or in fire until the victim no longer has the strength to escape and dies, he is liable even if he did not originally push him in. The same rule applies if one puts his hand over another's mouth and nose and releases him when the latter is convulsive and unable to live, or if one ties another up and leaves him in the cold or in the heat until he dies, or if one builds an enclosed space around another and deprives him of air, or if one puts another into a cave or a room and fills it with smoke so that he dies, or if one puts another into a room of marble and keeps a lamp alight there until he is killed by the foul air. In each of these cases the offender must be put to death on the victim's account inasmuch as he himself is deemed to have suffocated the victim.

10. But if one ties up another and leaves him to die of hunger and thirst, or ties up another and leaves him in a place where eventually cold or heat will come, and it does come and kills him; or if one puts a tub over another or loosens the plaster of the ceiling over another; or if one brings a snake near another to bite him; or, needless to say, if one incites a dog or a snake against another—the offender in each of these cases may not be put to death, although he is deemed a murderer. *He that avengeth blood* (Ps. 9:13) will require his blood.

11. Similarly, if one pushes another into a pit containing a ladder on which he can climb out, or if one shoots an arrow at another who holds a shield with which to defend himself, and someone else comes and removes the ladder or the shield, the rule is that neither may be put to death by the court. Even if the one who pushes the other into the pit is himself the one who removes the ladder, he is exempt from liability of death by the court; but blood will be required of him.

12. If one throws a pebble at a wall and the pebble rebounds and kills another, the thrower is liable for death by the court, seeing that the impetus of the stone came from him. Similarly, if ball players are duly warned and then kill someone, the rule is as follows: They are exempt if the victim was less than four cubits away, but they are liable if he was more than four cubits away, even if he was a hundred cubits away, provided that the ball had sufficient force to kill, as we have explained.

13. If one throws a stone into the air and it falls obliquely and kills another, he is liable. If one ties another up in a place from which he cannot escape and floods him with water so that he dies, he should be put to death on this account, provided that the victim dies because of the immediate force resulting from his act.

CHAPTER IV

1. If one intends to kill A and kills B instead, he is exempt from the penalty of death by the court, from the payment of compensation, and from exile, because the cities of refuge cannot receive him, as will be explained. Consequently, if one throws a stone into a crowd of Israelites and kills one of them, he is exempt from the penalty of death by the court.

2. If one intends to strike another on the hip and the weapon could not have inflicted a fatal injury on the hip but the stone strikes his heart and the blow on the heart is enough to inflict a

fatal injury and the person dies, or if one intends to strike another on the heart with a blow sufficient to inflict a fatal injury but the stone strikes the hip where it normally ought not to have inflicted a fatal injury and the person nevertheless dies, the rule is that the aggressor is exempt from the penalty of death by the court and need not go into exile, for if one kills deliberately, he is not exiled.

If, however, one intends to strike another on the hip with a blow sufficient to inflict a fatal injury on the hip, but his blow strikes the victim's heart and he dies, the murderer should be put to death. The same rule applies in all similar cases.

3. If one strikes another with a stone or with his fist, the effect on the victim must be appraised. If it is believed that he will live, the offender must pay compensation for the five effects of the injury and is exempt (from other penalties). Even if the victim then falls ill, gets worse, and dies as a result of the blow, the offender is exempt. If, however, it is believed that the victim will die, the assailant must immediately be put into prison and developments be awaited. If the victim dies, the assailant is put to death. But if the victim improves and recovers completely and is able to walk on his own accord in the street as does any other healthy person, the assailant must pay compensation for the five effects and is exempt (from the death penalty).

4. When Scripture says, *Upon his staff* (Exod. 21:19), it does not mean that he should be able to walk leaning on his staff or on another person, for even a dying person can walk leaning on a staff. The meaning of *Upon his staff* is that he should be able to walk relying on his health without requiring any help to support him.

5. If a victim is expected to die but improves somewhat and then grows worse and dies, the assailant must be put to death. No second appraisal need be made after the improvement, since there is good reason for attributing the death to the original blow.

6. If ten people strike a person, using ten sticks, and he dies, all are exempt from the penalty of death by the court, whether they

strike one after the other or together, for Scripture says, *Any man* (Lev. 24: 17), teaching that there is no death penalty until one person takes the whole life of another. The same rule applies if two persons push another into water or press him down under it, or if many people are sitting together and an arrow comes from among them and kills someone; in either case, all are exempt.

7. If ten people throw stones at a person, one after another, and none has sufficient force to kill him, but finally one person throws a stone that has sufficient force to kill, and he dies, the last person must be put to death on the victim's account.

If a condemned murderer becomes mixed up with other persons and it is not known which of them is the murderer, all are exempt. Again, if a murderer whose sentence has not been pronounced becomes mixed up with condemned murderers, all are freed from the death penalty, because sentence may not be pronounced except in the defendant's presence; however, all must be kept in prison.

8. If one commits murder without being seen by two witnesses at the same time, although they did see him one after the other; or if one commits murder in the presence of witnesses without first receiving a warning; or if the witnesses contradict each other in the cross-examination but not in the primary investigation—the rule in all such cases is that the murderer is put into a cell and fed on a minimum of bread and water until his stomach contracts and then he is given barley so that his stomach splits under the stress of sickness.

9. This, however, is not done to other persons guilty of crimes involving the death penalty at the hand of the court; rather if one is condemned to death, he is put to death, and if he is not liable, he is allowed to go free. For although there are worse crimes than bloodshed, none causes such destruction to civilized society as bloodshed. Not even idolatry, nor immorality nor desecration of the Sabbath, is the equal of bloodshed. For these are crimes between man and God, while bloodshed is a crime between man and man. If one has committed this crime, he is deemed wholly wicked,

and all the meritorious acts he has performed during his lifetime cannot outweigh this crime or save him from judgment, as it is said, *A man that is laden with the blood of any person shall hasten his steps unto the pit; none will support him* (Prov. 28:17). A lesson may be taken from Ahab, who worshiped idols and of whom it is said, *But there was none like unto Ahab* (I Kings 21:25). Yet when his sins and his merits were set in array before the God of all spirits (cf. Num. 16:22), the one sin that brought on him the doom of extermination and the weightiest of all his crimes was the blood of Naboth. For Scripture relates: *And there came forth the spirit and stood before the Lord* (I Kings 22:21); this was the spirit of Naboth, who was told, *Thou shalt entice him and shalt prevail also* (I Kings 22:22). Now the wicked Ahab did not commit murder himself but only brought it about. How much greater then is the crime of one who commits murder with his own hand!

10. It was at one time deemed meritorious to kill apostates—by this are meant Israelites who worship idols or who provocatively do other sinful things, for even one who provocatively eats carrion or wears clothes made of mingled stuffs is deemed an apostate—and sectarians, who deny the authenticity of the Torah or of prophecy. If one had the power to slay them publicly by the sword, he would do so. If not, one would plot against them in such a way as to bring about their death. Thus, if a person saw that such a one had fallen into a well containing a ladder, he would remove the ladder, giving the excuse that he wanted it to get his son down from the roof, and would bring it back afterward, and do similar acts.

11. But one may not procure the death of heathen against whom we are not at war, or of Israelite raisers of small cattle, or of similar people. It is, however, forbidden to save them from dying—for example, if any of them falls into the sea, one may not rescue him—for Scripture says, *Thou shalt not stand idly by the blood of thy neighbor* (Lev. 19:16), and none of these is *thy neighbor*.

12. This rule applies only to a sinful Israelite who persistently does evil deeds and repeats them continually, such as rearers of

small cattle who rob licentiously and persist in their wrongdoing. But if a sinful Israelite does not do wrong persistently but only does so out of self-indulgence—for example, if one eats the meat of carrion out of gluttony—it is a duty to rescue him, and it is forbidden to *stand idly* by his blood.

CHAPTER V

1. If one slays inadvertently, he must go into exile from the district where he has slain to a city of refuge. It is a positive commandment to send him into exile, for Scripture says, *And he shall dwell therein until the death of the High Priest* (Num. 35:25). Moreover, the court is warned not to accept ransom from one who has slain inadvertently, to allow him to live in his own city, for Scripture says, *Ye shall take no ransom for him that is fled to his city of refuge* (Num. 35:31).

2. If one slays inadvertently, he need not be exiled unless the victim dies immediately. But if one inadvertently wounds another, then even if the injury is judged to be fatal and the victim falls ill and actually dies, the slayer need not be exiled. For it is possible that the victim hastened his own death or that air got to the wound and killed him. Even if both windpipe and gullet of the victim are completely severed and he survives a short while, the slayer need not be sent into exile on his account. Consequently, if the victim does not move convulsively at all, or if he is killed in a place where no wind blows, such as in a closed stone room, the slayer must be sent into exile. The same rule applies in all similar cases.

3. If an Israelite inadvertently slays a slave or a resident alien, he must go into exile. The same rule applies to a slave who inadvertently slays an Israelite or a resident alien. Similarly, if a resident alien inadvertently slays another resident alien or a slave, he must be exiled, for Scripture says, *For the children of Israel and for the stranger and for the settler among them* (Num. 35:15).

4. If a resident alien slays an Israelite inadvertently, he must be put to death in spite of his inadvertence. For a human being is always deemed forewarned. Similarly, if a resident alien kills another resident alien, thinking that it is permissible to kill him, he is virtually a deliberate murderer and must be put to death on the victim's account, seeing that he intended to murder him. If a heathen kills another heathen inadvertently, the cities of refuge do not afford him asylum, for Scripture says, *For the children of Israel.*

5. If a son slays his father inadvertently, he must go into exile, and, similarly, if a father slays his son inadvertently, he must go into exile. This rule applies in the latter instance only if the father slays his son at a time when he was not teaching him, or when he was teaching him some craft unessential for him. But if one chastises his son to make him learn the Law or secular knowledge or a trade and the son dies, the father is exempt.

6. Similarly, if a teacher beats his pupil, or if a court official beats a litigant for not coming to court, and inadvertently slays him, he is exempt from exile, for Scripture says, *To chop wood* (Deut. 19:5), meaning for a private purpose, thus excluding a father who strikes his son, a teacher who chastises his pupil, and a court official, inasmuch as they slay inadvertently while performing a duty.

7. The initial procedure is that whether one slays a person inadvertently or deliberately, he must first go to (one of) the cities of refuge. The court of the city in which the slaying occurred then sends and brings him from there and tries him, as it is said, *Then the elders of his city shall send and fetch him thence* (Deut. 19:12). If he is condemned to death, he must be put to death, as it is said, *And deliver him into the hand of the avenger of blood* (*ibid.*). If he is judged exempt, he is set free, as it is said, *And the congregation shall deliver the manslayer out of the hand of the avenger of blood* (Num. 35:25). If he is condemned to exile, he must be returned to the place from which he came, as it is said, *And the congregation shall send him back to his city of refuge* (*ibid.*).

8. When the court sends him back, it provides two scholars for him, lest the avenger of blood kill him on the way, and tells them not to treat him as a murderer because the incident occurred through misadventure.

9. If the avenger of blood kills an inadvertent slayer outside the bounds of his city of refuge, he is exempt, for Scripture says, *Whereas he is not deserving of death* (Deut. 19:6).

10. It makes no difference whether the avenger kills him on the way, before he reaches the city of refuge, or whether he kills him when the two scholars guarding him are escorting him back.

If he enters the city of refuge and then leaves its confines deliberately, he has surrendered himself to death and the avenger of blood has the right to kill him. If anyone else kills the inadvertent slayer, he is not held liable on his account, for Scripture says, *There shall be no bloodguiltiness for him* (Num. 35:27).

11. If he leaves the bounds of his city of refuge inadvertently, and then one kills him, whether it is the avenger of blood or anyone else, the slayer must go into exile on his account. If one kills him within the bounds of the city of refuge, even if it be the avenger of blood who does so, he must be put to death on his account.

12. The altar affords asylum, for Scripture says of a deliberate murderer, *From my altar shalt thou take him to die* (Exod. 21:14), implying that an inadvertent slayer may not be killed at the altar. Consequently, if one slays inadvertently and takes refuge at the altar, and the avenger of blood kills him there, he must be put to death on his account, as is the rule if one kills him inside the city of refuge.

13. No altar can afford legally effective asylum except the top of the altar in the permanent Temple, and this affords asylum only to a priest actually engaged in sacrifice. But if he is a layman or a priest not actually engaged in sacrifice at the time, or if a priest engaged in sacrifice is not on top of the altar but only near it or holding its corners, the altar affords him no asylum.

14. If one is afforded asylum on the altar, he may not be left there but must be provided with guards and taken to his city of refuge.

The above rules apply only to one liable for exile (because of inadvertent murder). But if one is afraid that the king might have him killed under the law of sovereignty, or that the court might order his death as a special emergency measure, and he flees to the altar and gets near to it, he must be afforded asylum even if he is a layman. He may never be taken from the altar to die unless he has been condemned to die by the court on the basis of proper evidence and a prior warning, as is ever the rule regarding anyone executed by order of the court.

CHAPTER VI

1. There are three types of slayers without intent.

2. One slays inadvertently and in complete unawareness. Concerning him, Scripture says, *Who did not lie in wait* (Exod. 21:13), and the rule regarding him is that he must be exiled to (one of) the cities of refuge and rescued, as we have explained.

3. Another slays inadvertently in a manner that is almost an accident, such as when the death is the result of some unusual circumstance uncommon amid the greater part of human events. The rule regarding him is that he is exempt from exile, and if the avenger of blood kills him, the avenger must be put to death on his account.

4. Still another slays inadvertently but in a manner that approximates willfulness because there is present a circumstance tantamount to negligence, or because he should have been careful but was not. The rule regarding him is that he is not exiled, for exile cannot atone for him since his crime is a serious one, nor can any of the cities of refuge afford him asylum since they afford asylum

only to such persons as are condemned to exile. Consequently, if the avenger of blood finds him and kills him, no matter where, he is exempt.

5. What shall such a person do? He must constantly guard himself against the avenger of blood.

Similarly, if any person kills another in the presence of only one witness, or without warning, or in a similar manner, and is himself killed by the avenger of blood, there is no bloodguiltiness for him. For these cases are not to be deemed more serious than a case of unintentional slaying.

6. Thus, if one throws a stone into a public domain and it kills someone, or if one demolishes his wall beside a public domain and a piece of masonry falls and kills someone, the offender's act approximates willfulness whether the demolition is done by day or by night, and asylum is not afforded him. For this is deemed gross negligence, seeing that he ought to have looked carefully before proceeding to throw or to demolish.

7. If one demolishes a wall into a rubbish heap at night, the rule is as follows: If people are frequently to be found there, his act is regarded as approximating willfulness and he is not afforded asylum. But if people are seldom found there, his act is deemed one approximating an accident, and he is exempt from exile.

8. If the rubbish heap is usually used as a latrine at night but not in the daytime, and it happens that a person sits down there and a stone falls on him during the demolition and he dies, the demolisher should be exiled. But if the person comes and sits down only after the stone has already begun to fall, and it then falls on him and he dies, the demolisher is exempt from exile.

9. Similarly, if one throws a stone and after it leaves his hand another gets his head in the way and is struck by it, the thrower is exempt from exile, for Scripture says, *And lighteth upon his neighbor* (Deut. 19:5), excluding the case of one who gets in the path of the missile.

10. If one is slain inadvertently by his enemy, the slayer is not afforded asylum, for Scripture says, *And he was not an enemy of his* (Deut. 19:4), and an enemy is presumed to act in a manner approximating willfulness. By *an enemy* is meant one who has not spoken to the victim for three days or more because of enmity.

Similarly, if one runs into a corner and slays another there inadvertently, or if one bumps into another with his body, or if one intends to throw a weapon two cubits and it goes four, or if one believes that the slaying is permissible, or if one intends to kill a certain person and kills another, even if one intends to kill a heathen or an animal and it turns out to be an Israelite—the rule in each of these cases is that the act is regarded as approximating willfulness, and the slayer is not afforded asylum.

11. If one enters another's courtyard without permission and the owner kills him inadvertently, he is exempt from exile, for Scripture says, *Or who chances upon his neighbor in a wood* (Deut. 19:4). *A wood,* however, means any area which the victim was entitled to enter; hence the law imposing exile applies only to a place of this kind. Consequently, if one enters a carpenter's shop without permission and a block of wood springs up and strikes him in the face and kills him, the carpenter is exempt from exile. But if he enters with permission, the carpenter must be exiled.

12. If one is pulling a barrel up onto a roof and the rope snaps and the barrel falls on another and kills him, or if one is climbing a ladder and falls onto another and kills him, he is exempt from exile, for the latter is deemed the victim of a mishap. For this is not something likely to happen ordinarily, but is regarded as an exceptional occurrence. However, if one is letting the barrel down and it falls on another and kills him, or if one is descending a ladder and falls and kills another, or if one is flattening a roof with a roller and it falls onto another and kills him, he must go into exile. For when Scripture says, *And it fall upon him and he die* (Num. 35:23), it indicates that the object must fall in the way things fall, since falling objects commonly and frequently cause

damage; such an effect is probable, seeing that it is natural for heavy objects to fall swiftly. And inasmuch as this person has not been especially careful to see that everything was in proper order during the descent, he must go into exile. The same rule applies in all similar cases.

13. If a butcher is chopping meat and raises the hand holding the chopper behind his head and brings it down to break a bone in the way butchers do, the rule is as follows: If he kills another with the first motion, which consists of lifting the chopper in front and bringing it back behind himself, he need not go into exile. But if he kills another with the return stroke, which consists of lifting it from behind and bringing it down in front, he must go into exile. The general rule is as follows: Any inadvertent slaying caused by a downward movement entails exile; but an upward movement does not entail exile. Even a downward movement, if it is a preliminary requisite for an upward movement, does not entail exile.

14. Thus, if one is climbing a ladder and a rung slips from under his feet and he falls and kills another, he is exempt from exile. Similarly, if one intends to throw an object in one direction but it goes off in another, or if, without being aware of it, one has a stone in his lap and when he stands up it falls and kills another, or if a blind person slays inadvertently, the rule is that each of these is exempt from exile because in each case the slaying is regarded as approximating an accident.

15. If one has been aware of the stone in his lap but has forgotten it, and when he stands up it falls and kills another, he must be exiled, for Scripture says, *unwittingly* (Num. 35:15), implying that there was previous awareness.

If an axe slips from wood being chopped, the axman need not be exiled, because his slaying is not a direct act but only an indirect consequence of his act and is thus regarded as accidental. Similarly, if one throws a stone at a date palm to bring down dates, and some of the dates fall onto a child and kill him, the thrower is exempt, because the dates fall as an indirect consequence of his act. The same rule applies in all other cases having similar circumstances.

CHAPTER VII

1. If a disciple is exiled to a city of refuge, his teacher must be exiled with him, for Scripture says, *And he shall live* (Deut. 19:4), that is: make it possible for him to live on. Now life for scholars and for those who seek wisdom is like death when they are deprived of the study of Torah.

Similarly, if a teacher goes into exile, his school must be exiled with him.

2. If a slave is exiled to a city of refuge, his master need not provide food for him, but his earnings still belong to his master. However, if a woman is exiled to a city of refuge, her husband must still provide food for her, and he cannot tell her to keep her earnings for food unless they are sufficient for this purpose.

3. If a slayer condemned to exile dies before he is exiled, his body must be taken to the city of refuge. If a slayer dies in a city of refuge, he must be buried there. Then when the High Priest dies, the bones of the slayer may be taken from the city to his ancestral burial place.

4. If one of the levites who live in the cities of refuge dies, he may not be buried within the city or its bounds, because Scripture says, *And their open land shall be for their cattle and for their substance and for all their life* (Num. 35:3), meaning that it was given to them for the purpose of life, not for burial.

5. If a slayer inadvertently kills someone in his city of refuge, he must be exiled from one district of it to another, but he may not leave the city. Similarly, if a levite kills in his own city, he must be exiled to another of the levitical cities, all of which afford asylum, as will be explained. If, however, he kills outside the levitical cities and then flees to his own city, this affords him asylum.

6. If most of the inhabitants of a city of refuge are slayers, it cannot afford asylum further, for Scripture says, *And declare his cause in the ears of the elders of that city* (Josh. 20:4); but his cause must not be the same as their cause. Similarly, a city without elders cannot afford asylum, for Scripture says, *The elders of that city* (*ibid.*).

7. If a slayer is exiled to a city of refuge and its citizens wish to honor him, he must say to them, "I am a slayer." If they reply, "That makes no difference," he may accept the honor from them.

8. An exiled person may never leave his city of refuge, not even to perform a scriptural commandment or give evidence in a civil or a capital case, or even to save a life with his evidence, or to save someone from invading troops or from a river in flood or from a fire or from a fallen ruin. Indeed, not even if all Israel needs his help, as it did that of Joab, the son of Zeruah, may he leave the city until the High Priest dies. If he does leave, he surrenders himself to death, as we have explained.

9. There is no difference between a High Priest anointed with the anointing oil and one consecrated by wearing the High Priest's robes, or between one who is in active service and one who has been superseded; the death of any one of the four permits the slayer to return. The death of a priest anointed for the conduct of war, however, does not permit him to return, since such a one is regarded as an ordinary priest.

10. If a slayer is condemned to exile when there is no High Priest, or if one kills a High Priest when there is no other High Priest, or if a High Priest kills someone when there is no other High Priest, each of these must be exiled and may never leave the city of refuge.

11. If one is condemned to exile, and the High Priest dies before he has gone into exile, he is exempt from exile. If, however, the High Priest dies before a slayer is condemned, and he is sentenced after another High Priest has been appointed, he may re-

turn only after the death of the second High Priest, during whose term of office he was condemned.

12. If one is condemned and then it is discovered that the High Priest is the son of a divorced woman, or of a *ḥăluṣah,* it is as though he were condemned without there being a High Priest, for the status of the priesthood was voided, and the exile may never leave his city of refuge.

13. If a slayer returns home after the death of a High Priest, he is regarded as is any other person, and if the avenger of blood kills him, he must be put to death on his account. For his exile has atoned for his crime.

14. Yet, although atonement was effected for him, he may never resume any office he formerly held but must remain deprived of his honors throughout his life, because so great an offense occurred through his agency.

15. Although if one wounds his father deliberately he is still liable for death inflicted by the court, as is the rule when one murders another, if one inadvertently wounds his father or his mother he does not incur exile. For the Law condemns to exile only one who inadvertently takes a human life, as we have explained.

CHAPTER VIII

1. The injunction to set aside cities of refuge is a positive commandment, for Scripture says, *Three cities shalt thou separate for thee* (Deut. 19:2). The rule concerning cities of refuge applies only to the Land of Israel.

2. There were six such cities, three set aside by Moses, our Teacher, in Transjordan and three by Joshua in the Land of Canaan.

3. None of the cities afforded legally effective asylum until all six were set aside, for through the scriptural verse, *There shall be*

for you six cities of refuge (Num. 35:13), Moses, our Teacher, taught us that the three cities in Transjordan would not afford asylum until the three in Canaan were set aside. Why then did he set any aside? He thought: "Since a religious duty has come to me, let me carry it out."

4. In the time of the King Messiah three more will be added to these six, for Scripture says, *Then shalt thou add three cities more for thee beside these three* (Deut. 19:9). Where will they be added? Among the cities of the Kenites, Kenizzites and Kadmonites, concerning whose territory a covenant was made with Abraham, and who have not yet been conquered. It is of these that Scripture says, *And if the Lord thy God enlarge thy border . . . and give thee all the land which He promised to give unto thy fathers* (Deut. 19:8).

5. Moreover, it is the duty of the court to see that the roads leading to the cities of refuge are direct, to keep them repaired, and to have them made wide. All obstacles and obstructions must be removed from them, nor may there be left on the road any mound or hollow or stream, but a bridge must be built over it in order not to hinder a fleeing slayer, for Scripture says, *Thou shalt prepare thee the way* (Deut. 19:3). The width of a road to a city of refuge must be at least thirty-two cubits. "To the City of Refuge" was written at each crossroad, so that slayers could recognize the road and turn into it.

6. On the fifteenth of Adar each year the court must send officials to repair the roads. These must repair any place that is found to be damaged. Any court that is lax in carrying out this duty is regarded by Scripture as if it were guilty of bloodshed.

7. Similarly, the distance between each of the cities of refuge must be measured at the time they are designated, to ensure they are all evenly spaced, for Scripture says, *Thou shalt prepare thee the way and divide the borders of thy land* (*ibid.*).

8. A city of refuge may not be situated either in a small town or in a large city, but only in a town of medium size. It must be

situated only at places where there are markets and where there is a water supply. If there is no water supply, one must be provided. Such a city must be situated near other settlements. If the number of these diminishes, they must be increased. If the population of the city diminishes, priests, levites, and ordinary Israelites must be drafted into it. It is forbidden to spread snares in the city or to plait ropes there, so that an avenger of blood will not frequent the district.

9. Every city of the levites affords asylum, each one being a city of refuge, for Scripture says, *And beside them ye shall give forty and two cities. All the cities which ye shall give to the Levites shall be forty and eight cities* (Num. 35:6–7). Thus Scripture regards them as being all alike in so far as affording asylum is concerned.

10. What then is the difference between the cities of refuge especially designated to afford asylum and the remaining, levitical, cities? First, the cities of refuge afford asylum whether one enters knowingly or unknowingly, for as soon as the slayer enters, he is afforded asylum. But the other cities, of the levites, afford asylum only if entered knowingly. Then, too, a slayer who lives in one of the cities of refuge need not pay rent for his house; but one who lives in one of the other, levitical, cities must pay rent to the owner of the house (in which he lives).

11. The rule is that if a city affords asylum, its outskirts also afford asylum. If a tree stands within the limits of a city of refuge, and one of its branches protrudes outside the limit, asylum is afforded as soon as the slayer comes under this branch. If the tree stands outside the limit and one of its branches protrudes within the limit, asylum is afforded as soon as its trunk is reached, and if one kills a slayer there, he must be put to death on his account. But, although the border affords asylum, a slayer must not live there, for Scripture says, *And he shall dwell therein* (Num. 35:25), and not in the outskirts of the city.

CHAPTER IX

1. A slain person found lying on the ground, without any indication as to who killed him, must be left where he lies. Then five elders of the supreme court in Jerusalem must go out to it, for Scripture says, *Then thy elders and thy judges shall come forth and shall measure unto the cities which are round about him that is slain* (Deut. 21:2). Even if he is found right beside a certain city, so that it is a surety that this is the nearest city, it is a scriptural commandment to measure.

2. After measurements have been taken and the nearest city is determined, the slain person must be buried where he lies; the elders from Jerusalem then return home, and the court of that city must bring a heifer provided by its citizens and take it down to a valley with a swiftly flowing stream, this being the meaning of the scriptural expression *rough* (Deut. 21:4).

3. There they must break its neck from behind with a chopper, and the court of that city, together with all its elders, even if there be a hundred of them, must wash their hands at the place where its neck is broken and there in the valley say in Hebrew the following words: *Our hands have not shed this blood, neither have our eyes seen it* (Deut. 21:7), meaning, "We did not let this slain person come to us and send him away without food, nor did we see him and let him go away unaccompanied." Then the priests must say in Hebrew: *Forgive, O Lord, thy people Israel, whom Thou hast redeemed, and suffer not innocent blood to remain in the midst of thy people Israel* (Deut. 21:8), and they go away, and God forgives the blood, as it is said, *And the blood shall be forgiven them* (*ibid.*).

4. When they measure from the corpse, they must do so very carefully and must not measure the level distance only, in disregard of hills and valleys. They must measure only to cities having a court of twenty-three members, but need not measure to Jerusa-

lem, because Jerusalem need not bring a heifer for neck-breaking since it was never shared among the Tribes, and Scripture says, *In the land which the Lord thy God giveth thee to possess* (Deut. 21:1).

5. If the slain person is found near Jerusalem or near a city which has no court of twenty-three members, this is ignored and they must then measure to other neighboring towns. If it is found near the frontier or near a town with heathen inhabitants, no measuring at all need be done, because the presumption is that a heathen killed him.

6. The nearest town must bring the heifer only if its population is as numerous as that of the more distant towns. If, however, the population of a more distant town is greater than that of the nearer town, the principle of majority is followed and the more populous town must bring the heifer.

7. Although we should follow the principle of majority, on the authority of Scripture, and also the principle of proximity, the principle of majority takes precedence.

8. If the slain person is found midway between two towns that have an equal number of inhabitants, they must provide a heifer in partnership and each must make the following declaration: "If our town is nearer, this heifer belongs entirely to us, and let the citizens of the other town surrender their share to us as a gift, but if they are nearer, then the heifer belongs to them and we surrender our share to them as a gift." For it is impossible to be absolutely exact even in matters within human control.

9. From where must the measurement begin? From the slain person's nose. If the body is found in one place and the head in another, the body must be taken to the head and buried there. Similarly, in the case of every unclaimed corpse, the burial of which is a religious duty incumbent on anyone who comes upon it, the body must be taken to the head and buried there.

10. If several bodies are found side by side, the measurement should be made from the nose of each one. If one town is nearest

to all of them, it must bring one heifer for all of them. If the bodies are found one on top of the other, the measurement should be made from the one uppermost as they are lying there.

11. When Scripture says, *If one be found slain in the land . . . lying in the field and it be not known who hath smitten him* (Deut. 21:1), it means not strangled or still in the death throes, for these are not called *slain; in the land* means not hidden in a heap of stones; *lying* means not hanging on a tree; *in the field* means not floating in water; *and it be not known who hath smitten him* means that if it is known who smote him the ritual of neck-breaking is not performed.

12. Even if a single witness saw the slayer, or even a slave or a woman or one ineligible to give evidence because of a transgression, the ritual of neck-breaking was not performed. Consequently, when open murder became a common crime, the breaking of a heifer's neck was discontinued.

13. In cases where a single witness testified, "I saw the murderer," and another single witness contradicted him and said to him, "You did not see him," the ritual neck-breaking was performed. This, however, applied only if both came to court at the same time. But if one came and said, "I saw the murderer," he was held trustworthy as would be two witnesses in this particular matter, so that if another single witness later came and contradicted him, saying, "You did not see him," no heed was given to the second single witness, and the neck-breaking ritual was not performed.

14. If two witnesses came after a single witness had given his evidence, and they contradicted him and said, "You did not see him," this was regarded as two contradictory testimonies, and the rule was that the ritual neck-breaking had to be done. If a woman said, "I saw the murderer," and another woman said, "You did not see him," the ritual neck-breaking was performed, no matter whether both came together or they came one after the other. If two persons said, "We saw," and another said to them, "You did

not see," the rule was that the ritual neck-breaking need not be performed. But if one said, "I saw," and two others said, "You did not see," then the neck-breaking was performed.

15. The aforesaid applied only if all three were eligible witnesses or if all three were ineligible. But if one qualified witness said, "I saw the murderer," and two women or two ineligible persons said, "You did not see him," the rule was that no neck-breaking need be performed.

16. If two women or two ineligible persons said, "We saw the murderer," and another witness contradicted them and said, "You did not see him," the rule was that the ritual neck-breaking must be performed, for even a hundred women or a hundred ineligible persons, if contradicted by a single qualified witness, were regarded as one qualified witness contradicted by another.

17. If three women or three ineligible persons said, "We saw the murderer," and four women or four ineligible persons said, "You did not see him," the rule was that the ritual neck-breaking must be performed. The general rule is as follows: When ineligible persons offer contradictory testimony, the larger number is followed in all cases.

CHAPTER X

1. The rule concerning the neck-breaking of the heifer applies only in the Land of Israel and in Transjordan.

2. The heifer whose neck is to be broken must be two years old or less. If it is two years and a day old, it is deemed unfit. Blemishes do not render it unfit, yet if it is organically defective, it is deemed invalid because the same expression, *atonement,* is used with regard to it as with regard to sacrifices.

3. Any kind of work renders the heifer unfit as it does the Red Heifer, for Scripture says, *Which hath not been wrought*

with, and which hath not drawn in the yoke (Deut. 21:3). Why then is a *yoke* mentioned specifically after saying *which hath not been wrought with,* although this phrase includes a yoke together with various kinds of work? Because a yoke renders the heifer unfit whether worn while doing work or not. As soon as the heifer draws a yoke a handbreadth, it is deemed unfit even if one does not plough with it or do any work with it. But other kinds of exertion render it unfit only if it actually works.

4. Any act of labor done for the animal's own benefit—for example, if one spreads his coat over it to keep off flies—does not render it unfit. But any such act not specifically done for its benefit—for example, if one spreads his coat over it to be carried or does any similar act—does render it unfit, as we have explained in Laws Concerning the Red Heifer.

5. The heifer may have its neck broken only by day, for Scripture employs the same expression, *atonement,* with regard to it as with regard to sacrifices. The entire day is suitable for the breaking of its neck. Two heifers may not be used for the ritual at one time because scriptural commandments may not be performed in bunches.

6. No one may benefit from the heifer whose neck is broken and it must be buried at the place where the ritual is performed. Benefit from it becomes forbidden as soon as it is taken down to the valley, even before its neck is broken. If it dies or is slaughtered after being taken down, all benefit from it is forbidden and it must be buried.

7. If the witnesses are found to be conspirators, benefit from the heifer is permissible. Thus, if one witness says, "I saw the murderer," and two witnesses come and contradict him, saying, "You did not see him," and a heifer is designated and taken down into a valley for the ritual neck-breaking on the basis of their evidence, and then these two are found to be conspirators, the use of the heifer is permissible.

8. If the slayer is discovered before the heifer undergoes the ritual, it may return to pasture with the herd. If he is found after the ritual neck-breaking, it must be buried where it is, for it was originally brought because of doubt, and it has effected atonement for the doubt and has gone its way. As for the slayer, however, even if he is discovered after the ritual neck-breaking, he must be put to death, for Scripture says, *And thou shalt put away the innocent blood from the midst of thee* (Deut. 21:9).

9. The valley in which the heifer undergoes the ritual may never be sown or tilled, for Scripture says, *Which may neither be ploughed nor sown* (Deut. 21:4). If one does any work there on the land itself, such as ploughing or digging or sowing or planting or the like, he incurs a flogging. But one may comb out flax there or trim masonry there, for this is regarded as is weaving a garment there or sewing it, which is not work on the land itself. The reason that Scripture says *neither be ploughed nor sown* is to teach that just as sowing is done on the land itself, so the only kind of work forbidden there is work done on the land itself.

10. If the inhabitants of the nearest city delay in bringing the heifer for the ritual, they must be compelled to bring one even after several years have passed, seeing that those who are obligated to bring a heifer for the ritual, and who allow the Day of Atonement to pass without bringing one, must still bring one after the Day of Atonement.

CHAPTER XI

1. Making a parapet on one's roof is a positive commandment, for Scripture says, *Then thou shalt make a parapet for thy roof* (Deut. 22:8), provided that it is the roof of a dwelling. One is not enjoined to do so, however, for his storehouse or stables. Furthermore, any house less than four cubits square does not require a parapet.

2. If a house belongs to two persons in partnership, they must provide a parapet, for Scripture says, *If any man fall from thence* (*ibid.*), making the obligation depend only on the possibility of a person falling. Why then is the pronoun in *thy roof* expressed in the singular? To exclude the roofs of synagogues and lecture rooms, which are exempt because these are not made for dwelling in.

If the street is higher than the roof, one need not make a parapet, for Scripture says, *If any man fall from thence* (*ibid.*), and not "fall thereon."

3. The height of the parapet must be not less than ten handbreadths in order that no *man fall from thence.* And the barrier must be strong enough for a person to lean against without its falling. If one leaves his roof without a parapet, he disregards a positive commandment and transgresses a negative one, namely, *That thou mayest not bring blood upon thy house* (*ibid.*). But there is no flogging for breach of this prohibition, since it involves no action.

4. It makes no difference whether it be one's roof or anything else that is dangerous and might possibly be a stumbling block to someone and cause his death—for example, if one has a well or a pit, with or without water, in his yard—the owner is obliged to build an enclosing wall ten handbreadths high, or else to put a cover over it lest someone fall into it and be killed. Similarly, regarding any obstacle which is dangerous to life, there is a positive commandment to remove it and to beware of it, and to be particularly careful in this matter, for Scripture says, *Take heed unto thyself and take care of thy life* (Deut. 4:9). If one does not remove dangerous obstacles and allows them to remain, he disregards a positive commandment and transgresses the prohibition: *Thou bring not blood* (Deut. 22:8).

5. Many things were forbidden by the Sages because they are dangerous to life. If one disregards any of these and says, "If I want to put myself in danger, what concern is it to others?" or "I am not

particular about such things," disciplinary flogging is inflicted upon him.

6. The following are the acts prohibited: One may not put his mouth to a flowing pipe of water and drink from it, or drink at night from rivers or ponds, lest he swallow a leech while unable to see. Nor may one drink water that has been left uncovered, lest he drink from it after a snake or other poisonous reptile has drunk from it, and die.

7. The following liquids are forbidden if left uncovered: water, wine—even if it is diluted and has already begun to taste of vinegar—milk, honey, and fishbrine. One need not be particular in the case of any other uncovered liquids, however, inasmuch as no poisonous creature will drink them.

8. Garlic that has been crushed or a melon that has been cut into and is left uncovered may not be eaten. The same rule applies to similar victuals. Cooked wine and unfermented wine—the latter being wine within three days from the time of pressing—do not come under the rule of uncovered liquids. Similarly, heated wine or water or milk which has steam still rising from it, and all liquids into which other liquid falls from above drop by drop—provided that the dripping continues—are not subject to the rule of uncovered liquids, because reptiles are afraid of the splash of liquid and of steam and will not drink from these.

9. The liquid in which vegetables have been pickled or cooked, or in which lupines have been boiled, is not subject to the rule of uncovered liquids. For water in which pickled or well-cooked vegetables or lupines have been soaked, the rule is: If its taste has been altered, the rule of uncovered liquids does not apply; but if there was not enough of the vegetable to impart a flavor, it is forbidden. Similarly, water in which peaches or damascene dates have been rinsed for an invalid is forbidden if left uncovered.

10. Wine to which sharp condiments, such as pepper, or bitter flavoring, such as absinthe, have been added sufficiently to change

its flavor may be drunk if left uncovered. The same rule applies to other liquids.

11. All liquids that are forbidden when uncovered are so deemed whether left uncovered by day or by night, and even if one is asleep alongside the liquid, because a reptile is not afraid of one asleep.

How long does it take before such liquids are deemed forbidden when left uncovered? Long enough for a reptile to creep from under the handle of the vessel, drink, and return whence it came.

12. The amount of water required to be rendered forbidden when left uncovered is any quantity in which the poison is detectable and harmful. But if there is so much water that the poison will be lost in it, it remains permissible whether it is contained in vessels or in pools on the ground. The same rule applies to other liquids.

13. If a spring is flowing at all, it is not subject to the rule of uncovered liquids.

If an uncovered bottle is left in a chest or a box or a cupboard or in its own container or in a well even a hundred cubits deep or in a tower even a hundred cubits high or in a large, well-kept, and whitewashed room, it becomes forbidden. However, if one first examines the box or the cupboard before putting the bottle in, the liquid is permissible. But if there is a hole in any of these containers, the liquid is forbidden. The size of the hole must be large enough to admit the little finger of a small child.

14. If a barrel is uncovered, the rule is that even if nine people have already drunk from it without ill effects, the tenth may not drink. The Sages report a case in which the tenth person to drink died because the snake's venom had sunk to the bottom. There exists also a species of snake venom that floats on the top and another that remains suspended in the liquid. That is why the entire barrel is forbidden, even if the liquid is strained through a cloth. Similarly, if a melon is left uncovered, and nine people

have already eaten of it without ill effects, the tenth may nonetheless not eat of it.

15. Water left uncovered may not be poured out into a public domain or sprayed indoors to lay the dust or used for making mortar or for washing one's hands, face, or feet or given to one's own animal or to a neighbor's animal to drink. But it may be given to a cat to drink.

16. If dough is kneaded with water that has been left uncovered, the rule is that even if it is heave-offering, it must be burned, and even if the bread has already been baked, it may not be eaten.

CHAPTER XII

1. A domestic or wild animal or bird that has been bitten by a snake or any other poisonous creature, or that has eaten something poisonous to human beings—if eaten before it is assimilated in an animal's body—may not be eaten because of danger to life. Consequently, if a domestic or wild animal or bird is found with its leg cut off, then even though it may be permissible under the law prohibiting the organically defective, it is nevertheless forbidden under the law prohibiting the dangerous—lest one of the poisonous reptiles has bitten it—until after it has been tested. The method of testing is to roast the meat in an oven. If it does not shred or become in any way different from other roasted meat, it may be eaten.

2. Similarly, if figs or grapes or cucumbers or pumpkins or melons or apple melons—even if very large—have been pecked, they are forbidden whether they are plucked or are still attached. Moreover, even if they are in a vessel, the rule is that everything juicy which is found bitten is deemed forbidden, for possibly a snake or other poisonous creature has bitten it. Even if a bird or a rat is actually seen biting them, they are forbidden, for it may be biting a place where there is a previous bite.

3. The prohibition of exposed liquid does not apply to a fig or a grape from which the stem has been removed, and one may therefore eat figs or grapes at night without apprehension. A pecked fig that has dried and become a dried fig, or a pecked date that has been dried, is permissible.

4. One should not put small change or denar into his mouth lest they carry the dried saliva of one who suffers from an infectious skin disease or leprosy, or lest they carry perspiration, since all human perspiration is poisonous except that coming from the face.

5. Similarly, one should not put the palm of his hand under his arm, for his hand might possibly have touched a leper or some harmful substance, since the hands are constantly in motion. Nor should one put a dish of food under his seat even during a meal, lest something harmful fall into it without his noticing it.

6. Similarly, one should not stick a knife into a citron or a radish lest someone fall on the point and be killed. Similarly, one should not walk near a leaning wall or over a shaking bridge or enter a ruin or pass through any other such dangerous place.

7. Similarly, a Jew should not remain alone with heathens because they are suspect of murderous intentions. Nor should one travel on a journey in their company. If one chances to meet a heathen on a journey, he should keep him to his own right hand. If they are climbing an ascent or going down a slope, the Israelite should not be below the heathen lest the latter pounce upon him in order to slay him; rather he should keep himself above and let the heathen be below him. Nor should he bend down in front of a heathen lest the latter smash his skull.

8. If a heathen asks an Israelite how far he is going, he should mention a longer distance than the true one, as Jacob did with Esau, saying to him, *Until I come unto my lord unto Seir* (Gen. 33:14).

9. It is forbidden to buy medicine from a heathen unless hope of the invalid's recovery has been abandoned. It is forbidden to

receive medical treatment from a heretic even if all hope has been abandoned, lest one be attracted to his views. Animal remedies and remedies for an external wound, such as a poultice or a plaster, may be bought from a heathen. If, however, the wound is dangerous, the remedy may not be bought from him. Any wound for which the Sabbath may be profaned should not be treated by a heathen.

10. A heathen physician may be consulted on what drug or treatment is best, but the drug should not be bought from him.

11. One may not have his hair cut by a heathen in private lest the latter kill him. But a person of importance may do so because the heathen would be afraid to kill him. If one impresses upon the heathen that he is a person of importance in order to deter him from killing, he may have his hair cut by him.

12. It is forbidden to sell a heathen arms of any kind, or to sharpen his weapons, or to sell him a knife or collars or fetters or chains of iron or bars of Indian steel, or (to sell him) bears or lions, or anything that may be a public danger. Shields may be sold to heathens since they are solely defensive.

13. Just as the Sages forbade the direct sale of these things to a heathen, so did they forbid their sale to an Israelite who sells such things to a heathen. Weapons may, however, be sold to the local militia, since they protect the Israelite population.

14. Whatever should not be sold to a heathen should not be sold to an Israelite brigand, for to do so is to support a transgressor and lead him astray. Similarly, if one leads astray another who is blind to any matter by giving him bad advice, or if one encourages a transgressor who is blind and cannot see the true path because of his heart's desire, he transgresses a negative commandment, for Scripture says, *Before a blind man you must not put a stumbling block* (Lev. 19:14), which means that if one comes to you for advice, he should be given advice appropriate to his situation.

15. But beneficial advice should not be given to a heathen or to a wicked slave. Even to advise him to do a good deed is forbidden as long as he clings to his wicked ways. Daniel was tested only because he advised Nebuchadnezzar to give charity, as it is said, *Wherefore, O king, let my counsel be acceptable unto thee, and break off thy sins by almsgiving, and thine iniquities by showing mercy to the poor* (Dan. 4:24).

CHAPTER XIII

1. If, on the road, one encounters a person whose animal is crouching under the weight of its burden, he is enjoined to unload the burden from the animal whether the burden is suited to it or too heavy for it. This is a positive commandment, for Scripture says, *Thou shalt surely release it with him* (Exod. 23:5).

2. One may not unload the animal and then leave the other person helpless and go away; rather he must help him raise the animal up and reload the burden onto it, for Scripture says, *Thou shalt surely help him to lift them up again* (Deut. 22:4), which is an additional positive commandment. If one leaves the other helpless and neither unloads nor reloads, he disregards the positive commandments and transgresses a negative commandment, for Scripture says, *Thou shalt not see thy brother's ass,* etc. (*ibid.*).

3. If the passerby is a priest and the animal is crouching in a cemetery, he may not defile himself on its account, just as he may not defile himself in order to return lost property to its owner. Similarly, if one is an elder unaccustomed to loading or unloading, he is exempt, seeing that the act is not in keeping with his dignity.

4. The general rule is as follows: In every case where if the animal were his own he would load or unload it, he must load or unload another's. But if one is pious and does more than the letter of the law demands, even if he is a prince of the highest rank, still if he sees another's animal crouching under its burden of straw or sticks or the like, he should help unload and reload.

5. If one unloads and reloads an animal and it again falls down, he must again unload and reload, repeating the process even a hundred times if necessary, for Scripture says, *Thou shalt surely release* (Exod. 23:5), and *Thou shalt surely help him to lift it* (Deut. 22:4). He must therefore pace beside the other for a parasang unless the owner of the burden tells him that he no longer needs him.

6. From what point on does it become one's duty to help another unload and reload? From the moment when his seeing the animal can be deemed meeting it, for Scripture says both, *If thou see* (Exod. 23:5) and *If thou meet* (Exod. 23:4). What distance is this? The Sages estimated this distance to be 266⅔ cubits, which when multiplied seven and a half times is a *mil*. If he is more distant than this, he is not obligated to help.

7. The scriptural commandment requires one to help another unload without payment, but loading is a commandment for which one is entitled to be paid. Similarly, one is entitled to payment for pacing beside the owner for a parasang.

8. If one finds his neighbor's animal crouching, he is obligated to unload and reload it even if the owner is not with it, for Scripture says, *Thou shalt surely release* (Exod. 23:5), and *Thou shalt surely help lift it* (Deut. 22:4), meaning under any circumstances. This being so, why do the verses continue, *with him?* To teach that if the owner of the animal is present and he goes and sits down, saying to the one who has met him, "Since the commandment is incumbent on you, if you wish to unload it, do so by yourself," he need not do so, for Scripture says, *with him*. But if the owner of the animal is old or sick, one must load or unload it alone.

9. If the animal belongs to a heathen and the burden to an Israelite, the one meeting it is not obligated if the heathen is actually driving the animal; but otherwise he must unload and reload because of the trouble it is causing the Israelite. Similarly, if the animal belongs to an Israelite and the burden to a heathen, one

must unload and reload it because of the trouble it is causing the Israelite. But if both the animal and the burden belong to a heathen, one is obligated to assist him only in order to prevent ill feeling.

10. If one of a number of ass drivers has a weak-legged ass, the others should not get in front of him and leave him behind. But if it falls down, they may pass him.

11. If one ass is laden and another is mounted and the path is narrow, the rider must give way to the laden animal. If one is laden and the other unburdened, the unburdened animal must give way to the other. If one is mounted and the other is unburdened, the latter must give way to the former. If both are laden or if both are mounted or if both are unburdened, they must come to an agreement between themselves.

12. Similarly, if two boats crossing a river meet and will sink if both attempt to continue at the same time, but both can get across if they sail one after the other, or if two camels climbing a steep ascent meet and will fall if they try to advance together, but can manage to ascend one after the other, how must they proceed? Where one is unburdened and the other laden, the unburdened one must give way to the other. If one is near its destination whereas the other is still distant from its own, the former must give way to the latter. If both are near their destinations, or if both are distant from them, or if both are laden, they must compromise, seeing that they are in the same distress and one must compensate the other. It is with regard to these and similar cases that Scripture says, *In righteousness shalt thou judge thy neighbor* (Lev. 19:15).

13. If one encounters two animals, one crouching under its burden and the other unburdened because the owner cannot find anyone to help him load, he is obligated to unload first to relieve the animal's suffering, and then to load the other. This rule applies only if the owners of the animals are both friends or both enemies (of the person who comes upon them). But if one is an enemy and

the other a friend, he is obligated to load for the enemy first, in order to subdue his evil impulse.

14. The enemy mentioned in the Law (cf. Exod. 23:5) does not mean a foreign enemy but an Israelite one. How can an Israelite have an Israelite enemy when Scripture says, *Thou shalt not hate thy brother in thy heart* (Lev. 19:17)? The Sages decreed that if one all alone sees another committing a crime and warns him against it and he does not desist, one is obligated to hate him until he repents and leaves his evil ways. Yet even if he has not yet repented and one finds him in difficulties with his burden, one is obligated to help him load or unload, and not leave him possibly to die. For the enemy might tarry because of his property and meet with danger, and the Torah is very solicitous for the lives of Israelites, whether of the wicked or of the righteous, since all Israelites acknowledge God and believe in the essentials of our religion. For it is said, *Say unto them; As I live, saith the Lord God, I have no pleasure in the death of the wicked but that the wicked turn from his way and live* (Ezek. 33:11).

NOTES

References consisting of numbers only indicate passages found in the Code outside of the present volume, the numbers referring, respectively, to the book, the treatise, the chapter, and the section where the passage in question occurs.

Treatise I: Damage by Chattels

Chapter 1

1–4. These four sections offer a theoretical basis for the entire treatise. The individual statements cannot be assigned to definite rabbinic sources, although useful references can be given.

1. Cf. BḲ 1:4 and MRSY to Exod. 21:28 (131).
"any other domestic animal." Cf. BḲ 5:6.
2. Cf. BḲ 1:4; B., *ibid.*, 7a.
4. Cf. BḲ 1:4.
The somewhat vague definitions given in this section are made more precise below in Ch. 6.
"*mu'aḏ*, 'forewarned' "—a technical term coined on the basis of Exod. 21:29, *And warning hath been given* (*wĕhu'aḏ*) *to its owner*, and in rabbinic law extended to apply, as a rule, to the injuring animal or object rather than to its owner.
"*tam*, 'innocuous' "—used as the opposite of *mu'aḏ*.
"makes it a habit to repeat the abnormal action." Cf. BḲ 2:4.
"the particular action which it has made a habit"—that is, it is still deemed innocuous for other abnormal actions.
5. BḲ 1:4; B., *ibid.*, 16a.
6. BḲ 1:4.
"by goring, biting," etc. The implication is that they are deemed "forewarned" with respect to those actions for which other animals are regarded as innocuous and they pay for the full damage where other animals pay for only half. In cases, however, where other animals would be exempt altogether, as, for example, for eating produce in a public domain (below, Sec. 8), they too are exempt (MM).
7. BḲ 1:4.
"This is the rule," etc.—BḲ 1:2; B., *ibid.*, 13b.
8–9. Tos BḲ 1:9 (347) and B., *ibid.*, 14a.
10. B. BḲ 2b.
The main classes of injuries are those mentioned in Scripture: *horn* in Exod. 21:35, *tooth* and *foot* in 22:4. Damage caused in any other way is classed with the one of these three categories which it most resembles.
"subspecies of injury by the tooth"—B. BḲ 3a.
"soils produce"—with its droppings.
"subspecies of injury by the foot"—B. BḲ 3a and 17b.
"by swishing its tail"—B. BḲ 19b.

11. B. BḲ 19b.

"the injured party seizes property of the owner." The principle underlying this rule is that the court should not disturb the *status quo* unless the law definitely requires it. Hence if a problem is left unsolved by law, the court cannot interfere if one of the parties takes the law into his own hands. Some authorities, however, accept this ruling only where the facts cannot be ascertained. Where, as here, the law itself is in question, their rule is that judgment must be entered for the defendant (the injurer) whether there has been seizure or not.

Chapter 2

1. Cf. Alf, *ad* B. BḲ 2a.

"habitual to an animal . . . abnormal"—literally, "forewarned . . . innocuous."

2. B. BḲ 2a–3b.

"is the same"—literally, "resembles."

3. BḲ 2: 1; B., *ibid.*, 17b.

4. B. BḲ 19a.

"If an animal treads," etc.—BḲ 2: 1.

5. B. BḲ 19a.

"the owner is exempt"—because he can plead that, under the law, he is exempt from paying for damage by *foot* caused in a public domain, and that whether the pebbles sprang up as a result of a normal or an abnormal action is immaterial.

"a quarter of the damage." Compensation for damage by an abnormal action cannot exceed half the amount payable for the same damage—in this case damage by pebbles on private premises—when caused by normal action.

6. B. BḲ 19a.

7. B. BḲ 15b.

8. B. BḲ 15b.

"on the testimony of witnesses"—so that if the defendant confesses before witnesses testify, he is exempt. See below in Laws Concerning Theft, i, 5.

9. B. BḲ 18b–19a; Alf, *ad loc.*

"the half damage in the case of pebbles"—a monetary obligation that cannot be evaded by confession.

10. B. BḲ 18b.

"Poultry are deemed forewarned"—BḲ 2: 1; B., *ibid.*, 19b.

"a pit which moves." The thread, like any other impediment left on the public domain, is regarded as a pit (concerning which laws are described in detail below, Chs. 12–13). Since the poultry have moved the thread from its original site, it becomes a pit which has moved.

11. B. BḲ 19b.

12. B. BḲ 17b.

13. B. BḲ 17b.

14. B. BḲ 17b–18a.

15–16. BḲ 2: 3; B., *ibid.*, 21b–22a.

17–18. BḲ 2: 3; B., *ibid.*, 23a.

17. The rendering of this paragraph is based on the Oxford MS.

19. B. BḲ 24b.

"legally exempt but morally liable"—literally, "exempt in human law but liable in heavenly law."

20. B. BḲ 24b.

Chapter 3

1. BḲ 2: 2.

"benefits"—saves itself an ordinary meal.

2. B. BḲ 20a; Alf, *ad loc.*

Rashi, *ad loc.*, interprets the source differently and assumes that barley was eaten.

"At the cheapest (prevailing) rate." Cf. Maim's comment on BḲ 2: 2.

3. BḲ 2: 2; B., *ibid.*, 20a.

4. B. BḲ 20a. Cf. RABD and MM.

5. Cf. B. BḲ 23a.

6. B. BḲ 19b.

7. Tos BḲ 1: 8 (347); B. BḲ 19b.

"a dog eats small sheep"—B. BḲ 15b.

8. B. BḲ 19b–20a.

9. BḲ 2: 2; B. *ibid.*, 21a.

10. B. BḲ 20a.

11. BḲ 6: 1; B., *ibid.*, 57b–58a; Alf, *ad loc.*

"birth fluid"—i.e., if it begins to calve unexpectedly as a result of the fall.

"Similarly, if another animal crowds it," etc. Others consider that this is not negligence; see ḤM 394: 1.

12. B. BḲ 58a.

13. BḲ 5: 2–3; Alf, *ad loc.*

14. BḲ 5: 3; B., *ibid.*, 47b.

"In an actual case"—B. BḲ 48a.

15. BḲ 6: 3; B., *ibid.*, 59b.

"if it eats of it and suffers harm . . . he is exempt"—because the animal ought not to have eaten it (see above, Sec. 14).

Chapter 4

1. BḲ 6: 1; B., *ibid.*, 55b–56a.

"If brigands take a sheep out"—intending to steal the animal; see ḤM 396: 2.

2. B. BḲ 55b.

In this case the intention *is* to enable the animal to stray and cause damage. See, however, ḤM 396: 3.

3. B. BḲ 56b.

4. BḲ 4: 9.

"less than adequate care." Even a door able to withstand a normal wind is not considered adequate (MM).

"the owner being liable even if it kills a person." In a responsum (No. 340 of ed. Freimann, p. 306; see also KM), Maim. himself states that he added this sentence on the margin of his copy as an afterthought, intending it to follow "a gratuitous bailee is exempt," and that many copyists placed it wrongly after "they are exempt" at the end of the previous sentence. The printed editions still have the sentence misplaced, perhaps because MM explains it away as referring to damage by *horn,* for which adequate care is no defense (see below, vii, 1). The Oxford MS omits it altogether, but whether by oversight or because the copy was made before Maim. made the marginal addition cannot be ascertained.

5. BḲ 6: 2; B., *ibid.,* 56a.
6. BḲ 6: 2; B., *ibid.,* 9b and 56a.
7. B. BḲ 10a.
8. B. BḲ 40a–b.
9. B. BḲ 40b.
10. B. BḲ 13b and 45b.
11. B. BM 36a–b.

"to his son or to a member of his household"—B., *ibid.,* 36a–b.

"to an assistant"—B. BḲ 56b.

12. Cf. B. BḲ 40a.
13. BḲ 6: 2; B., *ibid.,* 58b.
14. BḲ 6: 2; B., *ibid.,* 58b–59a.

"But if it is a Persian or a similar palm"—B. BḲ 59a.

Chapter 5

1. B. BḲ 23b; Alf, *ad loc.*

"animal at pasture." Others say this section applies only to animals being kept for slaughtering on a market day; see RABD and ḤM 397: 2.

"For one is forbidden to cause damage willfully"—hence the owner of the sheep cannot plead he is prepared to pay for any damage caused.

2. BḲ 7: 7; B., *ibid.,* 79b.
3. B. BḲ 80b–81b.

"other than the stumps"—better perhaps "other than the prime shoots"; cf. Gen. R. 6: 21 (Theodor 287: 10).

For a different version of vi see ṬḤM 274: 6.

"across a boundary"—between two fields.

"within such a border"—within which no cemetery is permitted.

4. B. BḲ 81b.
5. B. BḲ 81b.
6. B. BḲ 81b.
7. B. BḲ 79b.
8. B. BḲ 80a.

"in their day"—in talmudic times.

9. BḲ 7: 7; B., *ibid.,* 82b–83a.
10. B. BḲ 80a.

"If a herder . . . repents"—and decides to give up rearing sheep.

Chapter 6

1. BḲ 2: 4; B., *ibid.,* 24a.
2. B. BḲ 24a.

"during a session of the court"—MRSY Exod. 21: 36 (136).

3. BḲ 4: 4; B., *ibid.,* 39b.

4. B. BḲ 39a.
5. BḲ 4: 4.
6. BḲ 4: 4; B., *ibid.*, 40b.
"these oxen"—i.e., oxen entrusted to a bailee or to the care of a guardian.
7. BḲ 2: 4; B., *ibid.*, 24a.
8. BḲ 4: 2; B., *ibid.*, 37a.
"From what point is its recovery assumed?" Above, Sec. 7.
9. B. BḲ 37a.
"with respect to all of them." Cf. MM.
10. B. BḲ 37a. See RABD.
11. B. BḲ 37b; cf. V, 1, viii, 6.
12. B. BḲ 37b.
13. See above, i, 11, note.

Chapter 7

1. BḲ 4: 9.
"Similarly, if it causes damage by an act with respect to which it is forewarned from the outset"—BḲ 6: 1.
2. B. BḲ 45b. See LM.
3. B. BḲ 33a.
"injury"—defined as in IV, i, 2, below.
"these other effects." See below, IV, i, 1 ff.
"for the damage"—so the Oxford MS.
"Consequently, if one's ox causes humiliation"—BḲ 3: 10.
"he is liable, as will be explained"—IV, iii, below.
"he would not have to pay, as will be explained"—II, iii, 1–2, below.
4. BḲ 5: 3.
"If it is innocuous, its owner must pay for half of the damage"—cf. Tos BḲ 5: 9 (353–4).
5. BḲ 5: 3; B., *ibid.*, 48b.
"the owner of a pit is not liable for damage to inanimate objects, as will be explained." See below, xiii, 1.
6. B. BḲ 48a.
"for damage to the courtyard"—or to the householder.
7. B. BḲ 48a.
8. B. BḲ 11a.
"*shall be his* . . . refers to the plaintiff"—and does not mean that it is transferred to the injurer.
"Depreciation of a carcass is borne by the plaintiff"—B. BḲ 10b.
"appreciation of the carcass is shared"—B. BḲ 34b.
11. B. BḲ 34a.
12. B. BḲ 34a.
13. B. BḲ 11a.

Chapter 8

1. BḲ 4:3.

"The law of compensation"—BḲ 1:2.

"subject to the law of sacrilege"—Lev. 5:14–16. See VIII, IX, ii, 2 ff.

"Consecrated animals which have become disqualified"—cf. B. BḲ 53b; P. *ibid.*, 1:2 (2a).

2. B. BḲ 13a.

"peace offering"—Lev. 3:11–17; *ibid.*, 7:28–43. See VIII, v, ix, 3 ff. Where specific parts of an animal belong to different owners, each pays in proportion to his share in the animal. The meat of the peace offering is regarded as belonging to the owner, the altar portions as belonging to the Sanctuary.

"as we have explained in the Laws Concerning Sacrilege." See VIII, IX, ii, 1.

"thank offering"—Lev. 7:12–15. See VIII, v, ix, 5 ff.

3. B. BḲ 13b.

"How is the compensation taken?"—if the animal is innocuous, so that the claim is against only the animal itself.

4. BḲ 1:2; B., *ibid.*, 13b.

5. BḲ 4:3.

The reasons given in this section appear to be the author's own. See RABD and MM; cf. also P. BḲ 4:3 (4b).

6. B. BḲ 33b.

7. B. BḲ 33b.

"become profane without redemption." The injured party therefore pays the Temple treasury a token sum as redemption before taking possession of the animal. Cf. MM, *ad loc.*

8. B. BḲ 33b.

9. B. BḲ 33b.

"From the finest of the defendant's property only"—and the plaintiff has no special claim to the animal that did the damage.

10. B. BḲ 7a–b.

11. B. BḲ 14b.

"It should seize inferior land"—Giṭ 5:2; B., *ibid.*, 50a–b.

"seized movable property during the lifetime of the defendant"—B. BḲ 14b.

12. Alf, *ad* B. BḲ 14b; XIII, III, xi, 11 (YJS, *2*, 120).

13. BḲ 1:3; B., *ibid.*, 14b.

"liability for ransom may not be collected, and an animal may not be killed." See below, Ch. 10.

"shepherds"—ordinarily unacceptable as witnesses. See XIV, II, x, 4 (YJS, *3*, 104).

14. Tos BḲ 3:6 (350); Alf, *ad* B. BḲ 47a.

Chapter 9

1. B. BḲ 47a.

2–3. BḲ 5:1; B., *ibid.*, 46a; Alf, *ad loc.*

4–5. B. BḲ 47a.

6. BḲ 3: 11; B., *ibid.*, 35b.

"an oath of inducement." See Shebu 40b and XIII, iv, i, 3 (YJS, 2, 191).

7. BḲ 3: 11; B., *ibid.*, 36a.

8. B. BḲ 36a.

9. BḲ 3: 11.

10. Cf. B. BḲ 35b.

"A scriptural oath." Cf. XIII, iv, i, 1 (YJS, 2, 190).

11. BḲ 3: 11.

"one who claims wheat from another person who admits owing barley." See XIII, iv, iii, 10 (YJS, 2, 202).

12. BḲ 4: 1.

"regarded as co-owners"—with respect to the second goring.

13. B. BḲ 36b.

14. BḲ 3: 8.

"half compensation of the surplus." From the examples given it is clear that the author has assumed that the balance or excess refers to the difference between the amounts that would be payable by each party if calculated separately. Another view is that the excess refers to the excess damage, and that half compensation is payable for the excess damage. Thus in the last example of the section, the compensation would be one half of the difference between a hundred and forty, and not ten. See Rashi, *ad loc.*

Chapter 10

1. Cf. BḲ 4: 5–6.

2. MRSY Exod. 21: 28 (131); cf. Ed 6: 1.

"What difference is there between an innocuous animal which kills"—BḲ 4:5.

3. B. BḲ 41a.

"fatally ill." See below, Sec. 7.

"mortally injures three human beings at one time." The three gored victims die only after the last one has been gored.

4. Mek Exod. 21: 29 (*3*, 85); MRSY Exod 21: 29 (132).

"Although the ransom is merely in the nature of atonement"—and not compensation, a bond can be exacted as if it were an ordinary debt.

"the court may forcefully exact bond"—B. BḲ 40a. Bond is not exacted from those liable to atonement sacrifices. See VIII, v, xiv, 17.

5. MRSY Exod. 21: 30 (133). See also B. BḲ 40a.

6. MRSY Exod. 21: 29 (132). See also B. BḲ 45a.

"a wild ox," etc.—BḲ 4: 7.

"Guardians need not pay ransom"—B. BḲ 40a.

7. B. San 78a.

8. San 9: 1; B., *ibid.*, 78a.

"The same rule applies if one incites a domestic or a wild animal." Cf. BḲ 4: 4.

9. BḲ 4: 6; B., *ibid.*, 44a–b.

"to pay a fine if it kills a slave"—B. BḲ 43b; see below xi, 1.

10. B. BḲ 48b.

"notices green vegetables in a pit." Rashi, *ad loc.*, says "at the mouth of the pit."

"forewarned with respect to rubbing its body against walls"—BḲ 4: 6; B., *ibid.*, 44a.

11. "Thus if one enters," etc.—B. BḲ 23b.

"to collect wages"—B. BḲ 33a.

12. B. BḲ 33a.

13. B. BḲ 26a.

Chapter 11

1. B. BḲ 40a.

"redemption of his life." Maim. accepts the view that the pronoun "his" refers to the person killed.

"the fine fixed by law"—Exod. 21: 32; BḲ 4: 5.

"a slave whose document of manumission has been delayed"—Giṭ 42b.

2. B. BḲ 42b.

"one who is half slave and half free"—Giṭ 42b. RABD and others admit this in the case of a bondwoman but not in the case of a male slave, whom they regard as one whose document of manumission has been delayed, and so covered by the previous section. Maim. appears to consider that the half slave can demand to be set free but remains legally half a slave until he receives his deed of manumission. See also below, IV, iv, 12, and the note thereon.

3. BḲ 5: 4; B., *ibid.*, 42a.

"the value of children." Cf. Exod. 21: 22 and below, IV, iv, 1 ff.

4. B. BḲ 49a.

5. Cf. BḲ 5: 4.

6. B. BḲ 44b.

7. B. BḲ 90b–91a.

8. B. BḲ 91a.

"If it is tried on the capital charge and escapes (from custody) it may not be tried on the money charge"—because its labor is not available to enable judgment to be enforced (MM). Others interpret the Talmud text as signifying that the owner of the ox fled from justice. See Rashi, *ad loc.*, and RABD.

9. B. BḲ 44b–45a.

"If a bailee returns it to its owner, this return is not recognized by law." The owner can therefore claim compensation for the loss of his bailment.

10. B. San 79b–80a; cf. also Zeb 8: 1.

11. B. San 80a.

"a sexual offense is committed with such an animal." The text has the euphemism "a crime was committed with it." Cf. Lev. 20: 15.

12. B. San 80a.

13. B. Ker 24a.

"are proved guilty of conspiracy." In the technical sense of XIV, II, xviii–xxi (YJS, *3*, 121–34).

Chapter 12

1. BḲ 5: 5, 7; B., *ibid.*, 50b.

2. BḲ 5: 5; B., *ibid.*, 49b.

"If, however, he declares both premises and pit ownerless." This is not stated explicitly in the Talmud but is accepted by all authorities except Rashi, *ad loc.*, who considers that he is liable in this case.

3. B. BḲ 48a.

"whether one digs a pit or purchases it or is given it as a present"—P. BḲ 5:7 (5a).

4. BḲ 5:6; B., *ibid.*, 52a–b.

"he is liable"—because he was negligent in his duty toward the oxen, since he should have expected the camels to weaken the cover.

5. B. BḲ 52b.

"he is exempt"—because the accident was not a consequence of his negligence. According to RABD he should be liable in this case because the principle that one is liable for accidents following negligence holds whether the accidents are consequences of the negligence or not.

6. B. BḲ 29b.

As long as the pit exists, the owner of the pit is responsible for seeing that it is kept covered. Once it has been filled in, however, this responsibility disappears, and the removal of the earth is equivalent to digging a new pit.

7. BḲ 5:6; B., *ibid.*, 52a.

8. B. BḲ 9b.

9. B. BḲ 30a.

10. BḲ 5:5.

11. B. BḲ 51b, with a reading different from that in current editions. Cf. MM.

12. B. BḲ 51a.

"If he fills in the handbreadth"—B. BḲ 51b.

13. B. BḲ 51b.

14–15. B. BḲ 50b.

16. BḲ 5:6; B., *ibid.*, 54a.

"If, however, a person or a normal animal is injured"—B. BḲ 28b.

"the owner must pay for the whole of the damage." RABD acquits the owner even from damage to a normal animal.

17. B. BḲ 51a.

18. BḲ 5:6; B., *ibid.*, 53a.

19–21. B. BḲ 53a.

"near the mouth of a pit." Cf. Rashi, *ad loc.*, 53a.

22. B. Ar 6a.

Chapter 13

1. BḲ 5:6; B., *ibid.*, 53b.

2. BḲ 1:1; B., *ibid.*, 3b & 28b.

3. B. BḲ 28b.

"and then renounces the ownership of the premises but not of the articles." The case where both are renounced is given above, xii, 2.

4. B. BḲ 48a.

5. BḲ 3:1; B., *ibid.*, 27b.

"it is not usual for persons to keep their eyes on the road." The pedestrian is therefore not guilty of negligence.

6. B. BḲ 27b.

7. BḲ 3: 1; B., *ibid.*, 29a.

"in effect abandoned property"—and he would normally be liable for any damage they cause.

8–9. BḲ 3: 4; B., *ibid.*, 31a.

10–11. B. BḲ 31a–b.

12–13. BḲ 3: 2; B., *ibid.*, 30a.

14–15. BḲ 3: 3; B., *ibid.*, 30b.

16–17. BM 10: 5.

"If any part," etc.—refers to this and the previous sec.

18. B. BM 118b.

"If the laborers are working jointly under contract." Each man is responsible not merely for the part of the work actually done by him, but also for the finished job. Cf. Rashi, *ad loc.*

19. BM 10: 4; B. BḲ 6b; B. BM 118a.

"and causes damage"—while falling. The case of damage after they have fallen is covered by Sec. 7 above (MM).

"even if he has not renounced ownership." This is the reading of the Oxford MS, the point being that he is ordinarily liable for damage done after articles have fallen only if he does not abandon his ownership of them. The printed editions of both text and MM have "Even if he has abandoned his ownership of them."

20. BḲ 3: 2; B., *ibid.*, 30a.

21–22. B. BḲ 30a.

23. B. BḲ 50b.

"Nor may one make a cavity"—BB 3: 8; B., *ibid.*, 60a.

"to dig a pit for public use"—B. BḲ 50a.

24–25. BB 3: 8; B., *ibid.*, 60b; Alf, *ad loc.*

26. BB 2: 14.

"A vacant space must be left"—B. BM 107b.

27. BB 6: 7.

Chapter 14

1. Cf. BḲ 6: 4.

"Conflagration is deemed one of the principal classes"—BḲ 1: 1.

2–3. BḲ 6: 4; B., *ibid.*, 61a.

4. B. BḲ 23a.

5. BḲ 6: 4; B., *ibid.*, 59b; Alf, *ad loc.*

6. BḲ 6: 4.

7. BḲ 6: 4.

"an unusual gust of wind"—BḲ 6: 4; P. BḲ 6: 4 (5c).

"If both a person and the wind fan it"—B. BḲ 60a. Cf. MM and KM.

8. BḲ 6: 4.

"If it consumes a cornstack"—BḲ 6: 5; B., *ibid.*, 61b.

9. B. BḲ 61b.

10. BḲ 6: 5.

"The kindler . . . is liable"—for the goat, since to tie a goat to a cornstack is "a normal use" for it. Moreover, the death of the slave is not a culpable slaying since the slave was free to escape. Cf. MM.

"he is exempt"—from liability for the goat. For the death of the slave is now a culpable slaying and so no claim for compensation can be brought.

11. B. BḲ 62a.

"the lender need pay only for the price of barley." Barley was cheaper than wheat.

12. BḲ 6: 5; B., *ibid.,* 62a.

"as will be explained." Cf. XIII, IV, i, 2 (YJS, *2,* 190).

13. BḲ 6: 6.

"whether or not the animal halts." Cf. B. BḲ 22a.

"Even his Ḥanukkah lamp"—and he is thus fulfilling a religious duty.

14. B. BḲ 55b–56a.

15. B. BḲ 23a.

"as we have explained"—above, vii, 3.

16. B. BḲ 3b.

Treatise II: Theft

Chapter 1

1. "worth a pĕruṭah or more." Cf. BḲ 9: 5; B. San 57a.

"Ye shall not steal"—so correctly in the Oxford MS, rather than Exod. 20: 13.

"must be repaid." See XIV, I, xviii, 2 (YJS, *3,* 50).

2. B. San 57a.

"however small"—even if it is worth less than a pĕruṭah.

"to steal in jest"—Sif Lev. 19: 11 (88c); B. BM 61b.

3. B. BḲ 79b; B., *ibid.,* 57a.

"Without the owner's knowledge"—i.e., without the owner being able to identify the thief. See next note.

"an armed brigand"—i.e., apparently, an armed brigand who keeps his identity secret, even though he makes no attempt to keep the theft secret. See, however, RABD, *ad loc.*

4. Cf. BḲ 7: 4.

5. Ket 3: 9; B. BḲ 75a.

6. BḲ 7: 1.

7. Sif Lev. 19: 11 (88c).

"a married woman." Cf. BḲ 8: 4.

8. Cf. BḲ 8: 4.

9. Yad 4: 7.

"chattels."—The Oxford MS has this sentence about slaves in the singular, which is tidier but not necessarily original.

"Should a slave become free." Cf. BḲ 8: 4.

10. MM states that he has been unable to find an explicit source for this section.

11. See below, III, ii, 2, and the notes there.

"if the thief has gone to expense"—B. BḲ 65a.

12. B. BḲ 66a.

13. B. BḲ 65a.

"a lamb and it grows into a ram"—B. BḲ 65b.

14. B. BḲ 65a.
15. B. BḲ 11a.
16. B. BḲ 68a.
17. BḲ 7:1; B., *ibid.*, 68a.
18. B. BḲ 68a.

Chapter 2

1. BM 4:9; Mek to Exod. 22:8 (*3*, 120); B. BḲ 76a.
2. BM 4:9; B., *ibid.*, 57b.
3. B. Bek 11a.

"before it has been redeemed"—Exod. 13:13.

4. Tos MSh 3:11 (91); B. Ket 30b.

The penalty for eating untithed produce or forbidden fat does not exempt the thief from liability for his theft.

5. B. Ḳid 58b.
6. BḲ 7:2, 4.

"must pay fourfold or fivefold"—i.e., to his father's estate.

"If his father dies before"—so that he becomes a part owner of the animal and is exempt as stated below, Sec. 13.

7. B. BḲ 69a.
8. BḲ 7:5, 2.

Fourfold or fivefold is paid only if the animal is slaughtered in a manner that is ritually valid as defined in V, III, i–iv.

"ṭĕrefah"—lit. "torn." A technical term for an animal which is organically defective and forbidden as food.

9. Tos BḲ 7:15, 16 (359).

"a fatally diseased animal"—*ṭĕrefah.*

10. Tos BḲ 7:14 (359).
11. B. BḲ 68a.

"all but a hundredth part"—BḲ 7:5; B., *ibid.*, 78b.

12. B. BḲ 78b.

"seizure by the plaintiff." See note above, on I, i, 11.

13. BḲ 7:5.
14. B. BḲ 78b.
15. B. BḲ 68b.
16. BḲ 7:5, 6.

"bailee or creditor"—so the Oxford MS.

17. B. BḲ 79b.

"goads the animal"—to get it to move away from where it is grazing.

18. BḲ 7:5.

Chapter 3

1. IV, IV, i, 11–14.

"or without receiving due warning"—XIV, I, xvi, 4 (YJS, *3*, 45).

"at the same time." Cf. Ket 31a; Ar 6b.

2. B. Ket 31a. Cf. also BḲ 3:10; *ibid.*, 7:2.

3. BḲ 7: 4.
"as we have explained"—in Sec. 1 above.
4. B. Ket 34b.
5. BḲ 7: 4; B., *ibid.,* 71a.
6. B. BḲ 71a.
"We have already explained"—above ii, 10.
7. BḲ 7: 2, 4.
"as we have explained"—above I, ix, 6.
8–9. B. BḲ 74b–75a.
10. B. BḲ 71b.
11. B. BḲ 5a.
12. Soṭ 3: 8; B. Ḳid 18a.
13. Mek to Exod. 22: 8 (*3*, 20).
14–15. B. Ḳid 18a.
16–17. The translator has been unable to find a specific source for either of these two sections. Cf. however, P. Soṭ 3: 9 (19b) and Tos Ket 10: 4 (272).

Chapter 4

1. BḲ 9: 8.
"himself is like a thief"—so the Oxford MS.
"butchers or sells"—B. BḲ 106b.
2. B. BḲ 105b.
3. B. BḲ 107b.
"is exempt from paying double"—even if he did not tamper with the deposit at all.
4. B. BḲ 106b.
"his own plea condemns him to pay for it"—and he does not pay double unless he tries to avoid liability altogether.
"a paid bailee"—who is liable if the bailment is stolen. See XIII, I, i, 2 (YJS, 2, 4).
"as will be explained"—below III, xiii, 10.
5–6. B. BḲ 108a.
7. B. BḲ 108a.
"seizes the fine." See note above on I, i, 11.
8. B. BḲ 108b.
9. B. BḲ 106b.
10–11. B. BḲ 118b; Alf, *ad loc.*
"coin." Text reads *sela'*.
12. BḲ 10: 8; B., *ibid.,* 118a, b; Alf, *ad loc.*

Chapter 5

1. Cf. BḲ 10: 9.
2. B. BḲ 115a.
"interest of market overt"—literally "the regulation of the market." The regulation protected the bona fide purchaser who might otherwise be afraid to buy goods for fear he should lose his money if they turned out to be stolen.

3. B. BḲ 115a; Alf, *ad loc.*
4. BḲ 10: 3.
"is on the authority of the Scribes"—Shebu 7: 1.
"the appropriate place." See XIII, iv, i, 2 (YJS, *2,* 190).
5. Shebu 7: 1, 4.
6–7. B. BḲ 115a; Alf, *ad loc.*
8. B. BḲ 115a.
"brings it to his creditor." Cf. MM.
9. B. BḲ 115a.
10. BḲ 10: 3; B., *ibid.,* 114b–115a.
"a kind usually lent or hired out." Cf. B. Shebu 46b.
11. B. BḲ 114b.
12. B. Shebu 46b.

Chapter 6

1. BḲ 10: 9; B., *ibid.,* 118b–119a.
"there is no presumption in such a case." The shepherd would not dare to steal so many.
2. B. BḲ 118b.
3–4. BḲ 10: 9; B., *ibid.,* 119a.
"orchard guards"—so the Oxford MS; see *Tos Yomṭob ad* BḲ 10: 9.
5. B. BḲ 119a.
6. BḲ 10: 10.
"three threads"—from the selvage, if they come out during the washing.
7. BḲ 10: 10, P., *ibid.,* 10: 12 (6c); Alf, *ad loc.*
"enough thread left to draw a needle through (cloth)"—i.e., twice the length of the needle, and thus enough to sew a stitch.
8. BḲ 10: 10; B., *ibid.,* 119b.
9. B. BḲ 119b.

Chapter 7

1. Cf. B. BB 89b.
2. Cf. B. BM 61b.
"a liability to pay." See XIV, 1, xviii, 2 (YJS, *3,* 50).
3. B. BB 89b.
"it does not involve action." See XIV, 1, xviii, 1, 2 (YJS, *ibid.*).
4. B. BB 89b.
"a coin that is defective"—B. BM 52b.
5. B. BM 52a.
"less than half, it must be clipped and destroyed." The words "it must be clipped and destroyed" are lacking in the printed editions but are clearly required and have been supplied from the Oxford MS.
6. B. BM 52a.
7. B. BB 89b–90a.
8. B. BḲ 113a–b.
9. B. BB 89b.
"*mĕśurah.*" See below, viii, 7.

10. B. BM 75a.

"are strict with one another." Each insists on an exact share of what is bought in common.

"correct measuring," etc. See III, 1, xxiii, 13.

11. Sifre Deut. 19: 14 (109a).

12. B. BB 88b.

"If one denies"—Sifra Lev. 19: 37 (91b).

Chapter 8

1. "filled with saffron"—B. BM 107b.

2. B. BM 107b.

"a ditch"—used as an irrigation canal, the banks being left unsown for the convenience of those who use the canal (Rashi, *ad loc.*).

3. B. BB 89b.

"because the rope shrinks." Cf. MM, *ad loc.*

4. B. BB 89b.

"tin"—so the Oxford MS and the Talmud.

5. B. BB 89b.

"a level"—used to level the top of dry stuffs sold by measure.

"too lightly"—and so be of disadvantage to the seller.

"too heavily"—and give the buyer short measure.

6. B. BB 89b.

"one side thick and one side thin"—so the Oxford MS, the Talmud, and ḤM.

7. B. BB 89b.

8–10. Kel 29: 4–6; B. BB 89a–b.

"the cord . . . the lines." The Hebrew word is the same for both. The former means the cord from which the whole balance was suspended, the latter the cords at the ends of the beam from which the stuff sold and the weights were hung.

11. Kel 29: 4; B. BB 89a.

12. B. BB 88b.

13. BB 5: 11; B., *ibid.*, 88b.

14. BB 5: 11.

15. B. BB 89a.

16. BB 5: 11; B., *ibid.*, 89a; Sifre Deut. 25: 14 (126b).

17. B. BB 90a.

18. BB 5: 10.

19. B. BB 89a; Alf, *ad loc.*

20. B. BB 89a.

Chapter 9

1. B. San 86a.

"There is no penalty of flogging." Cf. XIV, 1, xviii, 2 (YJS, *3*, 50).

2. San 11: 1; B., *ibid.*, 85b.

3. B. San 85b.

"he must separate him." The verse quoted may also be translated, *steal anyone from his brethren.*

4. B. San 85b.
5. San 11:1; B., *ibid.*, 86a.
6. B. San 85b.
"a slave"—San 11:1; B., *ibid.*, 86a.
7. San 8:6; B., *ibid.*, 72b.
"by day or by night"—Mek Exod. 22:2 (*3*, 102); P. San 8:8 (26c).
8. B. San 72b.
9. B. San 72a.
"regarded as is one who pursues another to kill him." See below, v, i, 6 ff.
10. B. San 72a–b.
11. P. San 8:8 (26c).
"surrounded by people or by witnesses." Cf. Mek Exod. 22:2 (*3*, 103).
12. See MM.
13. San 8:6; B., *ibid.*, 72b.
"is exempt from indemnity for articles which he breaks upon entering"—i.e., for damage done. He must, however, restore any property he steals.
"as we have explained." See above, iii, 1.

Treatise III: Robbery and Lost Property

Chapter 1

1. BḲ 9:5; cf. also B. San 57a.
"*pĕruṭah*"—the smallest fractional coin considered to possess monetary significance. It is defined in Ḳid 1:1.
"No flogging is incurred for breach"—B. Mak 16a; cf. XIV, 1; xviii, 2 (YJS, *3*, 50). The normal penalty for breach of an ordinary negative commandment was a flogging of up to 39 strokes. See XIV, 1, xvi ff. (YJS, *3*, 44 ff.).
"Even if he burns the robbed property"—so that restoration is now impossible and it might be thought that a flogging should be administered.
2. B. San 57a.
"Even a heathen"—B. BḲ 113a.
3. B. BḲ 79b.
4. Cf. B. BM 111a.
5. Cf. BḲ 9:1.
"he is liable for the repayment of its capital value only"—and never double, as may be the case with theft (see above, II, i, 4).
"takes a rafter by robbery and builds it into a structure"—Ed 7:9 (Giṭ 5:5).
"a rafter by robbery and uses it for the booth he builds for the Feast of Booths"—B. Suk 31a. The booth or *sukkah* (Lev. 23:42) cannot be dismantled during the festival without inconvenience and monetary loss, so that the regulation for the benefit of penitents mentioned earlier applies here too.
"has not been built in with mortar." If it was mortared into the booth, he can pay for it instead, since the booth is now a permanent structure.
6. B. BḲ 105a.
"because it was originally worth a pĕruṭah"—so that the commandment to

return the article taken by robbery applies to it and he must return either the article itself or its value.

"no significant robbed property remains in his hand." Cf. MM, *ad loc.*

7. BḲ 10: 6.

8. B. BḲ 118b., as interpreted by Alf.

"without awareness"—without knowing that he is counting restored stolen property.

"an empty purse." Since he has no reason to examine this purse, he will not know that it now contains money.

9. "transgresses the negative commandment." RABD, however, considers that there is no breach of the commandment if the other does finally consent to the sale, even though under pressure.

"even if he pays him a high price for it"—B. BM 5b.

"since it does not involve action." See YJS, *3*, 50. Since the actual sale is ultimately consented to, it cannot be regarded as an illegal *action*. Inasmuch as RABD assumes that there was no consent, so that the forced sale is to be considered an illegal action, his reason for the exemption from flogging is that the article so bought must be restored to its original owner.

"until he buys the object that he covets"—Mek. Exod. 20: 14 (*2*, 266).

10–12. MRSY Exod. 20: 14 (112).

11. *"houses."* The scriptural text has *fields*.

13. B. BḲ 119a.

"he taketh away the life." Our versions translate, *it taketh away the life*.

"Nevertheless, if property"—B. BḲ 94b.

"the robber wishes to repent and comes of his own accord." Cf. MM, *ad loc.*

"so as to encourage penitents in the right path." If a robber no longer possesses the things he actually took, the difficulty of finding sufficient money to pay for them all may deter him from repenting and remaining honest in the future. By urging the persons wronged to waive their claims, the Sages hoped to make penitence easier.

Chapter 2

1. B. BḲ 65a; *ibid.*, 111b.

"even if he has abandoned hope of recovering it." For although the property has become ownerless, his crime prevents the robber from acquiring it.

"even if the robber has died and it is now in the possession of his heirs." Inheritance is not regarded as a change of possession. Cf. below, Sec. 3.

"If, however, it becomes altered." Cf. BḲ 9: 1.

2. B. BḲ 111b.

"the robber acquires title to any improvement that takes place." Most other authorities consider this to be true even if the owner has not abandoned hope of recovery.

"the improvement is evaluated for him." For an example, see below, Sec. 6.

4. B. BḲ 96a.

"The person robbed may in turn exact the value of the improvement from the robber." Most authorities deny any such right of recovery. Cf. note above, Sec. 2.

5. B. BḲ 96a.

The rabbinic regulation enabling a purchaser to retain improvements did not extend to heathens.

"seizes the value of the improvement." See note to I, i, 11. The doubt concerns whether the regulation was meant to benefit any legal Israelite possessor or merely an Israelite purchaser buying from the robber.

6. "We have already explained." See above, Sec. 2.

"Thus if one obtains a cow"—BḲ 9: 1; B., *ibid.*, 95b.

7. BḲ 9: 1.

"or before there is any change." Maim. (unlike RABD) does not consider mere calving or shearing a change. The change intended here is doubtless a change from calf to cow, or lamb to ewe, which would entitle the robber to keep the animal. See below, Sec. 13.

8. B. Giṭ 55b.

10. B. BḲ 93b.

11. B. BḲ 96b.

12. BḲ 9: 1; B., *ibid.*, 93b, 96b.

"But . . . utensils"—so according to the Oxford MS, the Talmud and ḤM.

13. B. BḲ 96b.

"a growing palm." See B. BḲ 96a.

14. B. BḲ 96a.

"If he obtains a lamb by robbery." See B. BḲ 96b.

15. B. BḲ 11a.

16. Cf. B. BḲ 65a.

Chapter 3

1. B. BM 43a.

"the wine itself would have had to be restored." His action in breaking the cask has therefore deprived the owner of four denar worth of wine.

2. B. BḲ 65a.

3. B. BM 99b.

4. BḲ 9: 2; B., *ibid.*, 96b, 97a, 98b.

"obtained a utensil by robbery and broken it." Rashi and most other authorities regard all the cases of this section as cases of alteration.

"slaves . . . and they grow old." Slaves are not regarded legally as movable property but have the legal status of real property.

"leavened food . . . and it outlasts the Passover week." Its use is forbidden because it ought to have been disposed of before the Passover festival; see III, v, i, 4.

"abused"—(Lev. 20: 15), and so liable to be destroyed by order of the court.

"being taken to be stoned"—for having killed a human being. See Exod. 21: 28.

5. B. BḲ 98b.

"Consequently, if . . . he denies having it"—B. BḲ 98b. See below, vii, 1 ff.

"he is liable for payment." For although the property is intrinsically worthless, it is nevertheless regarded as equivalent to money, since its disappearance would make the robber liable for a money payment. According to RABD this is not true if the property is actually on the robber's premises at the time of the oath, for then there is not even a contingent liability for the payment of money.

6. B. BḲ 96b.

7–8. B. BḲ 97a.

9. B. BḲ 21a; Alf, *ad loc.*

"even if it is not usual for him to rent a place." The Tosafist RI holds that rent need not be paid in this case.

10. B. BḲ 101a.

"the amount by which he has depreciated the wool." If the dyed wool happens to be worth less than the original undyed wool, he must pay the difference.

"the improvement of the dye on the wool." The phrasing of the original is obscure, but the meaning is that the owner cannot claim the loss of his dyestuffs in addition, since these are in fact on the wool and he has not actually lost them.

"it may not be reclaimed from him." See above 1, i, 11.

11. BM 3:12; B., *ibid.*, 44a.

"Even if his action does not depreciate the value"—B. BM 41a; Alf, *ad loc.*

12. B. BM 44a.

"he is held responsible for accidental damage"—to the whole cask, although his intention was to take only one quarter-log. This is because the whole of the cask serves to preserve his quarter-log from deterioration until he needs it.

"similar object"—so according to the Oxford MS.

13. BM 3:12; B., *ibid.*, 44a.

"if the rest of the wine sours." It is assumed that the wine sours because the cask was broached.

14. B. BḲ 105b.

"before the court." These words are not in the Talmud and they are omitted by ṬḤM 294 and by ḤM 294:1. They are, however, in Me'iri, *ad loc.* (quoted in *Šiṭṭah Mĕḳubbeṣeṯ*) and so are undoubtedly part of our text.

15. BB 5:9; B., *ibid.*, 88a.

16. Shebu 7:2.

Chapter 4

1–2. Shebu 7:2; B., *ibid.*, 46a; Alf, *ad loc.* (first and second "Gates").

2. "to seize a pledge"—i.e., expressing the intention to seize property of the householder in satisfaction for a claim he has against him.

3. B. Shebu 46b.

4. B. Shebu 46a; Alf, *ad loc.* (third "Gate").

There is no definite presumption in this case that he is a robber.

5. Cf. Alf Shebu 46a (end of tenth "Gate").

"testifies that a person has entered"—with the intention of seizing a pledge (MM).

6–7. B. Shebu 46b.

8. The general ban of this paragraph is a Geonic provision not mentioned in the Talmud (MM).

9. Yeb 15:7; B., *ibid.*, 118b; Alf, *ad* B. BM 37a.

"robs one of five people"—and admits to having done so.

"But, according to the law of Scripture, a person is not obliged to pay if there is doubt"—because possession is taken as a presumption of ownership and is not disturbed without proof. Strictly speaking, therefore, all he should have to do is hand the amount taken by robbery to the court and leave it to the actual plaintiff to establish his claim.

10. BM 3: 3; Alf, *ad* B. BM 37a.

"If one says to two people"—without being sued by them.

"impose a penalty"—condemn him to pay both, as they did in the case in the previous section.

11. "an oath of inducement"—B. Shebu 40b.

"a scriptural oath"—Shebu 6: 1.

" 'the mouth that forbids is the same mouth that permits.' " The evidence that identifies the pledge as the property of the householder is the admission of the defendant. If we accept this admission, we should also accept his contention that he is entitled to recover his debt from the pledge. The rule itself is Mishnaic (Ket 2: 2).

"in the Laws Concerning Pleading." See XIV, IV, i, 2 (YJS, *2*, 90).

12–13. Alf, *ad* B. Shebu 46a (tenth "Gate").

13. The principle of this and subsequent sections is the following: If a litigant is prepared to contradict the evidence of a single witness by taking a scriptural oath, he is allowed to do so and go free; otherwise he must pay.

14. B. Shebu 47a.

15–17. There is no talmudic source for these sections (MM). Since, however, Maim. gives a dissenting opinion of his own in Sec. 16, it is probable that they are taken from a Geonic source.

Chapter 5

1. Cf. BḲ 10: 9.

2. Cf. B. Suk 27b, 31a.

3. "as must one," etc. See above, iii, 9.

"If one takes palm trees by robbery." Cf. B. BḲ 113b.

4–5. BḲ 10: 1; B., *ibid.*, 111b.

7. See above, II, v, 2 ff.

8. B. BḲ 119a.

9. BḲ 10: 1.

10. BḲ 10: 2; B., *ibid.*, 114a.

11. B. BḲ 113a.

12. Cf. B. BḲ 113b.

13. Cf. B. San 48b., the source for which is the story of Naboth's vineyard; see I Kings 21.

14. B. BB 55a.

15. B. BB 54b.

16. B. BM 73a.

"work like a slave"—e.g., make him carry his clothes to the bathhouse. Cf. XII, v, i, 7 (YJS, *5*, 248).

17. B. BḲ 113b.

Chapter 6

1. Tos Ket 8: 3 (270) quoted in B. BM 22a.

2. BḲ 10:2; P., *ibid.* (7b); B. BM 24a.

3. B. BḲ 114a.

"circumstantial evidence." The text has "defective proofs."

4. B. BM 107a.

5. See above, I, xiii, 14–15.

6. Tos BḲ 10: 24 (368); B. BB 46a.

7. San 3: 3; B., *ibid.*, 25a.

8. Tos Ḥul 10: 13 (512); BḲ 7: 7; B., *ibid.*, 83a.

"the pigeons belong to the owners of the vineyards." The reason given by Rashi (*ad loc.*) is that the vineyards enable the pigeons to wander long distances from their dovecotes without being lost.

9. BB 2: 5. Cf. Maim.'s Commentary, *ad loc.*

"its position is deemed legitimate." It is assumed that the original owner acquired the right to have it in its present position.

10. B. San 25b.

Many authorities deny that gaming winnings are regarded as robbery in the rabbinic sense and consider that gaming is forbidden only for the reason given in the following section.

11. B. San 25b.

12. Giṭ 5: 8; cf. also XII, II, i, 1–5 (YJS, 5, 110).

13. "A flowing river," etc. Cf. B. Er 46a.

"If a poor person is lopping"—Giṭ 5: 8; B., *ibid.*, 61a.

14–15. BḲ 10: 2; B., *ibid.*, 114b.

16. B. Giṭ 61a.

"add a fifth part." See Ch. 7, below.

Chapter 7

1–2. These secs. are Maim.'s own introduction to the chapter. The contents are drawn principally from Shebu 5: 1–5 and BḲ 9: 7.

3–6. Sifra Lev. 5: 22 (25b); B. BḲ 104b.

7. "to a heathen"—Sifra Lev. 5: 21 (24c).

"less than a pĕruṭah"—BḲ 9: 5.

"One-fourth part of the capital"—Sifra Lev. 27: 27 (114d).

8. B. BḲ 108b.

9. BḲ 9: 5; B., *ibid.*, 103b–104a.

10. BḲ 9: 6.

"He may give it neither to the son"—BḲ 9: 5.

"made him his agent in the presence of witnesses"—B., *ibid.*, 104a.

11. BḲ 9: 6; B., *ibid.*, 105a.

12. BḲ 9: 7.

"And shall add the fifth part more thereto." This verse is interpreted here in accordance with the Hebrew order, viz: "And as for its fifth part, he shall add thereto." This implies that it may be necessary to add something to the fifth part.

13. B. BḲ 108a.

From the fact that the singular form *ḥămišiṯ* has a plural possessive suffix in Lev. 5: 24, the inference is drawn that more than one fifth may be payable on a single capital sum.

Chapter 8

1. BḲ 9:5.
2. BḲ 9:9. The text of the Mishnah of Maimonides differed from that of Rashi. Cf. marginal note of Elijah of Wilna to B. BḲ 108b.
3. BḲ 9:9; B., *ibid.*, 109a.
"to his creditor . . . to charity"—so the Oxford MS.
4. B. BḲ 109a.
"he did acquire title to it"—by the death of the heirless proselyte. Cf. XII, II, ii, 1 (YJS, 5, 113).
5. B. BḲ 109b.
6. B. BḲ 110a.
"Nor may the priests divide unevenly"—*ibid.*, 110b.
"restitution for robbery from an heirless proselyte"—that is, they may not take a larger share of one property in return for allowing another priest to receive a larger share of a second property.
7. B. BḲ 110a.
"If the MAN" etc.—thus implying that an adult is being referred to; while the person robbed is described (Num. 5:7) as "him in respect to whom the robber hath been guilty," which includes minors.
8. B. BḲ 110b.
"as we have explained." See above, iii, 4.
9. B. BḲ 109b.
10. BḲ 9:11.
"as we have explained in the appropriate passage." Cf. VIII, VII, iv, 14.
11. BḲ 9:12.
"Even if the robber was a minor." The source for this statement is unknown to the translator.
12. B. BḲ 111a.
"hand it to the current watch"—so the Oxford MS.
13. BḲ 9:12.
14. B. BḲ 117b; 105a.
"legally regarded in the same way as land." Cf. above, II, ii, 2.
"as will be explained." See the next chapter.

Chapter 9

1. B. BM 14b.
"as we have explained." See above, i, 5, 7.
2. BḲ 10:5.
3. B. BḲ 116b.
4. B. BM 14b–15a.
"free property." Cf. XIII, III, xviii, 1 ff. (YJS, 2, 143 ff.).
5. B. BM 14b; Alf, *ad loc.*
6. B. BM 15a; Alf, *ad loc.*
"the capital sum"—the purchase price paid for the field.
7. B. BM 15a; Alf, *ad loc.*

"A buyer who is aware"—B. BM 15b; Alf, *ad loc.*

"If, however, the expenditure exceeds the value of the improvement"—Alf, *ad* B. BM 15b.

8. B. BM 14b.

"However, if he knows that the field was obtained by robbery"—B. BM 15b.

9. B. BM 15b–16a.

10. B. BM 16a.

"the court begins to advertise the robber's own property." Cf. XIII, III, xxii, 9 (YJS, 2, 161).

11. B. BM 16a.

"and then sells it to another buyer." Some authorities require both sales to have taken place before the robber's purchase of the property. Cf. Rashi, *ad loc.*, and ṬḤM 374.

12–13. B. BM 16a.

14–16. B. BB 47b–48a.

16. Cf. XII, I, x, 1 ff. (YJS, 5, 35 f.).

"Inasmuch . . . as proof"—so the Oxford MS.

Chapter 10

1–2. B. Giṭ 58b.

3. Giṭ 5:6; B., *ibid.*, 58b.

"either a quarter of the land or a third of the purchase price." The choice lies with the original owner.

4. B. BM 101a.

"the planter always having the disadvantage"—as defined above, ix, 5.

5. B. BM 101b.

7. B. BB 42a.

"A husband, with regard to his wife's property"—a wife who is a minor (MM). Cf. B. Ket 80a and IV, I, xxiii, 10.

8–9. B. BM 101a.

10. Ket 8:5.

"Let craftsmen come." The commentators know of no explicit source for this statement.

"craftsmen"—so the Oxford MS.

11. Cf. BB 1:4; B., *ibid.*, 6a.

"not yet taken an oath"—required of him in the preceding section.

12. B. Ket 80a.

"If the husband is himself a farmer"—capable of tending the land himself if necessary.

"but to their disadvantage"—just as it is for the husband himself. Cf. IV, I, xxiii, 9.

Chapter 11

1. Cf. B. BM 26b.

2. B. BM 26b.

"wicked," etc.—B. AZ 26b.

3. B. BḲ 113b.

"Furthermore, if one returns it," etc.—B. San 76b.

"in order to sanctify God's name"—P. BM 2: 5 (8c).

"involving a profanation of God's name"—B. BḲ 113b.

4–5. B. BḲ 113b.

"intend to test him"—to see whether he will return it or not.

6. Mak 2: 8; B. BM 24a.

7. B. BM 24a.

"which is chiefly frequented by Israelites"—e.g., a synagogue (MM).

8. B. BM 24b.

"all benefit . . . is forbidden"—because it must be assumed to have been dropped by a member of the majority, and the wine of a heathen is forbidden; see V, II, ii, 3.

9. B. BM 24b.

"may be retained as lost property"—but cannot, as a rule, be eaten. Cf. V, II, viii, 12.

10. B. BM 22b; cf. above, vi, 2.

11. Cf. B. BB 87b; B. BM 25b.

12. B. BM 27a.

13. BM 2: 8; B., *ibid.*, 30a–b.

14. B. BM 30b.

"he has already begun to perform the laudable act"—to restore the lost property, and must therefore finish doing so.

"If, after he returns it, it runs away again"—BM 2: 9; B., *ibid.*, 31a.

"He must continue," etc.—B. BḲ 57a.

15. B. BḲ 57a.

16. B. BM 31a.

17. B. BM 30b.

18–19. BM 2: 10; B., *ibid.*, 32a.

20. B. BM 31a.

Chapter 12

1. BM 2: 11.

2. BM 2: 11; B., *ibid.*, 33a.

"the equal"—in scholarship.

3. BḲ 10: 4; B., *ibid.*, 116a.

"the usual fee"—for his time lost; see Sec. 4 below.

"a hundred"—text reads *māneh,* equivalent to 100 zuz.

"Even if his own ass saves itself without help"—so that he did not actually lose it.

4. B. BḲ 116a.

"Similarly, if he was engaged in his trade"—BM 2: 9; B., *ibid.*, 31b.

"any laborer to refrain," etc.—i.e., the pay a person in his position would be willing to accept to take a holiday from work, which would normally be less than the amount he could earn by working. He is thus left free to restore the lost property, and this he must do without reward.

5. BḲ 10: 4; B., *ibid.*, 115b.

6–7. B. BḲ 116a.

8. B. BḲ 116b; Tos BM 8: 25 (389).

"to all"—Rashi, *ad loc.*, understands this to mean that each member of the party may take what was originally his, an interpretation accepted in ḤM 191: 1.

9–10. B. BḲ 116b; Alf, *ad loc.*

11. B. BḲ 116b; Tos BM 7: 13 (386–7).

"the usual custom"—i.e., the rule given above applies only when there is no usual custom.

12–13. Tos BM 11: 25 (397); B. BḲ 116b.

14. Tos BM 7: 14 (387); B. BḲ 116b.

"its load is lightened"—the cargo is pushed into the sea.

15. Tos BM 11: 26 (397); B. BḲ 116b.

Chapter 13

1. Cf. BM 2: 1.

"it becomes worth less"—B. BM 27a.

"a high rock outside Jerusalem"—B. BM 28b.

2. B. BM 25a, 28b; Alf, *ad* B. BM 25a.

"unmistakable marks of identification"—in this context, the measurements of an article of clothing or the dimensions or weight of another article.

3. BM 2: 7; B., *ibid.*, 28b.

"until the inquiring of thy brother." This is the translation of the verse assumed in the rabbinic interpretation quoted. The usual translation is "Until thy brother require it." In the Hebrew construction with the infinitive, "thy brother" may be either the subject or the object of the verb.

4. B. BM 28b.

5. B. BM 27b, 28b.

6–7. B. BM 28a.

"must be kept intact"—until Elijah comes (below, Sec. 10), i.e., indefinitely.

8. BM 2: 6; B., *ibid.*, 28a.

9. B. BM 28b.

"men of violence"—troops of occupation, presumably Roman.

10. B. BḲ 56b.

11. BM 2: 8; B., *ibid.*, 29b–30a.

12. BM 2: 8; B., *ibid.*, 30a.

13. BM 2: 8; B., *ibid.*, 29b.

"nor should two persons read in it at two different places." Rashi, *ad loc.*, says the reverse, namely that two may read at different places, but not at the same place.

14. B. BM 29b.

"because these are readily obtainable," etc. The owner will not be sufficiently attached to the ones lost to want these in preference to new ones.

15. BM 2: 7; B., *ibid.*, 28b.

16. B. BM 28b.

17. BM 2: 7; B., *ibid.*, 29a.

18. B. BM 29b.

"as we have explained." See above, Sec. 10.

19. Cf. B. BM 28b.
"in the public interest"—see Sec. 20, below.
20. Giṭ 5: 3; cf. B., *ibid.*, 51a; Alf, *ad loc.*

Chapter 14

1. BM 2: 5; B., *ibid.*, 27a.
2. Cf. BM 2: 1; B., *ibid.*, 24a.
3. Cf. BM 2: 2.
"if he hears the owner say, 'What a misfortune that I've suffered a loss of money' "—B. BM 23a.
4. B. BM 24a.
5. B. BM 22b.
"when he discovers that he has dropped it he will abandon hope"—because the coin is unidentifiable.
6. B. BM 26b.
"takes the denar"—intending to keep it and not restore it.
"as we have explained." See above, xi, 2.
7. B. BM 26b.
"as explained above." See above, Sec. 5.
8. B. BM 26b.
"even from among three people"—i.e., two or even three but not one.
"he must return it"—and cannot assume that discovery of the loss will lead automatically to abandonment.
"even if there is not in it a pĕruṭah worth for each." For it must not be assumed that they have equal shares in the coin. Cf. above, xi, 12.
9. B. BM 26b.
10. B. BM 25b.
"a coin will be spent"—unlike other property which is not presumed to be for sale.
11. B. BM 25a.
12. BM 2: 1; B., *ibid.*, 23b.
13. B. BM 23b.
"to promote peace"—B. Yeb 65b; Alf, *ad* B. BM 23b.
"Thus if, when studying." These examples are not talmudic.

Chapter 15

1. Cf. BM 2: 3.
"Even if he is in doubt"—BM 2: 3; B., *ibid.*, 25b.
"he acquires title to it"—RABD says he must hold it "until Elijah comes." Cf. also MM, ḤM 260: 9–10, and commentaries.
2. "Anything identifiable," etc. This paragraph continues the previous section.
"one finds an ass or a cow grazing"—BM 2: 9; B., *ibid.*, 30b.
"a vessel concealed in a rubbish heap"—BM 2: 3.
3. B. BM 31a.
4. BM 2: 9; B., *ibid.*, 30b, 31a.
"damage it might do to the land." Cf. above, xi, 20.

5. BM 2: 9; B., *ibid.*, 32a.

"a garment or an axe alongside a fence"—B. BM 31a.

6. BM 2: 3; B., *ibid.*, 25b.

7. BM 2: 3; B., *ibid.*, 25b.

8. BM 2: 1; B., *ibid.*, 21a, 23a.

"from the country"—literally, "from their respective regions." Cf. Rashi, *ad loc.*

9. BM 2: 2; B., *ibid.*, 23b.

"However, if the jars of wine or of oil have already been opened"—so that numerous sales of similar jars have taken place.

10. B. BM 23b.

"large sheaves"—B. BM 22b.

11. BM 2: 1; B., *ibid.*, 23b.

12. B. BM 21a.

"a ḳab̲ consisting of two or three species." According to our text the talmudic query concerned "a ḳab̲ of *either* sesame *or* dates *or* pomegranates." Cf. marginal note of the Gaon of Vilna to B. BM 21a and ḤM 260: 7.

13. BM 2: 2; B., *ibid.*, 25a.

14. B. BM 25a.

15. Maas 3: 4; B. BM 21a.

16. B. BM 22b.

"the owner renounces them"—although they are not spoiled by the falling.

17. B. BḲ 80b.

18. BB 2: 6; B., *ibid.*, 23b.

"the majority is decisive"—literally, "follow the (principle of) majority."

Chapter 16

1. B. BM 24a.

2. BM 2: 1, 2; B., *ibid.*, 25a.

3. BM 2: 2; B., *ibid.*, 25a.

4. BM 2: 4.

"as will be explained." Cf. XII, II, iv, 8–9 (YJS, *5*, 123).

5. BM 2: 4; B., *ibid.*, 26b.

"as we have explained." See above, xi, 7.

6. BM 2: 4; B., *ibid.*, 27a.

"from a merchant." The original owner of the produce, and so of the money, is therefore unknown.

7. BM 2: 3; B., *ibid.*, 25b–26a.

8. The reasoning of this section is not talmudic.

"concerning property lost," etc. Cf. above, xi, 10. The author argues that since loss to all persons is sufficient to deprive an original owner of his property right, it must certainly be a bar to the acquisition of a new title.

9. BM 2: 3; B., *ibid.*, 26a.

"the handle is an indication." If the handle is on the inner side, this indicates that the householder placed it there; if it is on the outer side, it was placed there by an outsider and so belongs to the finder.

10–11. BM 2: 3; B., *ibid.*, 26a.

"the treasure belongs to the most recent tenant"—who thus takes the place of the householder.

"three heathen"—but not three Israelites; cf. above, xiv, 8.

"into an inn"—frequented by a majority of heathen.

"even inside the house"—not concealed in a wall.

Chapter 17

1. BM 1: 4.

2. BM 1: 3; B., *ibid.*, 10a.

3. B. BM 10a.

"If two persons pick up lost property"—B. BM 8a.

4. B. BM 8a.

5. B. BM 8b–9a.

6. B. BM 8b.

"an heirless proselyte"—whose property is deemed derelict. Cf. XII, II, ii, 1 (YJS, *5*, 113).

7. B. BM 9a.

8. B. BM 11a.

"the four cubits of ground"—B. BM 10a.

9. B. BM 11a, b.

10. B. BM 10b–11a.

"so does she become divorced if it enters her courtyard." Cf. IV, II, v, 1.

"derives from the principle of agency." Cf. XII, II, iv, 8–9 (YJS, *5*, 123 f.).

11. BM 2: 4; B., *ibid.*, 11a.

"If one acquires the above creatures as a gift"—B. BM 12a.

12. Giṭ 5: 8.

"he need not pay a fifth part." Cf. above, vii, 1 ff.

13. BM 1: 5; B., *ibid.*, 12a, b.

"a maiden daughter"—between 12 and 12½ years of age. Cf. IV, I, ii, 1–2.

Chapter 18

1. BM 1: 6; B., *ibid.*, 13a; Alf, *ad loc.*

"he should not return it"—to either creditor or debtor.

"the note is certified"—i.e., it bears the certification of a court authenticating the signature of the witnesses.

"the creditor is nevertheless entitled to make seizure." Cf. XII, I, xix, 3 (YJS, *5*, 67) and XIII, III, xviii, 1 (YJS, *2*, 143).

2. B. BM 17a.

3–4. BM 1: 8; B., *ibid.*, 20b.

"by the scribe"—so the Oxford MS.

5. BM 1: 8; B., *ibid.*, 20b.

6. BM 1: 7; B., *ibid.*, 18b.

The law of this sec. must be read in conjunction with IV, II, iii, 9–11, where the legal validity, as distinct from the ownership, of the document is discussed.

7. B. BM 28a.

8. B. BM 19a.

9. B. BM 19a–b.

"To swindle B to whom he gave"—i.e., when the first donee secures possession on the strength of the document whose validity he now admits, they will come to some arrangement over sharing the proceeds.

"as will be explained." Cf. XII, II, ix, 15 (YJS, *5*, 144).

10–11. B. BM 19b.

12. Cf. B. BM 7b.

"either to the husband or to the wife"—so the Oxford MS.

13. BM 1: 8.

"*ḥăliṣah*"—the ceremony wherein the shoe of the brother who refuses to perform the levirate marriage is removed. Cf. Deut. 25: 5–11.

"refusal"—a document recording the protest of a minor fatherless girl against a marriage contracted for her by her mother and her brothers.

"The general rule is as follows." The formulation of the rule is the author's.

14. "and is not subject to mere suspicion"—just as an ordinary document would not be invalidated without proof, if the defendant pleaded one of the possibilities suggested above. For other opinions see ḤM 65: 16.

Treatise IV: Wounding and Damaging

Chapter 1

1. BḲ 8: 1.

"five effects." In what follows, the term "effects" refers to the items enumerated in this section for which compensation is payable.

"from the injurer's best property"—Giṭ 5: 1. See above, 1, viii, 10.

2. BḲ 8: 1.

"*for* signifies payment of monetary compensation"—Mek Exod. 21: 24 (*3*, 67).

3. "Moreover, Scripture says," etc.—B. BḲ 83b.

Maim. argues that Lev. 24: 20 cannot possibly be a commandment to inflict an injury on the person of the injurer because Num. 35: 31 shows clearly that it is permissible to take ransom instead. In the next section he applies the same argument to Deut. 19: 21. See below, Sec. 5.

5. MRSY Exod. 21: 24 (130).

6. "Although," etc. The meaning is apparently that in addition to the indications in Scripture (Exod. 21: 18–19 and Num. 35: 31), monetary compensation for injury is a matter of well-established legal procedure. See, however, Maim.'s views in his *Guide of the Perplexed,* III, 41 (tr. M. Friedlander, *3,* 194, and footnote).

7. Cf. MM, *ad loc.*

9. MT Deut. 25: 11 (168). The expression *Thou shalt cut off her hand* is here understood to mean, "make her pay compensation for the humiliation caused him."

10. BḲ 8: 1.

11. "forewarned"—Hebrew, *mu'ad;* see above, 1, i, 4.

"The rule that one who does injury while asleep must pay compensation applies"—P. BḲ 2: 8 (3a).

"and if the sleeper injures him, he is exempt." Most authorities explain this exemption as an indication that a person is not liable for damage caused purely by accident and without the least element of negligence on his part.

12. B. BḲ 27a.

"turns over to break his fall"—literally, "turns himself over." He clutches at the person injured in order to break his fall, regardless of the fact that he may injure him thereby (Cf. Rashi, *ad* B. BḲ 27a).

13. Cf. below, vi, 13–15.

14. B. BḲ 86a.

15. B. BḲ 26b.

16. B. BḲ 48a.

"the trespasser suffers accidental injury due to the owner"—who was unaware of the trespasser's presence (Rashi, *ad loc.*).

17. BḲ 3:7; B., *ibid.*, 32b.

18. B. BḲ 91a.

"Just as an appraisal of the capacity to harm must be made in the case of death." See below, v, iii, 1.

"for even"—according to the Oxford MS.

19. B. San 76b.

"If one throws a stone"—B. BḲ 33a.

"subsequently places himself within range"—i.e., after the missile was in flight.

Chapter 2

1–2. Tos BḲ 9:1 (363); P., *ibid.*, 8:1 (6b), quoted in Alf, *ad* B. BḲ 83b.

2. "on the head." It is assumed that the swelling does not interfere with his work.

"a spot that is not exposed." RABD adds the additional condition that the blow itself must not have been seen, for otherwise he will also have humiliation to pay for.

3. BḲ 8:1; B., *ibid.*, 85b.

4. B. BḲ 86a.

6. "no larger than a grain of barley"—so the Oxford MS.

7. B. BḲ 91a.

"legally exempt although morally liable." See above, I, ii, 19.

9. BḲ 8:1.

10. B. BḲ 85a.

"willing to pay"—the assumption being that the executioner of the king's decree is paid for the "service" of removing the limb and that in doing so he is free to choose a more painful or a less painful method.

11. B. BḲ 85b; Alf, *ad loc.*

"However, if one is deprived of a limb"—BḲ 8:1; B., *ibid.*, 85b.

"a cucumber watchman"—i.e., he is paid for enforced idleness at the rate appropriate to his future occupation, not his past employment.

12. B. BḲ 85b.

The *ḥereš*, deaf or deaf-mute, is assumed in rabbinic literature to be subnormal and unfit for any work at all.

13. B. BḲ 85b.

"pay him only his whole value"—that is, the several damages he suffered are estimated in bulk rather than calculated individually.

"If, however, the injured person seizes." See note above, 1, i, 11.

14–15. Tos BḲ 9: 3 (363).

17–18. B. BḲ 85a.

19. B. BḲ 85a.

"not as a result of the wound." RABD holds that in this case the medical expenses need not be paid either, and MM thinks that our text should be altered to agree with this view. KM considers alteration of the text unjustified and suggests that Maim. probably had a different reading in his copy of the Talmud.

20. B. BḲ 91a.

Chapter 3

1. BḲ 8: 1.

"Humiliation caused by an insignificant person," etc.—Tos BḲ 9: 4 (363).

2. B. BḲ 86b.

"If one humiliates another who is naked . . . he is exempt"—whatever the humiliation inflicted, because a person who is voluntarily naked is regarded as incapable of suffering further humiliation. Cf. Rashi, *ad loc.* The Tosafists, however, consider that a naked person humiliated by a slap, for example, is entitled to recover compensation for the humiliation.

3. BḲ 8: 1; B., *ibid.*, 86b.

"seizure by the heirs." See above, note on 1, i, 11.

4. "imbecile . . . deaf-mute"—B. BḲ 86b.

"proselyte"—*ibid.*, 88a.

"slave"—BḲ 8: 3.

"minor"—B., *ibid.*, 86b.

"Nevertheless, there is no comparison between," etc.—Tos BḲ 9: 4 (363). Cf. B., *ibid.*, 86a.

5. B. BḲ 91a.

"If one humiliates a scholar," etc.—P. BḲ 8: 6 (6c), quoted in Alf, *ad loc.*

7. " 'If one makes an honorable Israelite blanch,' " etc.—B. BM 59a.

8. B. BḲ 27b.

"the fixed sum covers the pain, the humiliation, the medical treatment, and the enforced idleness"—Alf. Rashi says it covers the humiliation only; others say it covers the pain only (cf. Hag. Mai.).

9. B. BḲ 27b; BḲ 8: 6.

"for tightening his fingers as though into a bunch." Rashi understands the talmudic expression to mean "for hitting him with an ass's saddle."

"if he gives another a stinging blow." Cf. Maim.'s Commentary to BḲ 8: 6.

"This is the amount one must pay for each act"—B. BḲ 37a.

10. B. BḲ 36b; B. Ḳid 11b.

11. BḲ 8: 6; B., *ibid.*, 91a.

Chapter 4

1. BḲ 5: 3.

"compensation for injury and pain to the woman"—B., *ibid.*, 49a. Some authorities consider that the compensation for the injury should be shared between husband and wife according to the formula of Sec. 15 below (cf. Rashi, *ad loc.*).

2. BḲ 5: 3.

"was worth"—if sold as a slave in open market. Cf. above, i, 2.

"the woman is given the value of the child as well." Cf. B. BḲ 49a. RABD and others consider that in this case the compensation still goes to the husband's heirs. The talmudic rule concerns a proselyte woman whose husband died before the accident. See Sec. 3 below.

3. B. BḲ 49a.

"the offender is exempt." A childless proselyte has no legal heir and all his property becomes ownerless at his death. So, too, all debts owed to him, including his claims for compensation, are automatically cancelled. See XII, II, ii, 1 ff. (YJS, *5*, 113 f.).

4. B. BḲ 49a.

"at the time of conception," etc.—since she was a slave or a gentile, no legal relation of paternity is established.

5. B. Ket 35a.

6. B. BḲ 42a.

The principle underlying this sec. may be stated as follows. If the action intended causes a death, there can be no claim for compensation for incidental damage, whether the death was intended or not. If, however, the action intended does not cause a death, all incidental damage must be paid for, even if there is also incidentally a death. RABD and others do not accept this distinction but say that as long as a death results from the action, there is no liability for compensation.

7. BḲ 8: 3.

For the death penalty when a parent is bruised, see Exod. 21: 15.

8. Cf. B. Shab 105b and III, 1, i, 17.

9. BḲ 8: 3.

"This principle is indeed true in every case except that of one who wounds another"—B. Ket 32b.

10. "Canaanite slave"—BḲ 8: 5.

"Hebrew slave"—*ibid.*, 8: 3.

"Even if the slave is treated with a (special) painful drug"—B. Giṭ 12b. The slave is not entitled to retain the difference between the actual cost of the treatment and the amount awarded as estimated medical expenses. See above, ii, 14.

11. B. Giṭ 42b.

"A fine is not payable"—if the slave is killed by an ox which is forewarned. See above, 1, xi, 1.

"Consequently, if one knocks out his slave's tooth"—the slave goes free but requires a document of manumission from his master. Cf. XII, v, v, 4 (YJS, *5*, 265).

12. B. Giṭ 42b.

Maim. assumes here that a slave who is half free—for example, if only one of his two masters has emancipated him—works one day for his master and one for himself until such time as his remaining master obeys the court's injunction to complete his emancipation. See XII, v, vii, 7 (YJS, *5*, 273) and Giṭ 4: 4. RABD and other authorities disagree and regard a male slave as free but requiring a document of manumission. But they accept the rule discussed in this sec. in the case of female slaves.

13. B. BḲ 86a.

14. B. BḲ 87b.

15. Ket 6: 1.

16. This sec. appears to be based on the Geonic decision referred to in it.

"in the same manner he pays for treatment of all her ailments." Cf. IV, 1, i, 2.

17. B. BḲ 32a.

18. B. BḲ 89a–b.

For the principal part of the marriage settlement and the supplements, see IV, 1, x, 7.

"at its present market value"—the price for which someone would be prepared to purchase it as a speculation, knowing that he will get nothing at all unless the husband dies first or the woman is divorced.

"a man is forbidden to keep his wife with him for a single hour without a marriage settlement." See IV, 1, x, 10.

19. B. BḲ 87b.

The law for minors in this section would seem to apply to boys only, the law for girls being that given above in Sec. 14.

20–21. B. BḲ 8: 4.

22. B. BḲ 27a.

"One's slave is regarded as his own person, but his animal is regarded as his inanimate property." Maim. makes his maxim apply to the injurer, viz: To injure a slave is like injuring his master; to do damage to an animal is like damaging inanimate property. RABD and the Tosafists, on the other hand, apply the maxim to the injured party, viz: It is one's duty to prevent injury to his slave in the same way that he must prevent injury to himself; but he need not prevent damage to an animal just as he need not prevent damage to inanimate property. They therefore understand the Talmud's examples reproduced here in the following way: if a slave is bound and helpless and the master sees someone place a burning coal on the slave's heart, it is his duty to remove it. If the same thing is done to his animal, he need not remove it but may allow the damage to take place and then claim compensation.

Chapter 5

1. BḲ 8: 6; B., *ibid.*, 91b.

"in the course of a quarrel"—rather than with benevolent intention, as when a surgeon makes a wound in order to promote cure.

2. B. San 58b; cf. Exod. 2: 13.

3. B. Ket 32b.

The pĕruṭah was the smallest fraction of the Palestine denar considered to be of monetary significance. Anything worth less than this was not regarded as transferable property.

"there is no compensation in this case." The penalty is therefore the same as that for transgressing any other prohibition, namely a flogging. Cf. XIV, 1, xviii, 1 (YJS, *3*, 50).

"liable for the penalty of death"—B. San 58b; not at the hands of a court, but only morally. Cf. XIV, v, x, 6 (YJS, *3*, 236).

4. Shebu 7:3.

5. B. Shebu, 46b.

6–8. The distinction between compensation for injury and pain and the other effects is attributed to R. Joseph ibn Migas (see MM). RABD disagrees and considers that all the effects should be treated alike.

9. BḲ 8:7; B., *ibid.*, 92a.

"rams of Nebaioth." See Isa. 60:7.

10. BḲ 8:7; B., *ibid.*, 92a.

11. BḲ 8:7; B., *ibid.*, 93a.

12. B. BḲ 93a.

13. BḲ 8:7.

Chapter 6

1. BḲ 2:6; B., *ibid.*, 27a, 31a.

2. Cf. BḲ 8:7–8.

3. B. BḲ 48a.

"deliberately." According to RABD he is also liable even for inadvertent damage if he is aware that the property is on the premises.

4. B. Mak 7b (Maim.'s reading differed from current edd.; see marginal note of R. Elijah of Wilna).

"A blow from Heaven." According to RABD we should regard the slipping of a firmly fixed rung as an act of God and the case of the rotted rung as entailing liability.

5. BḲ 3:1.

RABD points out that if the owner of the courtyard actually gave permission for the courtyard to be filled, he would be liable even for unintentional damage.

6–7. B. BḲ 28a.

8. BḲ 3:5.

9. B. BḲ 32a.

10. Cf. B. BḲ 3b; *ibid.*, 30a.

"mucus or phlegm"—B. BḲ 3b.

"damage caused by his 'pit.'" He will therefore not be liable for damage to articles soiled by the mucus or phlegm.

11. BḲ 6:6; *ibid.*, 9:3.

12. B. San 76b.

Many authorities (e.g., Naḥmanides)regard these cases as analogous to those of indirect damage dealt with below in vii, 7–12, and not as analogous to shooting with an arrow. Cf. MM, *ad loc.*

13. This sec. is an introduction to the cases recorded in the next three secs. and is implicit in them.

14. B. BḲ 10a (with a variation in reading from that of the current editions).

According to Rashi, *ad loc.*, another case altogether is intended: the adding by a single individual of bundles of twigs to another person's fire, causing it to spread and burn property.

15. B. BḲ 10b.

16. B. BḲ 53b.

The underlying principle of this sec. is that where damage is caused by several persons jointly, some of whom are exempt from compensation for the particular kind of damage caused, the whole of the liability must be borne by the remaining persons. In particular, the following rules of compensation apply: only a human is liable for the four additional effects of an injury (see I, vii, 3); only a human is liable for compensation for a child born prematurely (I, xi, 3); the owner of a pit is exempt from paying for slaying a person or for damage to inanimate objects (I, xiii, 1), or for damage to a dedicated animal which has become unfit for sacrifice (I, xii, 17); no ransom of thirty shekels is paid by a person who slays a freeman or a slave, since this is a capital offense (II, iii, 1); thirty shekels are payable when an ox kills a slave (I, xi, 1).

Chapter 7

1. B. Giṭ 53a.

"damage that is not discernible." The food or other articles suffer no physical change but become ritually forbidden for the use to which they would normally be put.

2. Giṭ 5: 4.

"forbidden libation wine"—wine manipulated by a heathen, thus forbidden to Israelites.

"from his best property"—B. BḲ 5a.

3. B. Giṭ 53a.

"the compensation may not be collected from his estate"—B. Giṭ 44b.

"inadvertently"—Giṭ 5: 4.

4. Giṭ 5: 4; B., *ibid.*, 53a.

"invalid"—i.e., an offering one proposes to eat after its prescribed time or outside its prescribed place. Cf. Lev. 7: 18.

"does work with a Heifer of Purification." The Red Heifer, whose ashes were used in purification from ritual uncleanness communicated by a corpse, was rendered unfit if work was done with it. See Num. 19: 1 ff.; cf. X, II, iv, 17 (YJS, *8,* 109).

"or with Water of Purification." See X, II, vii, 1 (YJS, *8,* 116).

5. B. Giṭ 53a.

In the examples of this section the offender is the cause of the disqualification of the heifer or the water but does no action (the introduction of the heifer into the stall does not in itself disqualify the heifer, since it is introduced for a legitimate purpose, namely, to suckle). He is therefore only morally liable. RABD disagrees with all these rulings concerning the heifer and the Water of Purification and says that the offender is always exempt, provided that his action is done for some personal benefit (in this case the benefit from the work done) and not to inflict damage.

"or if he diverts his attention from Water of Purification." See X, II, x, 5 (YJS, *8,* 128).

6. "the wine does not become forbidden"—B. Ḥul 41a.

"and must pay compensation"—B. Giṭ 52b.

"he becomes liable for compensation from the moment he lifts up the wine." The act of lifting the wine for his illegal purpose constitutes robbery.

7–8. Alf, *ad* B. BḲ 26b.

9. B. BḲ 98b.

10. B. Ket 86a.

"B is released from the debt, as will be explained." See XII, I, vi, 10–12 (YJS, 5, 26).

"if A's heir forgives the debt"—after A's death.

"from his best property"—and not merely from the estate, since it is he himself who caused the creditor's damage, even though indirectly.

11. Giṭ 4: 4; Alf, *ad* B. BḲ 98a.

"to manumit the slave"—to write him a bill of emancipation.

"pushes another's coin." If he actually lifts the coin he is liable for direct damage. For this and the other cases of this section, Maim. follows Alf, who reverses decisions of Rabbah. See above, Secs. 7–8.

"causes its value to be reduced." As a result of the blemish it cannot now be used as a sacrifice, for which a higher price would be paid.

"flattens"—without actually reducing its weight.

The cases of Secs. 7, 8, and 11 are the subject of extensive controversy among the authorities. RABD accepts the decision in the last three cases but rejects the others; some Tosafists reject them all. Most authorities would also include under damage caused indirectly the laws for dealing with the informer, which Maim. places separately in the next chapter.

12. B. BḲ 26b.

13. B. BḲ 91b.

"he is exempt, inasmuch as this was to be done in any case." The burden of proof is transferred to the owner of the ox or the tree.

14. B. BḲ 91b.

"covers the blood"—Lev. 17: 13.

"ten gold pieces." This is the sum actually imposed by R. Gamaliel in a case where an outsider covered the blood before the slaughterer could do so. The authorities referred to regarded this as a fixed fine (cf. above, iii, 8–9) unlike Maim., who looked upon it as the amount considered appropriate in this particular case.

15. B. BḲ 10b–11a.

"as we have explained in the case where one's ox inflicts damage." See above, I, vii, 8 f.

16. B. BḲ 5a.

"the fine of one guilty of rape"—Exod. 22: 15–16; Deut. 22: 19, 29.

17. B. BḲ 62a.

"as does one robbed." See above, III, iv, 1 ff.

18. B. BḲ 62a.

"A villainous person." The Hebrew *'annas* signifies a person who gets his own way by employing force and terrorism and who is too powerful to be sued by ordinary legal process.

"However, if the plaintiff seizes property." See above, note on I, i, 11.

19. The source of this sec. is a decision of R. Joseph ibn Migas disputed by RABD; see XIII, II, v, 6 (YJS, 2, 66 f.).

"provided that his claim . . . . to take an oath." This passage, omitted in the edd. (*homoioteleuton*), is preserved in the Oxford MS (though hardly, it seems, in the exact wording of Maim.).

Chapter 8

1. Cf. B. BḲ 5a.; *ibid.*, 11b.
For the definition of "villainous person," see note on vii, 18, above.
2. B. BḲ 117a.
"for one who saves himself by appropriating another's property must repay it"—B. BḲ 117b. He cannot claim exemption from payment on the ground that he is right not to endanger his life for other people's money. Cf. also below, Sec. 13.
3. B. BḲ 117a.
"the king applies constraint." From the context of the incidents in the Talmud and the interpretation of the later commentaries (e.g., SMA to ḤM 388), it is evident that the levies in question are not regular and legal taxes but extortionate demands, such as those of an enemy occupying power whom it is a duty to resist. For the rule when the demand is a lawful one, see Sec. 6 below.
4–5. B. BḲ 117a.
6. P. BḲ 10: 6 (7c).
"seized"—or "arrested."
7. B. BḲ 62a.
"If the plaintiff seizes property." See above, note on I, i, 11.
8. Alf, *ad* B. BḲ 62a.
"a stringent oath"—holding a sacred object.
"deemed wicked"—*raša'*. Cf. XIV, II, ii, 10 (YJS, *3*, 107).
9. B. Giṭ 7b.
10. B. BḲ 117a.
11. "The Maghrib"—Moorish Spain, North Africa, and Egypt. For an interesting account of informers in Spain illustrating this sec., see A. A. Neumann, *The Jews in Spain, 1*, 130–8.
12–14. B. BḲ 117b.
15. B. BḲ 117b.
This decision appears to conflict with that stated above, III, xii, 14. MM points out that in the latter case the ship is not overloaded but the danger comes from outside and so all must contribute to ward it off (cf. III, xii, 10). Here, on the other hand, the danger is due to the extra load, which can therefore be regarded as the pursuer.

Treatise V: Murder and Preservation of Life

Chapter 1

1. San 9: 1; B., *ibid.*, 52b.
"human being." The Oxford MS has "a single Israelite"; cf. below, Sec. 16.
"death by the sword"—i.e., decapitation.

2. Sif Num. 35: 19 (218); B. San 45b.
3. B. Mak 12a.
4. B. Ket 37b.
5. Sif Num. 35: 12 (216); B. Mak 12a.
6. San 8: 7; B., *ibid.*, 72b.
7. Sif Deut. 25: 12 (126b); cf. also B. San 74a.
8. Sif Deut. 25: 12 (126b).
9. Oh 7: 6; B. San 72b.
10. San 8: 7; B., *ibid.*, 73a.
11–12. B. San 73a.
13. B. San 74a.

"deserves to be put to death"—i.e., is morally guilty of murder and will be punished by God.

14. B. San 73a.
15. Sif Deut. 25: 12 (126b).
16. San 4: 5.

"because breach of them involves no action." Cf. XIV, I, xviii (YJS, *3*, 50).

Chapter 2

1. San 9: 2.
2. B. Ḳid 43a; B. San 77a.
3. Cf. B. BḲ 91b; Gen R *ad* Gen 9: 6 (ed. Theodor, pp. 324–5).

"the verb *require*"—seeing that in all three instances the verb is used in the first person singular, referring to God.

4. Cf. XIV, v, iii, 10.

"Similarly, if the court deems it proper" etc.—B. San 46a.

5. Cf. San 9: 5.

"In a fortress or a prison"—literally, "in the siege and in the straitness." Cf. Deut. 28: 53.

6. Nid 5: 3; B., *ibid.*, 44b.
7. B. San 78a.
8. B. San 78a.

"suffers from a fatal organic disease"—Heb. *ṭĕrefah*. When used technically of animals this term signifies an injury or anomaly of a vital organ sufficient to render the animal unfit for food even if properly slaughtered. Because these injuries were regarded as fatal, the term is applied by transference to fatal human injuries. In the context of this sec. it has no precise technical meaning, but is defined by our author as a disease which physicians testify is not normally curable.

"every human being is presumed to be healthy." Cf. B. Mak 7a.

9. B. San 78a; cf. XIV, II, xx, 7 (YJS, *3*, 128 f.).

"(Deut. 19: 19)." The phrase quoted occurs a number of times in Deuteronomy, the first being Deut. 13: 6. The above reference was preferred because its context is the law concerning conspiratorial witnesses.

"conspirators." Cf. XIV, II, xviii f. (YJS, *3*, 121 f.).

10. Mek Exod. 21: 20 (*3*, 56).

"he must go into exile"—B. Mak 8b.

11. Cf. Mek Exod. 21:14 (*3,* 37); San 9:2.

"If an Israelite"—so the Oxford MS; edd. prefix "formerly."

"a resident alien"—Heb. *ger tošab̲,* a heathen who resides among Israelites and abstains from idolatry but is not a proselyte.

"does not suffer capital punishment"—but is guilty of the crime of murder. See Mek, *loc. cit.*

"yoke"—so the Oxford MS.

12–13. Mek Exod. 21:21 (*3,* 61–2).

12. *"his property"*—his money.

"By a day or two"—Mek Exod. 21:21 (*3,* 61).

15. B. BḲ 90a.

"owned by him." This is a reference to ***under his hand*** in Exod. 21:20, which is understood to mean, "While in the owner's possession."

16. Mek Exod. 21:20 (*3,* 57); B. BḲ 90a.

Chapter 3

1–7. The first seven secs. of this chapter are based on Sif Num. 35:16–20 (217–8), but the arrangement and formulation are the author's own.

4. Cf. B. San 76a.

5. Cf. San 9:2.

7. "as the Sages have stated in the case of a pit." See above, I, xii, 10.

8. SZ Num. 35:16 (333).

9. San 9:1; B., *ibid.,* 77a.

10. San 9:1; B., *ibid.,* 77a.

"puts a tub over another"—so that the victim dies when he has used up all the air in the tub. This differs both from the case in Sec. 9 above, where the victim is walled up with no air at all, and the case where a lamp is put in with him to use up the air. For in the latter cases it is the slayer who deprives the victim of air, but in the former it is the victim himself who uses up the air in the tub before he begins to suffocate and the slayer's action is less direct.

11–12. B. San 77b.

"the pebble rebounds and kills another"—this being the intention of the thrower.

13. B. San 77b.

"because of the immediate force resulting from his act." Cf. Rashi, *ad loc.* The stream of water kills the victim as soon as it is released by the offender.

Chapter 4

1. San 9:2; B., *ibid.,* 79a–b.

"as will be explained." See below VI, 6.

"into a crowd of Israelites." This case is not actually stated in the Talmud. Cf. B. San 79a.

2. San 9:2.

"the weapon . . . the stone." This change of expression occurs in the text.

3. B. San 78b.

"compensation for the five effects of the injury." See above, IV, i.

"the assailant must immediately be put into prison"—Mek to Exod. 21: 19 (*3*, 54).

4. Mek to Exod. 21: 19 (*3*, 53).

5. San 9: 1; B., *ibid.*, 78b.

6. B. San 78a.

"Any man"—Heb. *kŏl*, here interpreted as "the whole."

"and an arrow comes from among them"—*ibid.*, 80a.

7. Cf. B. San 78a.

"If a condemned murderer becomes mixed up with other persons"—San 9: 3; B., *ibid.*, 79b.

"except in the defendant's presence." This rule is here taken to signify that the court must know the individual on whom sentence is being pronounced.

8. San 9: 5; B. San 81b.

"although they did see him one after the other." Each saw him commit a murder. Rashi, *ad loc.*, says both witnesses saw him commit the same murder from different vantage points, so that they cannot have him condemned to death. See XIV, II, iv, 1 (YJS, *3*, 89).

"cross-examination . . . primary investigation"—the queries and cross-examination to which witnesses are subjected. Defined in XIV, II, i, 4–6 (YJS, *3*, 82 f.).

9. As far as the translator is aware the law of this sec. is not stated explicitly in any of the ancient sources.

10. B. AZ 26a–b.

"provocatively"—even when ritually permissible alternatives are available, as opposed to the sinner who does wrong to gratify his appetite. See below, Sec. 12.

"mingled stuffs"—Deut. 22: 11.

"sectarians"—according to the Oxford MS.

11. Tos BM 2: 33 (375).

"raisers of small cattle." See next sec. and above, I, v, 2.

12. B. AZ 26b.

Chapter 5

1. Mak 2: 1.

2. B. Giṭ 70b.

"the victim hastened his own death"—by his struggles. According to RABD this possibility is considered only in the special case of severed throat organs mentioned next. It is in any event ignored where the charge is one of deliberate murder (KM).

3. Mak 2: 3; B., *ibid.*, 8b.

4. Sif Num. 35: 15 (216); B. Mak 9a.

5. Mak 2: 3.

"The rule is applied in the latter instance only," etc.—Mak 2: 2.

6. Mak 2: 2.

"beats a litigant for not coming to court." RABD asserts that this should be "who administered the flogging prescribed by the court." See Mak 3: 14.

7. Mak 2: 6; Sif Deut. 19: 11 (108b).

8. Mak 2: 5; Tos, *ibid.*, 3: 5 (440).

"and tells them." This is Maim.'s reading of the Talmud text. Our text (B. Mak 10b) would have the scholars tell the avenger.

9–10. B. Mak 10b.

"It makes no difference"—continuing the preceding section.

"and then leaves its confines deliberately"—Mak 2:7.

11–13. B. Mak 12a.

14. B. Mak 12a. Cf. also B. San 48b–49a.

Chapter 6

1–5. These introductory paragraphs provide a rationale for the variety of cases that follow.

5. "or in a similar manner"—i.e., a deliberate murder not punishable by death on technical grounds.

"a case of unintentional slaying"—i.e., the case of Sec. 4.

6–8. Mak 2:2; B., *ibid.*, 8a.

7. "into a rubbish heap"—to which people might go to relieve themselves.

9. Mak 2:2; Sif Deut. 19:5 (108b).

10. Mak 2:3; B., *ibid.*, 7b.

"one runs into a corner"—carrying a dangerously exposed implement. Cf. Rashi, *ad loc.*

11. Mak 2:2; B. BḲ 32b.

12. Mak 2:1; B., *ibid.*, 7b.

"For falling objects," etc. This is the author's own explanation of the difference between the cases. Observe the Aristotelian statement that it is natural for heavy things to fall down *quickly;* this does not, however, affect the argument.

13. B. Mak 7b.

"The general rule is as follows"—Mak 2:1; B., *ibid.*, 7b.

14. B. Mak 7b; B. BḲ 26b; Mak 2:3.

15. B. BḲ 26b.

"If an axe slips," etc.—Mak 2:1; B., *ibid.*, 8a. Cf. KM, *ad loc.*

Chapter 7

1. B. Mak 10a.

2. Tos Mak 2:8 (p. 440).

3. B. Mak 11b.

4. B. Mak 12a.

"and for all their life." The standard translations render this verse *and for all their beasts,* which would make the inference that follows meaningless.

5. Mak 2:7; B., *ibid.*, 12b.

"as will be explained." See below, viii, 9.

6. B. Mak 10b

7. Mak 2:8.

8. Mak 2:7.

"as we have explained." See above, v, 10.

9. Mak 2:6. Cf. Rashi, *ad loc.*, for the entire section.

"anointed for the conduct of war"—Deut. 20:3.

10. Mak 2: 7; B., *ibid.,* 11b.
11. Mak 2: 6.
12. B. Mak 11b.
"hăluṣah." Cf. Deut. 25: 9–10.
14. Mak 2: 8.
15. Sif Num. 35: 11 (215).

Chapter 8

2. Deut. 4: 41–43; Josh. 20: 7–8.
3. Mak 2: 4; B., *ibid.,* 10a.
4. Tos Mak 3: 10 (441).
"the Kenites"—Gen. 15: 19.
5. Mak 2: 5; Sif Deut. 19: 3 (108a).
"The width of a road," etc.—B. BB 100b.
"was written at each crossroad"—Tos. Mak 3: 5 (440).
6. Shek 1: 1; B. MḲ 5a.
"regarded by Scripture"—Deut. 19: 10.
7. B. Mak 9b.
"and divide"—Heb. *wĕšillašta,* "trisect," hence space evenly. The latter half of the quotation is missing from the printed editions but is clearly necessary (cf. the Talmud source cited) and has been supplied from the Oxford MS.
8. Tos Mak 3: 8–9 (441).
9. B. Mak 10a.
10. B. Mak 10a; B. Mak 13a.
11. Mak 2: 7; B., *ibid.,* 12a–b.

Chapter 9

1. Soṭ 9: 1.
"Even if it is found right beside," etc.—Tos Soṭ 9: 1 (312).
2. Soṭ 9: 5; B., *ibid.,* 45b.
3. Soṭ 9: 5–6; Sif Deut. 21: 6 (112b).
"in Hebrew"—Soṭ 7: 2.
"without food"—so causing him to become a brigand and leading to his death (Rashi, *ad loc.*).
4. B. Er 58b.
"must not measure the level distance only, in disregard of hills and valleys." Cf. Rashi, *ad loc.* Hills and valleys were ignored in measuring the Sabbath limit; see Er 5: 4; and III, 1, xxviii, 16.
"only to cities having a court of twenty-three members"—Soṭ 9: 2; B., *ibid.,* 45b.
5. Soṭ 9: 2; B., *ibid.,* 45b.
6–7. B. BB 23b.
"principle of proximity." Cf. Deut. 21: 3.
"takes precedence." And where the two rules give conflicting results, the principle of majority is followed.
8. Soṭ 9: 2; B. Bek 18a.

" 'If our town,' " etc. The text uses the third person plural indiscriminately throughout the declaration.

9. Soṭ 9: 4.

"If the body is found in one place," etc.—Soṭ 9: 3; B., *ibid.*, 45b.

"unclaimed corpse, the burial of which . . . incumbent on anyone who comes upon it"—because the dead person's own near relatives are unknown.

10. "found one on top of the other"—B. Soṭ 45a–b.

11. B. Soṭ 45b, 47b.

12. Soṭ 9: 8–9.

13. Soṭ 9: 8; B., *ibid.*, 47b.

14. Soṭ 9: 8.

15–17. B. Soṭ 47b.

Chapter 10

1. Sif Deut. 21: 1 (111b).

2. Par 1: 1; Soṭ 9: 5; P., *ibid.*, 9: 5 (23d).

"organically defective"—Heb. ṭĕrefah.

"atonement is used"—Deut. 21: 8.

"sacrifices." Cf. YJS, *4*, 221.

3. B. Soṭ 47a.

"the Red Heifer." See Num. 19: 1 ff., and X, II, i, 7 (YJS, *8*, 98).

4. Cf. Par 2: 3.

"as we have explained"—Cf. X, II, i, 7 (YJS, *8*, 98).

5. Meg 2: 5; Tos Neg 1: 13 (619); B. Soṭ 8a.

6. AZ 8: 9; B. Ker 6a; *ibid.*, 25a.

7. Tos Ker 4: 3 (566).

8. Soṭ 9: 7.

9. Soṭ 9: 5; B., *ibid.*, 46b.

10. Tos Ker 4: 3 (566).

"must still bring one after the Day of Atonement"—unlike private individuals liable to a guilt offering for a doubtful transgression, who would be exempt under similar circumstances. See Ker 6: 4.

Chapter 11

1. Sif Deut. 22: 8 (116a).

"One is not enjoined to do so, however, for his storehouse or stables." The source given states that these are liable; see KM.

2. B. Ḥul 136a; Sif Deut. 22: 8 (116a).

3. Sif Deut. 22: 8 (116a); cf. BB 4: 1.

"no flogging . . . since it involves no action." Cf. XIV, I, xviii, 1 (YJS, *3*, 50).

4. Sif Deut. 22: 8; cf. B. BḲ 15b.

6. Tos AZ 6: 6 (469); B. AZ 12b.

7. Ter 8: 4; Tos, *ibid.*, 7: 12 (37–8).

8. B. Beṣ 7b; B. AZ 30a; 12a; Tos Ter 7: 15 (38); 7: 13; B. AZ 30b.

9. Tos Ter 7: 13 (38).

10. B. AZ 30a.

11. B. AZ 30a; B. Ḥul 10a.
12. Ter 8: 5.
13. Tos Ter 7: 16 (38).
14. B. AZ 30b.
15. Tos Ter 7: 14 (38); B. AZ 30b.
16. Tos Ter 7: 13.

Chapter 12

1. Ḥul 3: 5; B., *ibid.*, 59a.
"organically defective." See note above, x, 2.
2. Ter 8: 6; Tos Ter 7: 17 (38); B. Ḥul 9a.
3. B. AZ 30b.
"A pecked fig that has dried," etc. The commentators do not indicate the source of this statement.
4–5. P. Ter 8: 6 (45d).
"the palm of his hand under his arm." According to RABD the source really says, "A slice of meat or bread under his arm"—because of the perspiration.
6. P. Ter 8: 6; B. RH 16b; B. Ber 3a.
"lest someone fall on the point." According to RABD, the objection is to the use of the fruit as a sheath, a disrespectful use.
7. AZ 2: 1; Tos, *ibid.*, 3: 4 (463).
8. Tos AZ 3: 4.
"unto Seir"—when in fact he stopped at Succoth. The idea is that the heathen will postpone his attack because he thinks he has plenty of time, and the Israelite will leave him earlier (Rashi, *ad* B. AZ 25b).
9. B. AZ 27b.
"Animal remedies," etc.—AZ 2: 1; B., *ibid.*, 27a–b.
10. B. AZ 27a.
11. AZ 2: 1; Tos, *ibid.*, 3: 5 (463); B., *ibid.*, 29a.
12. AZ 1: 7; Tos, *ibid.*, 2: 4 (462); B., *ibid.*, 15b–16a.
13. B. AZ 15b.
"to the local militia"—*ibid.*, 16a.
14. B. AZ 15b; Sif Lev. 19: 14 (88d).
15. B. BB 4a.

Chapter 13

1. BM 2: 10.
2. B. BM 32a; Mek Exod. 23: 5 (*3*, 165).
3. Sif Deut. 22: 4 (115a–b).
4. B. BM 30b; cf. above, III, xi, 13–17.
5. BM 2: 10; B., *ibid.*, 31a, 33a.
6. Mek Exod. 23: 5 (*3*, 165).
7. B. BM 32, 33a.
8. Sif Deut. 22: 4 (115b).
9. Mek Exod. 23: 5 (*3*, 166); B. BM 32b.
10. Tos BḲ 2: 10 (349); Alf *ad* B. San 32b.

11. Tos BḲ 2: 10 (349).
12. Tos BḲ 2: 10 (349); B. San 32b.
13. B. BM 32b.
14. B. Pes 113b.

"if one all alone sees." If there is more than one witness, the miscreant can be punished by the courts, and it is unnecessary to harbor a private hatred.

LIST OF ABBREVIATIONS

Sources and Commentaries

Alf—Alfasi
B.—Babylonian Talmud
Gen R.—Genesis Rabbah (ed. Theodor, Berlin, 1912)
Hag. Mai.—*Hăḡahoṯ Maimuniyyoṯ* (on *Mishneh Torah*)
ḤM—*Ḥošen Mišpaṭ* (Lemberg, 1898)
KM—*Kesef Mišneh* (on *Mishneh Torah*)
LM—*Leḥem Mišneh* (on *Mishneh Torah*)
Mek—*Mĕḵilta dĕ-Rabbi Ishmael* (ed. Lauterbach, Jewish Publication Society, 1933)
MM—*Maggiḏ Mišneh* (on *Mishneh Torah*)
MRSY—*Mĕḵilta of Rabbi Simeon ben Yoḥai* (ed. Hoffmann, Frankfurt a.M., 1905)
MT—*Miḏraš Tanna'im* (ed. Hoffmann, Berlin, 1908)
P.—Palestinian Talmud (ed. Krotoschin, 1866)
RABD—Rabbi Abraham Ben David (12th Century)
Sif Deut.—*Sifre* (ed. Friedmann, Vienna, 1864)
Sif Lev.—*Sifra* (ed. Weiss, Vienna, 1862)
Sif Num.—*Sifre* (ed. Horovitz, Leipzig, 1917)
SMA—*Sefer Mĕ'iraṯ 'Enayim* (on ḤM)
SZ—*Sifre Zuṭa* on Numbers (ed. Horovitz, Leipzig, 1917)
ṬḤM—*Ṭur Ḥošen Mišpaṭ*
Tos—*Tosefta* (ed. Zuckermandel, Jerusalem, 1937)
YJS—Yale Judaica Series

Tractates of Mishnah and Talmud

Ar—*'Ăraḵin*
AZ—*'Ăḇoḏah Zarah*
BB—*Baḇa Baṭra*
Bek—*Bĕḵoroṯ*
Ber—*Bĕraḵoṯ*
Beṣ—*Beṣah*
BḲ—*Baḇa Ḳamma*
BM—*Baḇa Mĕṣi'a*
Ed—*'Eduyyoṯ*
Er—*'Eruḇin*
Giṭ—*Giṭṭin*
Ḥul—*Ḥullin*
Kel—*Kelim*
Ker—*Kĕriṯoṯ*
Ket—*Kĕṯubboṯ*
Ḳid—*Ḳiddušin*

Maas—*Maʻaśĕroṯ*
Mak—*Maḵḵoṯ*
Meg—*Mĕḡillah*
MḲ—*Moʻeḏ Ḳaṭan*
MSh—*Maʻăśer Šeni*
Neg—*Nĕḡaʻim*
Nid—*Niddah*
Oh—*'Ŏhaloṯ*
Par—*Parah*
Pes—*Pĕsaḥim*
RH—*Roš Haššanah*
San—*Sanheḏrin*
Shab—*Šabbaṯ*
Shebi—*Šeḇiʻiṯ*
Shebu—*Šeḇuʻoṯ*
Sheḳ—*Šĕḵalim*
Soṭ—*Soṭah*
Suk—*Suḵḵah*
Ter—*Tĕrumoṯ*
Yad—*Yaḏayim*
Yeb—*Yĕḇamoṯ*
Zeb—*Zĕḇaḥim*

GLOSSARY

Denar (denarius)
a coin of silver or gold, the silver denar being one twenty-fifth part of the gold denar

Five Effects
The five heads under which compensation for injury was payable, viz: Injury, Pain, Medical Treatment, Loss of Earnings, Humiliation

Forewarned (Heb. *mu'aḏ*)
a. an animal whose owner has been warned in court that it has caused damage with its horn three or more times and that he is liable to pay full compensation for any future damage; b. by transference used of any object prone to cause damage for which the owner must pay full compensation

Four Effects
a. the Five Effects (see above) with the exception of injury; b. the Five Effects with the exception of humiliation

Geonim (singular: *ga'on,* Excellency; plural: *gĕ'onim*)
the title borne by the heads of the Babylonian academies in post-talmudic times until about the twelfth century

Ḥăliṣah (literally: the drawing off—of a shoe)
the ceremony which released a widow whose husband had died childless from levirate marriage (see Deut. 25: 5–10)

Ḥăluṣah
a woman who has performed *ḥăliṣah*

Hin
a liquid measure equal to 3 *ḳaḇ* or 12 *loḡ*

Innocuous (Heb. *tam,* "perfect, innocent")
the contrary of "forewarned"

Ḳaḇ
a measure of capacity equal to one sixth of a *sĕ'ah*

Ḳor
a measure of capacity equal to thirty *sĕ'ah*

Litra
a liquid measure equal to ½ of a *loḡ*

Loḡ
a liquid measure equal to ¼ of a *ḳaḇ*

Mĕśurah
a measure of capacity equal to one thirty-sixth of a *loḡ*

Mil
a measure of distance (cf. v, xiii, 6)

Mina
100 *zuz* or *denar*

Mu'aḏ
see Forewarned

Oath, of inducement
an oath imposed by the court in cases where scriptural and mishnaic law did not prescribe an oath, and sworn informally, i.e., without holding a scroll of the Law or some other sacred object

Oath, scriptural or quasi-scriptural
an oath prescribed by scriptural or mishnaic law and sworn holding a scroll of the Law or phylacteries

Pĕruṭah
the smallest fraction of a denar of monetary significance equal to 1/192 of the denar

Resident alien
a gentile who has accepted the belief in One God

Sĕ'ah
a measure of capacity

Sela'
a silver coin equal to four denar

Tam
see Innocuous

Ṭĕrefah (literally: torn—by a beast or bird of prey)
the meat of an animal or bird one of whose vital organs has suffered a mortal injury as defined in V, III, x, 9

Zuz
another name for the silver denar

INDEX

YALE JUDAICA SERIES

SAADIA GAON: The Book of Beliefs and Opinions. Translated by Samuel Rosenblatt

THE BOOK OF CIVIL LAWS (*The Code of Maimonides, Book 13*). Translated by Jacob J. Rabinowitz

THE BOOK OF JUDGES (*The Code of Maimonides, Book 14*). Translated by Abraham M. Hershman

THE BOOK OF OFFERINGS (*The Code of Maimonides, Book 9*). Translated by Herbert Danby

THE BOOK OF ACQUISITION (*The Code of Maimonides, Book 12*). Translated by Isaac Klein

FALASHA ANTHOLOGY. Translated by Wolf Leslau

KARAITE ANTHOLOGY: Excerpts from the Early Literature. Translated by Leon Nemoy

THE BOOK OF CLEANNESS (*The Code of Maimonides, Book 10*). Translated by Herbert Danby

Date Due